ETERNAL VISION

ALSO BY DAVID TAYLOR
Operation 10/40 Window

LEADER'S EDITION

DAVID TAYLOR

ETERNAL VISION

SEEING LIFE FROM HEAVEN'S PERSPECTIVE

TAYLOR PUBLISHING GROUP
PASADENA
www.taylorpublishing.info

Copyright © 2005 by David Taylor. All rights reserved. No portion of this book may be reproduced, stored in a retrieval system, or transmitted in any form or by any means—electronic, mechanical, photocopy, recording, or any other—except for brief quotations in printed reviews, without the prior permission of the publisher.

The publisher may be contacted at tp@finishthetask.org.
The author may be contacted at ev@finishthetask.org.

Unless otherwise indicated, Scripture quotations used in this book are from the Holy Bible, New International Version (NIV). Copyright © 1973, 1978, 1984, International Bible Society.

Other Scripture references are from the following sources:

New American Standard Bible (NASB), copyright © 1960, 1977 by the Lockman Foundation.

The King James Version of the Bible (KJV).

The Integrated Gospel (ING), copyright © 2004 by the Taylor Publishing Group.

Library of Congress Control Number: 2005902439
ISBN 0-9762933-0-7 (pbk.)

Printed in the United States of America
05 06 07 08 09   WPN   9 8 7 6 5 4 3 2 1

To the Staff of the Frontier Mission Fellowship

ಌ

May the God of hope fill you
with all joy and peace
as you trust in him,
so that you may overflow with hope
by the power of the Holy Spirit.

Romans 15:13

CONTENTS

Introduction ix

One • 1
Getting Perspective

Two • 13
Staying Focused

Three • 33
Eternal Glory

Four • 47
The Real Danger

Five • 65
Where Your Treasure Is

Six • 85
Only One Way?

Seven • 103
Satan's Final Defeat

Eight • 125
Bringing Back the King

Nine • 143
The Blessing

CONTENTS

Ten • 163
Courage Under Fire

Eleven • 187
Radical Discipleship

Twelve • 205
Just Ask!

Thirteen • 223
Spiritual Realities

Fourteen • 239
Growing in Faith

Fifteen • 263
Satan's Top 5 Lies

Sixteen • 279
Getting Direction

Seventeen • 297
I Am Resolved

Eighteen • 313
Final Countdown

Appendix 1 • 323
10/40 Window Prayer Calendar

Appendix 2 • 338
Frontier Mission Fund

Notes • 339

INTRODUCTION

Wouldn't it be incredible if you could see life from heaven's perspective, even for just one day? I believe that one day would change the rest of your life. If you could walk with Jesus and ask him, "Lord, what are you up to? And how can I help out while I'm here on earth?" The answer to that question alone would set your life on a whole new course. But that's only the beginning; after all, you have the whole day! It would be the best-spent day of your life.

Well, here is the opportunity to do something like that. This is a book that can literally change your life if you let it. Learning to think the way heaven thinks is the most important transformation that can happen in anyone's life. The ability to think clearly affects everything about us. In essence, you are as you think. This wonderful and mysterious ability is the part of us that has been made in the image of God. And so it is the part of us that Satan seeks most to destroy.

I am convinced that the enemy has done everything in his power to keep this book out of your hands. But for whatever reason, he has not succeeded. You are well on your way to doing something that will mark a before and after period in your life. I feel so strongly about this I would encourage you to pray before each reading, asking the Lord Jesus Christ to open the eyes of your heart to the message of each chapter. In fact, *I don't recommend reading this whole book in a single day!* The subject matter is too serious and important to be hurried through. So take your time. One or two chapters a day is a good pace.

The *Leader's Edition* is designed to be used along with the shorter *Class Edition*. The latter has condensed chapters and a study guide for use in discipleship groups, Sunday school classes, and house-church fellowships. The *Leader's Edition* goes into more depth and will be helpful to facilitators.

Finally, I would love to hear from you. Let me know what happens and how I can be praying for you (ev@finishthetask.org). We are in this together and soon we will be standing before him, face to face, in all his glory. Let us press ever onward toward that day and work to see it come! (2 Pet. 3:12).

David Taylor
January 2005

CHAPTER ONE

GETTING PERSPECTIVE

*"Take hold of the eternal life to
which you were called." (1 Tim. 6:12)*

What is the most important thing I can do *now* as a follower of Jesus that I can never do again throughout *eternity*?

Have you ever asked yourself this question? It is perhaps the most important question you can ask yourself at the present time. In Christ, I have all the time of eternity to do an endless number of things. All my dreams and desires will be fully met far beyond what I could ever imagine possible. But is there something I must do *now* for Jesus that I will never be able to do again? Is this one thing the priority of my life, is it my passion and heart's desire, or could it be that I am missing out on what might be the most incredible opportunity I will ever be given?

That is the idea behind this book, and I think you will be amazed at how much Scripture has to say about it. In the span of eternity our presence in time is but a tiny blip on the screen. But where we are in eternal history is far more significant than we could ever understand or appreciate. All time before us and all eternity ahead of us will point to the time in which we are now living. Incredible as it may seem, according to Scripture, we have been given the opportunity to participate in the last battle of the last war that *eternal* history will ever know.

Opening our eyes to this reality was the number one thing Jesus came to accomplish. He came to set us free through an act of love never before witnessed in any previous age and never to be repeated again. He was sent to refocus our vision, to deliver us from demonic bondage, and to build an army of the Kingdom with one very focused mission: to bring about an absolute and final end to Satan's rebellion and influence in this universe.

With this in mind, it should come as no surprise that Satan also has one objective for you and one standing order for all of his demons. His goal for you is simple: *Just stay out of the action.* Don't move. Stay put. Keep quiet and keep the TV guide handy. The greatest tragedy that can happen to any believer is to go through life and not recognize the time in which he lives—like someone from the 10th century walking around on the streets of Manhattan today without a clue what's going on. In the same way, Satan doesn't want you to recognize your place in eternal history.

Scripture tells us Satan is filled with fury because he knows his time is getting short (Rev. 12:12). Jesus told us an "end" is coming, and there is no more frightening prospect for the enemy than this impending reality. It is the end of a heavenly rebellion that has ravaged the lives of billions over the centuries and continues to this day. But according to Scripture, it is coming to an end, and you and I as followers of Jesus have a unique and urgent assignment in this final campaign. For there is one reason and *one reason only* why Jesus has not returned up until this moment. He said, "This gospel of the kingdom *will be* preached and *must first* be preached in all the world as a testimony to all nations *and then* the end will come" (Mt. 24:14;

Getting Perspective

Mk. 13:10). The last battle of the last war that eternal history will ever know centers on the fulfillment of the Great Commission. Indeed, this *is* the last battle!

Now depending on where you stand, this can be a very exciting reality. The Bible doesn't tell us how long Satan has been in rebellion against God, but it does tell us his days are coming to a rapid and final ending. And that is why you and I, if we consider ourselves followers of Jesus, are Satan's greatest enemy and worst nightmare. Coming to understand this, and learning to see your life in the context of this heavenly war, is the most important thing that can happen to any believer at the present time.

Without a doubt, opportunity is winding down for the enemy. But for us it is just beginning. We are on the verge of something so incredible it will forever divide eternal history like B.C. and A.D. Generations before us have looked forward to our day and have longed to see it come. They are watching us from above and cheering us on. They are in the stands and they are rising to their feet. The roar of their triumph is deafening as the finish line comes closer into view. The final trumpeter is moistening his lips and filling up his lungs. And there at the end, an angel stands ready with a massive chain. With it he will bind the authority and power of Satan and cast him into the lake of fire.

WE ARE WINNING!

The most exciting reality of our day is how close we are to fulfilling the Great Commission. No other generation has been as close as we are today. Now as never before, it is especially critical that each of us pay careful attention to what is happening in our world. We need to be alert and focused, ready and waiting, prepared and willing to go anywhere and do anything that might be necessary to finish the task of world evangelization.

Now we are all very busy people. We have errands to run, people to answer to, bills to pay, and a whole shopping list of things we may never get around to unless we get a fully paid vacation for two years. We all know the feeling. Sometimes life itself is just too overwhelming to think about anything beyond just getting by. But we need to wake up and realize what's going on. Satan wants our eyes focused on things that seem urgent, but don't really matter.

Jesus is inviting us to a celebration, a wedding feast. Like the wedding he told us about 2,000 years ago, many people are too busy to make it (Matt. 22:1-14). And some people who would like to be there aren't getting ready. They had many excuses back then. Much like today. I'll learn to pray *tomorrow*. I'll get into the Word *after work*. I'll start supporting missionaries *when I can afford it*. I'll just be a missionary where I am and *hope someone notices*.

The sad thing is, these people won't have much to celebrate on that awesome day when Jesus comes to take us home. What an awkward bunch they will be, as they are called to celebrate something they had nothing to do with! Jesus warned us that these people would be called "least in the kingdom of heaven," for they disregarded his commands and lived as they pleased (Matt. 5:19).

Scripture clearly warns us about two kinds of believers who will be living in the end-times. Jesus told a parable about ten virgins who were awaiting the coming of the bridegroom (Matt. 25:1-13). They were people like us. They read the signs of the times, they understood his coming was near, but some of them were getting ready and others were not. Some of them were filling up on the oil of the Holy Spirit, and others were hoping to just get by on what they had and take from the others if they needed it. But it didn't work out that way. They were gambling with eternity and the odds were against them, infinity to one. For in the end, the issue is not how much you know about his coming, or how many books you have purchased on the subject, but the issue is, *What are you actually doing about it?*

We live in an age where the second coming of Christ is one of the hottest topics around. It's not surprising because the signs of the times are everywhere. Turning on the news is like reading Scripture. The eyes of the whole world are focused on Israel, just like the Bible said they would be in the end-times. The nations surrounding Israel are preparing for war against her, just as the Bible said would happen (Zec. 14:2). But at the same time, something else is happening—exactly as was promised. This you may not read about in the news. But all over the world, the Great Commission is rapidly being completed. Breakthroughs into new areas and untouched regions, languages and peoples are happening at a speed never before seen in any other generation.

Yet the amazing thing is, this great progress, which is the most exciting thing going on in our generation, is being organized and implemented by a relatively small minority of believers. Only a few are aware of this great achievement and even less are actually participating in it. Remarkably, only a fraction of those who claim to follow Jesus are on board with his program for this generation.

However, this should not surprise us. Jesus told us it would be like this. He asked his disciples, "When the Son of Man comes, will he find faith on the earth?" (Luke 18:8). It's a good question, because we live in an age of great paradox. We believe Jesus is coming soon, but so many don't have a clue what that means for their lives. Like the ten virgins waiting for the bridegroom, many are running out of oil and they don't even recognize it.

Eternal Vision

George Barna, a well-respected Church researcher of many years, just concluded another study of evangelicals in America. His findings show evangelicals declining in America from 12% ten years ago to 5% today. Now this does not mean there are less people going to church. People are still in the pews and still warming benches. But what it does mean is that people who believe in basic scriptural principles, such as Jesus being the only way to salvation, are rapidly decreasing in number.[1]

The "love of many" is growing colder as the days grow steadily more evil and the remaining hours slip fast away before our Lord's second coming. The enemy is waging war against our capacity to fulfill the Great Commission as never before. In the subtlest ways possible, he is gradually eroding the foundations of holiness, purity and faithfulness to the Word of God. He has only one objective and that is to shut us down altogether. He doesn't care about anything else. He knows exactly what awaits him when the Great Commission is finished. He has only one focus and he will never lose it. Can you just imagine what it might be like to work for this guy? Imagine the intensity of someone who is fighting to escape eternal judgment and his end is only moments away!

There is no doubt in my mind that Satan takes the Great Commission far more seriously than we do. Millions of people have bought into his lie that the lost are going to be okay. Millions of believers have written off the Great Commission as a relic from the past. Millions have succumbed to the brain washing of a cleverly organized campaign to eliminate from our hearts and minds any passion for those who are perishing. We have told ourselves, "They're going to be okay. There is good in every religion. Don't they all believe in God anyway? You know if I were God I would find a way to save everybody. What's so hard about that?"

GETTING PERSPECTIVE

But here is what the Bible says and I would encourage you to memorize this. These are the words of Jesus to the apostle Paul. These words will rise up and come to life and they will accuse many in this generation. Jesus said:

> "I am sending you to them
> to open their eyes and turn them
> from *darkness to light*
> and from the *power of Satan to God*,
> so that they might *receive forgiveness* of sins
> and a place among those
> who are sanctified by *faith in me*."
> (Acts 26:17-18)

From this heavenly mandate we can learn three important things. First, the lost *are* in darkness. Second, as if that were not enough, the lost *remain* under the power of Satan. And third, the whole reason we are being sent, the whole purpose of our going, is so that—and mark those words—*so that* they might receive forgiveness of sins. The Great Commission is not an option. It is a rescue operation where the lives of billions are at stake. It's the only priority we've been given and if it's not your top priority, you need to ask yourself *why not* and *whose program am I following?*

NEW VISION

I once asked a friend, "If you could go to heaven and ask God one question, what would it be?" Immediately she replied, "I would ask him what I am supposed to do with my life." What an awesome heart! I think everyone would like a clear answer to that question (well, I hope so anyway). And while I can't tell you specifically what

God has planned for you, I know this much, until we enter into eternity, God's plan for you will involve your participation in fulfilling the Great Commission and preparing the way for his coming. It's the only thing on the agenda!

The Kingdom's objective for our time is not a mystery. It is clear and focused: every person in every language, tribe and nation must be given an opportunity to say *Yes* to Jesus and become his disciple. Therefore, if you are in the Kingdom this is your mission statement also. The issue is not whether you are to be involved, but *how*.

Since God is our commander, he is the one who will be setting up opportunities for each believer to make the greatest impact possible in bringing the gospel to all people, everywhere. If we want to be effective for Jesus we have to think in these terms:

> How can I use the gifts God has given me,
> combined with the opportunities he has opened up,
> to further the *completion* of the Great Commission
> in the *greatest* possible way?

If this becomes the focus of your life, no matter where you are, you will make an eternal difference. Most people miss out because they refuse to ask the question. They refuse to put Jesus on the throne of their life. They simply don't want to find out. But what a sad way to blow off the most incredible moment of your eternal life in Christ!

The fact is, these are very exciting times to be alive. You don't want to be left out! Most people don't understand or aren't aware of the significant things that are going on all over the world to "hasten his coming" (2 Pet. 3:12). We have to ask God to open our eyes and lift them up to the harvest fields. Did you know that we are in the

Getting Perspective

midst of the greatest harvest the world has ever known? More ethnic groups have seen the Church established among them in the 20th century than in all other centuries combined! This is a very frightening reality for the Devil. But very exciting for us! It means we are close. *Very close*. For the first time in history we are only a few years away from seeing the gospel proclaimed in every nation, tribe and tongue. Jesus said this *will* happen. He said not only will this happen, but it *must* happen before the end can come (Mt. 24:14; Mk. 13:10). Everyone in the final generation before the Lord's return will be given an opportunity to give their lives to Jesus.

That final generation may very well be the one we are living in today. The signs of the times are exciting. The gospel is accelerating with tremendous speed in a way that no other generation has ever witnessed. In the first century after Christ there were 400 unbelievers for every one believer. Today there are only 10 unbelievers for every one believer! Most people find this hard to believe. But it's true. There are over 550 million evangelical Christians in the world today. 90% of these live in the non-western world and are the result of missionary efforts over the last century. This means that believers are now strategically spread out all over the world. They live in every country and major city, and speak a total of over 4,000 languages. Close to 300 million evangelicals have come to Christ as a direct result of missionary sending all over the world. And while this is tremendous, we must keep in mind that much remains to be done. There is still an urgent and costly rescue operation under way and the lives of billions are at stake.[2]

In our world today, there are 2.7 billion persons who live with virtually no access to the gospel. They live among the least evangelized peoples of the world—receiving the least amount of organized missionary effort. In a region known as the 10/40 Window (so called because it is between ten and forty degrees latitude—see map), 1.3 billion Muslims, 800 million Hindus and 500 million Buddhists live in absolute darkness and Satanic bondage. Missionaries have identified close to 2,000 tribes and ethnic groups that have yet to see a disciple-making movement established among them. In India alone there are over 500,000 villages without a church. They have never heard of Jesus, they don't know what he has done for them, and unless someone goes they will never know. Among those in the 10/40 Window, fifty thousand people will die every day, most of whom never had someone come live among them to share Christ's love.[3]

In almost every country in the 10/40 Window, missionary work is greatly restricted. You can't show up in these countries and say, "I'm here to tell your people about Jesus—the only way, the truth and the life." *Visa denied! Confiscate his luggage and put this guy back on the plane!* In many countries it's illegal to share your faith. In over a dozen countries, Christians are greatly persecuted and many are imprisoned for following Christ. But in all of these countries the gospel is being preached. The Holy Spirit is working. And you can be a part of it on your knees in prayer and intercession, and perhaps one day, if the Lord opens the door, by going in a creative way to let the light of Christ shine through you in a land of great darkness.

There is a war going on and the lives of billions are at stake. This is not the time for timidity. This is not the time for living in comfort and security. This is the time for risking everything to rescue those for whom Christ died. This is the eternal moment for being willing to go anywhere and do anything for the sake of the Kingdom. This is *not* the occasion for saving one's life. I often wonder, "What exactly are people saving their lives for anyway?" What a shock it must be that death comes just the same! This is the *only* opportunity you

10/40 WINDOW

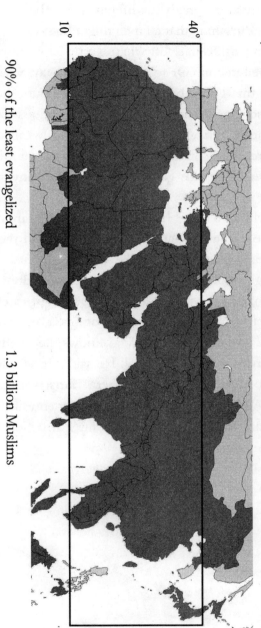

- 90% of the least evangelized
- 50,000 die every day without Christ
- 85% of the poorest of the poor
- 90% of the world's "restricted" countries

- 1.3 billion Muslims
- 800 million Hindus
- 500 million Buddhists
- 2,000 least-evangelized ethnic groups

will *ever* have to give your life away for the sake of the One who gave up everything that all men might be saved.

So let's ask ourselves: what exactly is *our* responsibility to those in our generation? Or to put it another way, what is *my* responsibility, now that I have been rescued, to seek out others who might also need rescuing? I believe the answer is obvious to anyone with a listening heart. Quite simply, we are not only called, but we are quite *able* to reach all of them. There is no reason why we cannot give every person in this generation a personal invitation to become a follower of Jesus.

So why don't we? If Jesus were walking among us today, where might he lead us? What might he ask of us? If the apostle Paul were here today, what might he be doing—where might we find him? You might look for him in the jungles of Indonesia, searching with determination for that lost tribe. You might catch him cruising the Ganges River into the heartland of India, on his way to some unevangelized Hindu village. Who knows, he might even be dodging bullets in an inner city school. He said, "It has always been my ambition to preach the gospel where Christ was not known" (Rom. 15:20). And he lived his life to the very end like these words really mattered. May his prayer and his life's ambition become the heartcry of this generation!

CHAPTER TWO

☙

STAYING FOCUSED

"I press on towards the goal to win the prize for which God has called me heavenward in Christ Jesus." (Phil. 3:14)

*T*he closer we get to the end, the closer we need to pay attention to our Heavenly Coach. If you've ever played on a championship team, or had the privilege of coaching one, you know what this means. The final few moments of a game can be the most crucial. Each player needs to stay focused and work as a unit with the others. In the midst of all the pressure, and in spite of any surprises, a winning team has to keep it together and focus on the game plan. The job of the coach is to make sure that happens.

Jesus did something like this with his team in Matthew 24, just two days before he would go to the cross. His disciples asked a good question. "Tell us," they said, "what will be the sign of your coming and the end of the age?" (Matt. 24:3). Notice they were not looking for "the signs" (plural), but *the sign* (singular). They wanted something so clear, no one could possibly miss it.

So Jesus took the opportunity to give them a glimpse into the future. He spoke directly to a generation that would be living in the last days and he made it clear what their world would be like. In a way, his words are even more relevant today than they were two thousand years ago. The description he gave us has proven to be accurate in every detail. Pick up any newspaper on any given day and you will practically be reading a description from Matthew 24. Violence fills the headlines. Terror, uncertainty, and natural disasters fill all the earth. Injustice prevails. Evil men have their way. Christians are being hounded, persecuted and martyred in dozens of countries.

Now to the triumph-seeking disciples, this may have sounded a little disappointing. But a perfect world was *not* the sign he gave them. He left his disciples no grand illusions of creating a utopian world, free of disease, suffering and war. Rather, he said wicked and evil men would triumph until the end. The love of many would grow cold. There would be famines, civil unrest and international turmoil up until the last moment of the final hour of the final day (Matt. 24:6-8).

But then in the middle of all this, Jesus stops and gives a warning. He adds, "See to it that you are not alarmed. Such things much happen, but the end is still to come" (v. 6). In other words, these things are not the main event. In fact, they are the distractions. Or to put it like a football coach might say it, "Whatever happens out there, keep your eye on the ball. Watch for the diversions. Stick to the game plan."

In the same way, Jesus wanted his disciples to remain focused. They would not be able to stop the terrible things coming in the days ahead. But just the same, they were not to bury themselves in underground bunkers and disappear. They had a job to do, a special focus to keep until the end. And so as requested, they were given a clear and definite sign that would guide them to the finish:

THE SIGN OF THE TIMES

> This gospel of the Kingdom *will be* preached,
> and *must first be* preached,
> in all the world as a testimony to all nations
> *and then* the end will come.
> (Matt. 24:14; Mark 13:10)

The sign Jesus left his disciples was the fulfillment of the Great Commission. It was like a measuring stick that would let us know how close we were to the end. This assignment had to be completed, and then, and only then, would he return. In effect, Jesus was throwing the ball back in their court. He was saying, "Finish what I've started and I'll be back." In other words, *Don't wait around for the end—get out there and do something about it!*

Certainly there will be famines and earthquakes and wars (and every generation can point to such things). But the final stroke on heaven's end-time clock will be something so unique, no other generation can claim it. The result will be a great multitude that no one can count—from every "nation, tribe, people and language"—standing before the throne, worshiping the Lamb (Rev. 7:9).

Everything else that we do will perish. All other endeavors will be forgotten. All else will fail. But not the Great Commission. It is the *only* assignment we've been given to *complete*. That is why Scripture says we are to "look forward to the day of God and *speed its coming*" (2 Pet. 3:12).

Now this priority focus does not exempt us from speaking out against evil and fighting injustice wherever we find it. We should, and we must, oppose every work of the evil one. But we must always keep the big picture in perspective. We must not be distracted from doing the one thing which *only we can do*. Our assignment is to go make disciples of all nations. The World Health Organization is not going to do this for us, nor is the United Nations. *Nor can they.* What's more, these organizations will not succeed in eradicating poverty, disease, injustice and war. As long as Satan is on the loose, as long as people are under his control and living under the curse of sin, this world will go from bad to worse. We live in a condemned world that awaits a final judgment from the Lord. Our only lasting hope is his return. He is the only one who will give us a "a new heaven and a new earth." Not the United Nations. Not the European Union. And certainly not the Americans!

Jesus will return the moment his global mission is completed. This means the timetables of history have been turning in perfect alignment with our obedience and faithfulness to the Great Commission. Two thousand years ago this assignment was given, and true believers in Christ have come a long way in fulfilling it. The finish line is well within view, and his coming has never seemed so close. We all know it and feel it. But how many, I wonder, are actually doing something about it? How many are in the race, running faithfully to the end? And how many are merely spectating, with popcorn and binoculars in hand?

The truth is, most of us still need to wake up, take a deep breath, and smell planet earth. The place is rotten to the core, but how many have become accustomed to the stench! We need to pull ourselves together and get on board with God's program for this generation. This is not a time for wondering. It's a time for knowing. We need to recognize why we're here and get moving with that purpose.

If the love of many is sure to grow cold before the end, we ought to make sure we are white hot and getting hotter. All of us need to seriously re-examine the direction our lives are headed in and cut out all distractions, hindrances and foolish desires. As time begins to run out for this world, we need to keep our eyes on Jesus and find out what he wants done. We need to ask and we need to listen. We need to remember what this place is all about and how we ought to live in light of his soon coming. We need to protect our eternal vision by living holy lives and learning to pray in faith and perseverance. We need to remember who we are and what we've been called to be, and why it matters.

REMEMBERING WHERE WE ARE

Heaven's Hall of Fame is filled with people who came to understand where they were living and who made up their minds to live accordingly. Trapped in enemy occupied territory, they refused to cower beneath the radar, but instead they resolved to resist and fight and pursue the enemy. Think of Hitler's Nazi Germany or Stalin's communist regime, and you're just getting warm. What might it mean to live in such places as a follower of Jesus?

It's a challenging question, because the world we live in, when viewed through spiritual lenses, makes Nazi Germany look like a walk in the park. Hitler in his worst moments could never have conceived what Satan and his demons do to billions of people all over the world, day and night without pause or mercy. If only we could see our world the way heaven sees it, even for a brief moment, we could never go about our lives, business as usual. We would be immediately challenged to join in heaven's rescue operation and engage the enemy, though it cost us all we possess. We would be compelled to set aside all other ambitions and desires, personal plans and petty agendas, and fight hard until the last battle was won and the Great Commission was finally finished.

The Bible tells the story of such people, who saw this world for what it was, and who refused to ignore or set aside the implications of this reality for their lives. Scripture says, "They were stoned; they were sawed in two; they were put to death by the sword. They went about in sheepskins and goatskins, *destitute, persecuted and mistreated.* They wandered in deserts and mountains and in caves and holes in the ground" (Heb. 11:37-38).

The great missionary Paul said of himself and his fellow believers, "To this very hour we go hungry and thirsty, we are in rags, we are brutally treated, we are homeless . . . up to this moment we have become the scum of the earth and the refuse of the world" (1 Cor. 4:11-13). I don't know about you, but I think we have a lot to learn about what it means to follow Jesus. If this were the description on the wanted ad, how many today would sign up? Can we really identify with these guys? Would they feel at ease with our modern, comfortable Christianity?

Somehow these guys just got it. They saw the oppression. They heard the cries. They felt the suffering of those around them. They knew exactly where they were and what mattered most in a place like this. They chose to understand it. They lived in a reality that very few, even today, remotely understand. They saw the spiritual barbwire, the invisible watchtowers, and the shrouded prison guards. They smelled the stench of death all around them. They saw this world as a Satanic controlled prisoner-of-war camp, where the only thing that mattered was resistance against the enemy and rescuing those within. There was nothing else to live or die for. Only one struggle. One purpose. One mission. One rescue operation.

So the question begs itself to be asked, *are there really two kinds of believers?* Those who work hard and those who take it easy? Those who risk their lives and those who shrink back? Those who fight against the tyranny of this evil age and those who comply with it?

Staying Focused

What does Scripture mean when it says, "*Everyone* who wants to live a godly life in Christ Jesus *will be* persecuted?" (2 Tim. 3:12). Is there something about truly following Jesus that demands a life of conflict with the world? Are we all called to the same fellowship as those who went before us and refused to settle down here? Those who *could not* close their eyes and shut their ears to a world that was dying? Is God still calling? Is he calling me? Is he calling you?

During World War II, Americans were asked to consecrate themselves to a *wartime lifestyle*. Not everyone could make it out to the frontlines, but each had a part to play. They were asked to buy war bonds, grow Victory Gardens, and conserve metal and rubber. Families bought world maps and put them up in their dining rooms. Each night they would listen to the radio and get the latest reports, placing pins on the map to mark the progress of the Allied efforts. They were asked to send their sons and daughters. They were asked to pray. They were asked to volunteer. It was an all-out mobilization effort to stop a madman from enslaving the world.

I think that's a great example of how we are called to live today as followers of Jesus. We have become members of a Kingdom that has launched a full-scale assault against the forces of darkness. We are in a war like no other, and our lives must reflect that reality. We can't just spend money any way we like. We can't just take a break for ten years and let others pick up the slack. We can't just use our talents as if they were ours to gamble. We're gambling with people's lives! During WWII the entire country mobilized for war because they understood what was at stake. Every industry, every scrap of metal, every skill was subject to the urgency of the cause. Signs on the highways read, "Is this trip really necessary?" People would confront each other if they saw something out of line and say, "Hey, don't you know there's a war on?"

Eternal Vision

We can learn a lot from this period about how Jesus intended his disciples to live and think. Jesus came to put an end to a rebellion that has enslaved the lives of billions of people. Signing up to follow Jesus is signing up to fight in this cause. Wherever there are people created for worship who are being held captive by Satan's dark regime, that's where the cause is and that's where we're headed. It's a full-scale mobilization of all that is required to rescue as many people as possible and get out of here before this world heads into its final meltdown. It's as simple as that. The complete dedication of our hearts, minds, talents and resources is being asked of us. No less is worthy of the cross that saved us. Nothing less is required for those who seek to be His followers.

Now perhaps this idea is new to you, as it once was to me. No one ever told me in the beginning that becoming a Christian was signing up to fight in this war. I was told about the cross and it was the most wonderful message I had ever heard. But no one told me about *my* cross, the one I was supposed to pick up every day. No one warned me about a struggle that is *not* against "flesh and blood," but against "the spiritual forces of evil in the heavenly realms" (Eph. 6:12). No one explained to me that this was a life and death matter for billions of ruthlessly corrupt and tirelessly evil spiritual beings. No one ever cautioned me that the moment I signed up to follow Jesus I immediately became a mortal enemy of all of them!

But now that I know, I need to ask myself: Am I taking this war as seriously as my enemy does? When Jesus called people, he didn't hesitate to tell them what they were getting themselves into. On the first day of his conversion, Jesus confronted the apostle Paul with this reality. He said, *I am sending you to open their eyes and to turn them from darkness to light and from the power of Satan to God* (Acts 26:17-18). He said the same thing to a group of fishermen on the lake shore,

Staying Focused

"Follow me, and I will make you fishers of men!" You couldn't change his mind or the subject. He was, and is, a recruiter for a global rescue operation.

Signing up to follow Jesus is signing up for his mission, his cause. It means we are under his command. Scripture says, "No one serving as a soldier gets involved in civilian affairs—he wants to please his commanding officer" (2 Tim. 2:4). As soldiers under a heavenly commission, we have an obligation to stay focused on our Commander's objectives. Can you imagine an officer in the heat of battle suddenly forgetting who he is, where he is, and what he's supposed to be doing? It sounds ridiculous, but it can happen to the best of us if we turn aside from where Jesus is leading us. We need to ask ourselves: If Jesus is my commander, am I really free to pursue whatever it is I want to do down here? Does his cause take precedent over my career? Should his heart overrule my personal desires?

The fact is, 2.7 billion souls remain without the gospel message in their language and culture. Now why is that? What has gone so wrong with our concept of who Jesus is that we would allow such a thing to happen in our generation? Two thousand ethnic groups still await faithful messengers to show them the way. If the Great Commission is God's priority, what does that say about our priorities? Are we following his program, or do we have some other, perhaps more pressing, agenda?

We really ought to see all of this from his perspective. He gave *everything* for us! He left it all! He was completely sold out to save us. He was all passion. All heart. All commitment. Somewhere, something has broken down between us—we just don't get it! If the President of the United States asked the Marines to deliver a personal message to every person living today, how long do you think it would take them? Probably only a few years or less. But here we are, acclaimed followers of the supreme Allied Commander of the Universe, and we have yet to fulfill the mission we have been given! Do the Marines actually have more loyalty and sense of obligation to their earthly commander than we do to our Heavenly Commander? What other conclusion can we make but that this is *absolutely* the truth?

So let's do some wondering together: Are we willing to consecrate ourselves to a wartime lifestyle today—to do whatever it takes to finish the Great Commission? Are we willing to think it through, and refuse to settle for shallow, lukewarm answers? Do we really want to know what Jesus expects from us, and once we get it, are we prepared to accept it?

If we're willing to start the journey, perhaps one good place to begin is in Hebrews, chapter 11. Here we find the most incredible list of first-place winners ever compiled. Emmy nominees, Nobel Prize winners and Olympic champions will all be forgotten, but not the people on this list. Their names are etched in the eternal pillars of God's Hall of Faith. Here we find a sacred fellowship of all those who finished the race and received their reward.

What made them so different?
What set them apart from their generation?

As you study their lives, one thing will begin to stand out. Each of them had a simple faith in God's heavenly promise—an enduring conviction about the eternal significance of what we do here in this life. Scripture says, "They were longing for a better country—a heavenly one. Therefore, God is not ashamed to be called their God" (Heb. 11:16). Generally speaking, it wasn't the rich and powerful, the well spoken of and appreciated that made it on his list. It was the people who were headed somewhere, and they weren't afraid to move against the flow of popular opinion or man-made tradition. They didn't go looking for persecution or the glory of a martyr's death. But they knew what God wanted done and they were determined to do it no matter what.

I'm convinced that anyone who wants to make it into God's Hall of Faith will find life increasingly uncomfortable down here. That is why the Bible tells us that friendship with the world is hatred toward God (Jas. 4:4). And I think you will find that as people begin to follow Jesus, the things of this world become dimmer and darker and altogether unattractive. Now, more than ever, we ought to heed the advice of those who made it out of here with honor. They said, "Live your lives as strangers here in reverent fear. *Do not* love the world or *anything* in the world" (1 Pet. 1:17; 1 John 2:15). They left us a dozen letters to warn us. They wrote to our generation and they said, "Don't forget what this is all about. This is not a playground, a vacation spot, or a retirement village. In the eyes of heaven it is a war zone, a toxic wasteland, a brutal concentration camp. It's the most spiritually dangerous place there has ever been or ever will be. And you *must* live accordingly."

REMEMBERING WHAT TIME IT IS

Have you ever thought about what makes the difference in the lives of those who will be ready for Christ's second coming and those who are in for a big surprise? Clearly there are going to be two kinds of Christians living in the last days—those who are working hard to see Jesus return—and those who have their own mission, their own sacred plan which no one must interrupt. But Jesus came to disrupt careers. He came to empty bank accounts. He called to anyone who would listen, "Repent! The Kingdom of God is at hand." And yet very few paid any attention, though he was King of Kings and Lord of Lords.

James wrote to the wealthy people of his day, "Now listen, you rich people, weep and wail because of the misery that is coming upon you. . . . You have hoarded wealth in the last days" (Jas. 5:1-2). Apparently these people didn't know what time it was. It wasn't time to hoard wealth. It was time to give it away—to put it to good use for the Kingdom's final campaign. Jesus came to set in motion this very special time. He called it the "end of the age"—a period of history that was going to be different from all those preceding it and one that would require a change of lifestyle and attitude.

I was once talking with a wealthy lady, who was also a believer, and I challenged her with what Jesus said about wealth: "Woe unto you who are rich, you have already received your comfort. Sell your possessions and give to the poor, provide purses for yourself that will not wear out, a treasure in heaven that will not be exhausted" (Luke 6:24; 12:33). She replied, "But what about Solomon, and Abraham, and David? Were they not all wealthy?" Sure enough they were. But the difference, I explained, is that Jesus is here. This is not the time for business as usual. We have entered into the final phase of the last war that eternal history will ever know. And in this final phase, lifestyles have to change—radically. There are no exceptions.

Now if you are a wealthy person reading this, you may object. But on what basis? Make sure it's solid, because if it's not, you will have no one to blame but yourself when you stand before the Lord. Only in the eyes of eternity can the few pieces of paper or the few bits of data on a bank's hard drive—that mean so much to us—be seen in their proper light. The fact is, you will never know if wealth is your master until the day you ask yourself, "Am I willing to give it all away?" And that's exactly the question Jesus is asking you to make. Only when you've come to terms with this question will you be in a position to make wise Kingdom investments with what has been entrusted to you. When Jesus says, "Sell your possessions and give to the poor," he is not saying be irresponsible with what you own. He is simply saying: "At the present time, don't live on what you don't need. Use the extra you have to invest in eternity."

A lot of lifestyle issues get cleared up quickly when we begin to understand where we are on God's timetable. It's like my family when we were growing up and our parents would leave us on our own for a few hours. The moment we heard that car rolling up the driveway, we knew our parents were coming home and the party was over. It's kind of the same thing here: if we knew Jesus was coming back tomorrow, how might that change things? How might we reorganize our priorities, our finances, our lifestyles? Are we doing anything that we would be ashamed of, were he to come today? Are we *not* doing some things that we *should* be doing?

To be sure, these are tough questions for even the most saintly and committed! And we all need to have answers for them. But let's take them one step further. Jesus coming back tomorrow is fairly simple. We clean up our lives and get our priorities straight and in 24 hours we're out of here. Not a bad deal. But what about ten years? What about a whole lifetime? What if you knew for sure that you would live to see Jesus come back at some point in your life, but you weren't told exactly when? Would you be hanging in there? Would you have forgotten?

This may sound a little radical, but there is one way to know for sure you will remain on track with God's program. Why not think of every new day as an extended bonus to reach more people with the gospel and invest in eternity? Daily taking up your cross is about just that: living each day as though it were the absolute last to honor and serve the Lord here on this earth—because one of these days *will be* the last one! Live that way, one day after the next, and you'll be right in step with the heartbeat of the Father.

John Wesley, one of the most famous evangelists in England during the 18th century, was once asked what he might do differently if he knew Jesus was coming back at noon the next day. He said, "Not a thing." Then he took out his schedule and told his friend exactly what he would be doing tomorrow. All his appointments remained intact; he had no need to readjust his lifestyle! He was already doing everything he could to serve his Commander-in-Chief. He was already living in such a way that he might help the most people possible prepare to meet the Lord.

So here's the question: Is everyone called to be John Wesley? Are we all called to this same singular focus, *reaching as many lost people as possible with our lives?* Is this rescue operation really the only thing that matters right now? Well, look at it this way, if everyone *did* live like John Wesley, it would only be a matter of a few years before the Great Commission would be completed and everyone on the planet would be reached with the gospel. Is that worth it? A few years of radical living so millions of lost people can enjoy eternity with us?

Some people say, "We can't all be radicals!" But this misses the point. If we were all radicals, there would be no radicals. It would just be normal. It would be heaven, for that is what heaven is, the eternal sanctuary for God's radicals. The Bible calls them the Holy, the Set-Apart, the Saints. We would call them the Radicals. But whatever you want to label them, it would be Biblical. It would be Satan's worst nightmare and heaven's delight.

The Radical Paul was given some wisdom about this by the Lord. He said, "What I mean, brothers, is that *time is short*. From now on those who have wives should live as if they had none; those who mourn, as if they did not; those who are happy, as if they were not; those who buy something, as if it were not theirs to keep; those who use the things of this world, as if not engrossed with them. For this world in its present form is passing away" (1 Cor. 7:29-31).

Now you can just imagine what might happen if someone were to say these words today. Marriage counselors would walk out. The businessmen on the church board would call an emergency meeting. This guy would not be invited back. But of course that would be a mistake. Scripture is not saying that married people should ignore each other. No one is suggesting that personal property is a bad thing. But the apostle is trying to put things in their proper perspective. He's asking, "Are you happy—well, watch out, what are you happy about? Are you sad—well, wake up, what are you sad about? This world is passing away and we all need to sober up. Stay alert. Remain focused. Be on your guard. Are you depressed? Snap out of it. Are you happy-go-lucky? Open your eyes. Are you single? Marry carefully. Are you financially set? Think again. Is that your mission in life?"

You see, all of these are temporal values when viewed from the eternal perspective. Success in God's mission will go to those who keep their eternal vision by learning to manage their temporal distractions (explain this diplomatically to your spouse!). If married people place their marriage before the Lord's agenda, it's nothing short of idolatry. And the one who seeks to save his marriage in this way will lose it. The right thing done the wrong way becomes the wrong thing. But it doesn't have to be that way. To the contrary, those who are married should work together to advance the Kingdom. Indeed, marriage can greatly enhance your effectiveness in the Lord's work. So marry carefully! Because the opposite is also true.

The overall point is basic: *the time* takes precedent over *the ideal*. In the ideal world you have heaven. But we are not there yet. We are at war. And things are very different. Not only are we at war, but we are in the final phase of that war. There will be storms like never before. Hardships and disasters will go from bad to worse. But through it all, "This gospel of the Kingdom *will* be preached and *must first* be preached in all the world as a testimony to all nations, *and then* the end *will* come" (Matt. 24:14; Mark 13:10). Christ's victorious kingdom will prevail and all nations will be reached; it's only a matter of time—and not much more at that!

REMEMBERING WHO YOU ARE

The most incredible thing that happens when you put on your eternal lenses is you get to see who you really are in Jesus. Not surprisingly, this is the one Satan wants to keep most out of focus. You are not a threat to the enemy on your own. You are a victim and a captive. But in Christ you are the most dangerous person in the world. Now I think some of us need to be reminded of this. I know I do!

Heavenly Reminder

"For though we live in the world,
we do not wage war as the world does.
The weapons we fight with
are not the weapons of the world.
On the contrary, they have divine power
to *demolish* strongholds.
We demolish arguments and every pretension
that sets itself up
against the knowledge of God."
(2 Cor. 10:3-5)

Staying Focused

In Christ we have become agents in a heavenly war. On our own we are mere "flesh and blood." But in Christ, we have been lifted up into the heavenlies as agents of his life-changing power. We are stronghold busters and heavenly lie-detectors. We carry the Light that expels the darkness and brings freedom to the captives.

Jesus said, "I have given you authority to overcome *all the power* of the enemy. *Nothing* will harm you" (Luke 10:19). This is the vision heaven wants us to see. It is the eternal side of who you are that makes Satan a little more than afraid. In fact, he is down right terrified of you discovering who you are in Christ. Fortunately for him, most believers are living at only a fraction of their true potential. The Bible says that Christ is able to do "immeasurably *more than all we ask or imagine*, according to his *power* that is at work within us" (Eph. 3:20). This, and this alone, is what makes Satan worried when he thinks about you. But most people never bother to find out what it means.

Jesus said to his disciples, "Wait in Jerusalem until you receive what was promised . . . you will receive *power* when the Holy Spirit comes upon you" (Acts 1:4,8). Up until this moment, all the disciples could think about was getting political power for themselves. But on the day of Pentecost, all of that changed. When the Holy Spirit's power filled their lives, they stood before a hostile crowd, boldly proclaimed the gospel, and saw 3,000 souls rescued from the power of Satan to the power of God in a single day.

Now that's what Christ intends for his Church! That's the future as he sees it. But how many are living like it? How many would rather settle for less? How many are content with the tyranny of shallow Christianity? One thing is certain, nowhere in Scripture do we read, "The disciples of Christ must limit their activity to attending a gleaming white, steepled church in the middle of suburbia, once a week for an hour or two." It's not in my Bible and I hope it's not in yours. But if our lives are a reflection of what we truly believe, then it might as well be one of our most cherished doctrines.

If we want our lives to make an eternal difference, our passion for Jesus must come from something far deeper than a casual commitment to church meeting participation. It must come from a desire to love him so much we would go anywhere and do anything for the sake of his Kingdom. If there is a need and we're able, then we're there. That's why we're here. Jesus didn't come here to be analyzed in theological laboratories. He came here to challenge people to take up their cross and obey him by serving those whom he came to rescue.

He is calling us, *each one of us*, to follow him into the places where his heart is broken. He is saying, "Come and open your eyes. Then let me fill them with tear drops from heaven for a world that is dying." That's what eternal vision is all about. It's seeing the world clearly through tear-stained lenses. Only then will you begin to understand who you are and what you can become in Christ. For the more you die to yourself and your desires, the more Christ will live in you, and the more he lives in you, the more he will change the world around you.

The sooner we start seeing ourselves and others in this way, the better. Jesus sees our potential. He sees Christians that need to be activated. He sees the best in all of us and he knows how to get us there. Our Lord wants every one of us to be eternal harvesters, winning hundreds, even thousands to Christ with our lives. That's the power we've been given. That's why we're here. That's how heaven sees us. And the truth is, if knowing Jesus does not leave you with a passion to make him known, then you don't really know him. You're in touch with the wrong person!

Staying Focused

When Jesus has invaded your life, you will know it. There are no shortcuts to following him. There is no substitute for full surrender. We have to kneel at the foot of the cross before we can stand and say, "I know him." There's no other way. But how many are willing? How many are asking, "Lord Jesus, take control. Have your way in me. Whatever you want me to do, whoever you want me to be, it's all yours. You're the captain of this ship from now on"?

It's absolutely impossible to make that decision without being changed for eternity. *You will know the difference!* The temporal things that seem so important now will soon become so tasteless and boring, you will never look back on them again. That's when living really begins. It's when Christ wraps you in his arms and says, "Welcome home. I missed you. Now let's get to work!"

So why wait? After all, it's not going to be Harvest Time ever again, throughout all the ages of eternity. You have nothing to lose, except what you cannot keep anyway, and everything to gain, which you can never lose. That's who you are in Christ, and don't let anyone tell you otherwise. You alone must make the choice, and you alone must answer for it.

Let no one deny you the glory of living for Jesus 100%.
Let nothing stop you from *being* who Christ died to make you.

CHAPTER THREE

ETERNAL GLORY

"I consider that our present sufferings are not worth comparing with the glory that will be revealed in us." (Romans 8:18)

John Paton was called by God to take the gospel message to some of the most dangerous people on earth. Many thought he was making a great mistake. Surely he would be killed and eaten by depraved savages on some Pacific island not yet on any map. Why waste a useful life on such people? One day an elderly gentleman came to him and solemnly warned him, "John, if you go, you will surely be eaten by cannibals." With a twinkle in his eye he responded, "Friend, you are advanced in years now, and your own prospect is to be laid in the grave, there to be eaten by worms; I confess to you, that if I can but live and die serving and honoring the Lord Jesus, it will make no difference to me whether I am eaten by cannibals or worms."[1]

John Paton's statement has always amazed me. But I suppose it is exactly what Jesus expects from his disciples. The great missionary Paul had the same perspective. Though he was beaten, stoned almost to death, chased from town to town, shipwrecked and left to rot in a dungeon, he left us these incredible words: Be joyful *always*. Give thanks in *every* circumstance; pray *continually*.² Have you ever wondered how he did it? How did a guy who endured every hardship imaginable end up so incredibly happy? How did he sit in the bottom of a dungeon and give thanks? What did he understand that allowed him to rise above every circumstance he faced?

Perhaps one of his greatest spiritual secrets can be found in a letter to the Corinthian church. He writes:

> "Though outwardly we are wasting away,
> yet inwardly we are being renewed day by day.
> For our *light and momentary* troubles
> are achieving for us an *eternal* glory
> that far outweighs them all."
> (2 Cor. 4:16-17)

Have you ever found yourself thinking, "Lord, what am I doing here? There must be more to life than just getting up every morning, trudging through the day, eating wretched TV dinners, and then dropping dead into bed—only to do it all over again a few hours later?" If that sounds familiar, you're in good company. God made you to think that way. And in this passage, Scripture tells us exactly what he's up to.

You are here for a very special reason, and it has nothing to do with those microwavable, frozen TV dinners with half the fat. (If you're a Weight Watchers fan, you might want to ignore this next part.) It doesn't matter what you look like on the outside. Yes, we should take care of our bodies! But that's not our mission in life. *Our reason for being here is an eternal one.* "For what is seen is temporary, and what is unseen is eternal" (2 Cor. 4:18).

Eternal Glory

Though it is hidden from us now, God is at work as a master craftsman. He is molding and shaping us according to his purposeful design. Moment by moment, he is working on the eternal part of who you are. Like infants in a womb, our spirits are growing and developing, being transformed from one likeness into the next—even "from glory to glory" (2 Cor. 3:18). Some of us are learning to listen to that still, quiet voice and trust in His gentle assurances. And others are choosing to ignore His lead and go their own way. But eventually we all have to "graduate" from this place, and that's the whole idea. Safe and comfortable as this place may seem, we can't stay in here forever. We have to give up who we thought we were and leave behind what we know. But God helps us along—just like an unborn baby, it gets a little cramped and uncomfortable around here towards the end!

When you realize where we are in God's eternal plan, it changes the way you think about every situation you have ever been in or will ever face. If the entire reason we're here on this planet is to be developed for eternity, then everything that happens to us can be seen in this incredible light. We can truly be joyful and thankful in every circumstance, because we understand God's purpose behind it all. Everything that happens to us is for our eternal benefit. There is method to the madness. There is a reason for the obstacle courses, the long detours into what seems like nothing at all, the boss who fired you last week, and the crazy driver who just swerved in front of you, sending your car into the mud. If you're a believer, you can see all of this for what it is. You're in God's basic training camp, and he's shaping you for an eternity of glory with him.

Years from now (perhaps a lot of years for some of us!), I'm sure we will all look back with fond memories on old *Camp Stuck in the Mud* and say, "What a place! Lord, I just want to thank you. You sure knew what you were doing down there." And the sooner we realize this, and just became thankful for everything, the better off we will be. In fact, many people are actually cheating themselves, and shortchanging the eternal glory God has planned for them, by deliberately making a decision to resist his plan and stay out of the action. The Bible says, "Star differs from star in splendor. So will it be in the resurrection" (1 Cor. 15:41-42). Even as we live this day, our spirits are being shaped by what we allow to influence them, and especially by what we worship. Is it money, is it power, is it status? Or is it the love, joy and peace offered us in Christ?

The choice is ours. The Master Craftsman has an eternal plan at work in your life. And compared with eternity, the difficulties we are asked to face are truly "light and momentary." Through them, Christ is renewing us day by day, fashioning a work of art that will shine like the stars in the heavens. This is what Christ wants you to see, and when you give your life to him, your vision will never be the same. It will stretch deeper and wider and farther than you could ever possibly imagine or even know to desire.

OFF WITH THE BLINDERS

The older and more mature we become, the more our Heavenly Coach wants us to focus on what is important in the light of eternity. When he sees this world he is not impressed by what impresses us. Presently, his vision is focused on one thing only, and yet most people never see it. We're so busy spinning on the merry-go-round, we don't even have time to see it. But when Jesus saw humanity he didn't just see a mass of people. He saw individuals who were being "harassed and helpless like sheep without a shepherd" (Matt. 9:36). He saw Satan's handiwork and it moved him to great compassion and prayer. He saw people in darkness and under the influence of

Satan's power and deception. He saw people being manipulated by evil spirits. He saw our wretchedness. Our shame. Our spiritual deformity. When he saw it he wept. He pleaded with his disciples that they might see it: "Open your eyes and look at the fields. They are ripe unto harvest!" He said, "The harvest is plentiful but the workers are few. Ask the Lord of the harvest, therefore, to send out workers into his harvest field" (John 4:35; Matt. 9:37-38).

Anyone who has ever been a farmer can sense the urgency here. This is one of the most moving and powerful statements in the Bible. Jesus is literally saying, "I need your help!" As incredible as that may seem, Jesus wants us to understand how important we are to his mission. Unless we do our part, he can't do his. It's that simple. When we finally confront ourselves with this reality—with our responsibility to join with him in the harvest, to ask and seek, and to get out there and bring it in—we will finally begin to understand the heart of Jesus. He *longs* to save people. It's all he's thinking about, day and night.

Chuck Pierce, founder of World Vision, once asked, "Let my heart be broken with the things that break the heart of God." I can think of no greater prayer for a believer to pray than this one. It's basically saying, "Lord, I want to be like you. Fill my heart with your desire." The Lord answered Chuck's request, and as a result, many others saw what heaven allowed him to see. That's my prayer as well. I'm asking God to take off the blinders. A heart that's not broken for those without Jesus is a heart that has closed its eyes to spiritual realities.

The gift of spiritual sight is exactly what Christ died to bring us. He wants to open our eyes. So I'm asking, and I intend to keep asking until I receive all that Christ has for me. Some of us are going through life peeping and squinting. But what an awesome gift it would be if you could look at an elderly, believing lady, who has been praying and fasting for God's purposes all her life, and see what God sees? You would see a giant. (And it might scare ya a bit, so be nice.) Or equally, if you could see past the charm, talent and beauty of those whom the world admires most and see what Jesus saw when he looked at the great people of his day. (You might lose your lunch on this one, so eat lightly before viewing!)

Seeing the world through heaven's eyes compels us to change everything about ourselves: our prayer life, our concern for others, our sinful habits, and who we choose to admire. Once we have seen the power and devastation of sin, can we so easily sin again? Once we have witnessed its horror in the lives of others, can we possibly be indifferent about the condition of the lost?

This world is full of spiritual leprosy patients who are not only blind, deaf and dumb, but fumbling their way through a minefield. Billions today are being held captive by a strongman that makes Adolph Hitler look like a schoolyard bully. But how many ever come to see this holocaust as Jesus sees it? Or really want to? How many share his concern that each day 50,000 souls are perishing among the 2.7 billion least evangelized in the 10/40 Window? How many will let their hearts be broken with this reality? Not many ever make it there. But that's the goal and that's where Jesus wants us to be.

Your Camp Instructor wants to transfer your thinking about this world and take it to the next level—that you might understand what is actually the *real and more permanent* world we are heading into. For this present world is "light and momentary." It is transitory. It will vanish and hardly be remembered. But what happens here will go on, it will ripple into eternity. That's what Jesus sees, and that's what we must learn to see as well if we are going to be effective for him.

The amazing thing is, when you start to *act* like the realities of the

Bible are true, your vision starts to focus—or perhaps better put, it starts to "clear up." When you behave like people around you are spiritually dying without Christ, you actually begin to see them the way heaven sees them. Satan's goal is to spiritually blind us, and he starts from the moment you enter his world. It is only when you begin to *live* like spiritual realities matter that he must flee and his deceptions with him. The reason we remain lifeless and without passion for the lost is simply because we aren't trying to reach them. If you wait for the passion to come before you go, you'll never go anywhere. But set out with Christ and you will soon watch *his* passion flow into you like a river of love and unshakeable conviction. You simply have to experience his great love to believe it and want others to receive it.

NEW ATTITUDE

A missionary colleague of mine was once approached with a job offer that far exceeded anything he had ever dreamed possible. It was a tempting offer, because just a few days before he had decided to give his life for missionary service. So he couldn't help wondering why this was happening—why now? What was God up to? Now looking back, he can see why God allowed him this opportunity. It was a chance to strengthen his resolve and seal his commitment. Though a little confused at first, after praying about it he knew what to do, and there was no doubt in his mind. When the company representative sat him down and offered him the package of a lifetime, my friend looked him in the eyes and said, "No thanks, I've decided to become a missionary." He recalls, "You could have seen his jaw drop to the floor."

My friend never regretted making that decision. It was no turning back. When you set out to follow Jesus, the first thing he will do is give you a new attitude on life—a new perspective on what sacrifice is all about. The world doesn't understand Kingdom sacrifice. It can't, it never will. Don't expect it to. The world has its eyes glued to a mirror that only reflects the fleeting rays of earthly glory. They can't see the part of them that God wants them to see. By default, those who have their minds set on a temporal perspective will ridicule what comes natural to you. They'll shake their heads and say, "What a waste. He had such a promising career ahead of him." But that's okay, love them anyway. They have no other choice but to think as they do.

Jesus said to his disciples, "In this world you will have trouble. But take heart! I have overcome the world" (John 16:33). Your Camp Instructor has been there and back again. Jesus didn't come here with this one under his belt. He landed here without any trophies or medals. He left the glory and power behind. He told his angels to stand down and stand back. He checked his sidearms at the door, so to speak, and walked in empty-handed.

Yet to the surprise of all the hosts of darkness, he still overcame! He lived a perfect life, without fault or sin. Have you ever wondered how he did it? What made the difference between his life and those of his peers? How did he pull it off? The answer is positively life-changing. The one thing different about Jesus was simply this: He had heaven's perspective. *He knew why he was here, where he was going, and why his faithfulness mattered.* He knew what life was all about and he saw God's purpose behind everything. He understood what it would take, and he knew what lay on the other side of the cross.

So the Bible says, "Fix your eyes on Jesus, the author *and* perfecter of our faith." For he endured the cross, "scorning its shame," and he did it all "for the joy set before him" (Heb. 12:2). If we graduate from this earthly camp without realizing what we're here for, we have surely lost a great reward—the joy and freedom Jesus knew when he overcame all the best Satan had to offer him.

We are not here to build great palaces of comfort, or excel in a particular career, or break the world's record in discus throwing. While there is nothing wrong with any of those things in and of themselves, they are going to make poor summaries of our performance when we stand before our Commander on graduation day. Success in this training program is not to be measured in terms of what we have accomplished. But rather, it will be measured in terms of *who* we have become in Christ, and as a result of this, what *he has accomplished* through us. That's why we're here—to become instruments of God's love and grace through whom his Kingdom authority will be administered.

Yes, it will be difficult. This camp isn't designed for your comfort. And yes, it will likely be painful. (But try not to think of that too much!) Every athlete knows the rule. In this camp it's the same: No earthly pain, no heavenly gain! But through it all, try to remember what Jesus taught his disciples: "Whatever happens, I'll be there, I'm in control of it all." And so he says, "Do not worry about your life—what you will eat; or about your body, what you will wear . . . For the pagan world runs after all such things. . . . But *seek first* his Kingdom and all these things will be given to you as well (Luke 12:22-34; Matt 6:33). So just relax and enjoy the ride. You're in very good hands! The same hands that formed the universe are holding yours now. And rest assured, your Heavenly Father knows how to take care of his own. The safest place you can possibly be is in the center of his purpose and will for your life.

So in the end, you will see this place for what it really is. Problems, impossibilities, hopeless situations—that's the whole purpose of this camp! It's why we worship; it's why we pray; it's why we study his promises. We just want to know him, because in knowing him we become more like him, and as we become more like him we are changed forever in the light of his glory.

As you begin to see life in the spiritual dimensions, you come to understand what "light and momentary" really means. Compared with the reality of Satanic power in people's lives, compared with all eternity with or without Jesus, what we are being asked to do for a few short years really isn't so bad. Sacrifice, when viewed through spiritual lenses, is an outsider's perspective. Compared with what we are gaining, the so-called sacrifice is a small investment. Not only that, our investment is completely risk-free! Jesus says give me a few years and I will fashion you for eternity. I will give you a part in the greatest campaign of eternal history. I will empower you to make an enduring mark on the eternal destiny of an entire generation. What more could you ask for!

THE POWER OF SACRIFICE

If you could ask Satan what is the one thing he hates the most, he would point you to the cross. Satan hates sacrifice with a passion. In the realm of spiritual warfare, sacrifice is like a nuclear bomb. When we are brought low, Christ is lifted up. In fact, worship goes way beyond just singing songs on Sunday. Worship is any form of sacrifice where God gets the glory. And when we worship, Satan trembles, demons run for dear life, and darkness retreats into its sinister cave. Then the lies begin to crumble, the deceptions start to lift, and the bondages loosen their grip.

Time after time God has used sacrifice to bring praise to his name and advance the Kingdom's presence in the dark domains of this world. When Jim Elliot and four of his missionary companions were martyred in the jungles of South America, many people were shocked at what proceeded from this seemingly dark event. What Satan intended for evil, God used for good. The story of their heroism challenged an entire generation to heed the call of Christ. Instead of fear and cynicism, God's people responded with courage and conviction to fill the ranks of their fallen comrades.

Recently, I met with a missionary who is now vice president of World Vision. He recounted to me how God used the martyrdom of Jim Elliot in his life. He was in college, in India at the time, and seeking the Lord's will for his life. When news came of Jim Elliot's martyrdom, the Holy Spirit moved powerfully upon him and four others. They felt the Lord calling them to form an organization to send more missionaries into the harvest fields of the world. They formed a prayer group and called it the Friends Missionary Prayer Band (FMPB). From their one example over thirty years ago, close to 1,200 prayer bands have been organized all throughout India, continuing to this day. From these groups, hundreds of missionaries have been sent out to some of the most unreached areas of the nation.

The ripple of Jim Elliot's martyrdom stretches far into eternity. One story in particular is the most amazing I have ever heard. One of the five founders of FMPB is named Patrick Joshua. I had the privilege of meeting with him as well, not too long ago. (In all honesty I must say this guy is the most humble person I have ever met! His life is filled with the presence and power of Christ. I walked away from that meeting a changed person.)

During our time together, he recounted to me the following story that broke my heart but stirred my will. He told me of one of the fiercest, most unreached tribes in India, the Maltol tribe. FMPB had already sent many missionaries there and each had died of cerebral malaria soon after their work began. Remarkably, Patrick's son, whom he had named Jim Elliot, received a call to preach the gospel to this group. It wasn't an easy decision to let him go. But God had called him. So the answer was a definite, "Yes, you must go." Despite the danger, Jim Elliot Joshua sensed God was going to do something tremendous among this group. He knew not how, but he knew the miracle was close at hand. And indeed it was, but it would come at great sacrifice. After a short time of ministry, he too contracted cerebral malaria (a disease that causes hemorrhaging of the brain). Despite the incredible pain, he decided to continue ministering among them. Throughout the ordeal he persevered in showing Christ's love and sharing the gospel with as many as possible until the Lord took him home. When the tribesmen saw this, they were greatly moved. These missionaries were not afraid to die for what they believed. So they asked for more. Soon a great revival broke out among them that continues to this day. Close to 20,000 have come to know Jesus. The government leaders in that area were shocked and amazed for this group was the most troublesome tribe in India!

Jesus said, "Unless a kernel of wheat falls to the ground and dies, it remains only a single seed. But if it dies, it produces many seeds" (John 12:24). There is no evil that can overwhelm the love of God. He can turn every tragedy into hope, and every sacrifice into glory. Whenever his people have gone the distance, God has always moved in ways that far exceeded their greatest expectations.

My life and family have also been touched by the sacrifice of a young missionary, who died almost a century ago. His name was William Borden. He was born into a wealthy, prestigious family and could have done anything with his life. But while he was studying at Yale, he received a call from God to go to China as a missionary.

After graduation, he gave away his entire inheritance and signed up with the China Inland Mission, which had been founded by Hudson Taylor to reach the millions of unevangelized in China's interior. William Borden felt called to reach the Muslim Uighurs (a tribe of 9 million today), so on his way to China he stopped over in Egypt for a brief consultation. But while he was there, he contracted spinal meningitis and died very suddenly. It wasn't long before the press picked up the story. Within a few days, the whole Christian world had heard about his life. The result was stunning. As with Jim Elliott, many hundreds testified how God called them into missionary service upon hearing what had happened to him.

My dad was one of them, though in a delayed sort of way. While my grandma was reading a book called *Borden of Yale*, she was so inspired she dedicated my father to be a missionary, though he was still in the womb! (She never told him about it until years later when it actually happened.) My dad said all his life he felt God leading him into missionary service, though his parents never pressured him in that way. Only later did he understand the reason. Apparently the Lord takes baby dedications seriously! Now, today, I and many of my brothers and sisters are also in full-time missionary service.

It really is amazing what God will do through the willing sacrifice of his people. The apostle Paul said, "Christ's love compels us, because we are convinced that one died for all . . . that those who live should no longer live for themselves but for him who died for them and was raised again" (2 Cor. 5:14-15). Christ's love *compels* us to give everything for his glory. And when we are following in the footsteps of Jesus, what he will do through a life of sacrifice will shock even the greatest critic. It will ripple through the generations and thunder into eternity.

When Jesus went to the cross, the disciples thought it was all for nothing. Jesus knew better. When Paul and Silas were chained in prison, many thought the Lord had abandoned them. They knew better. They understood what was going on. God was getting them ready for something even greater and more incredible than had ever been seen before.

So instead of complaining, they just started praising. They could have said, "Lord, what have you done to us! You sent us here to preach the gospel; now how are we supposed to do that in here!" But they soon realized God wanted them to simply worship him in that dark place. And, oh, did they worship! Their praises reached the heavens and shook the earth below. The jailer brought them out and asked only one thing, "Sirs, what must I do to be saved?" (Acts 16:30). His whole family believed and a new church was born in that city.

From beginning to end, missions is all about God. His glory. His worship. His faithfulness. "Therefore," Paul declared, "I will boast all the more gladly about my weaknesses, so that Christ's power may rest on me" (2 Cor. 12:9). All great men and women of God have come to this same conclusion. *When we are in our greatest position of weakness, He is in the greatest position of power in our lives.*

So don't lose heart. When your world falls apart and you feel like a dismal failure—once again, don't forget, *You're not alone.* Peter was there. Paul was there. Anyone who has done anything lasting for the Lord has been there. God never let any of them down, and he's not going to start with you.

> "For the Kingdom of God is not a matter of talk, but of power. That is why, for Christ's sake, I delight in weaknesses, in insults, in hardships, in persecutions, in difficulties. For when I am weak, then I am strong."
> (1 Cor. 4:20; 2 Cor. 12:10)

CHAPTER FOUR

⁓

THE REAL DANGER

"It will be good for those servants whose master finds them ready, even if he comes in the second or third watch of the night." (Luke 12:38)

Never before have so many people been praying for the salvation of Muslims, and never before have so many been responding to the gospel. There are 1.3 billion Muslims in the world today, and they are some of the most difficult people to reach with the gospel. But conservative estimates indicate that well over one million have come to know Christ in the last twenty years![1] Something supernatural is happening today in Muslim lands that is completely unexplainable apart from God. All over the world, in recent years, thousands of Muslims have been receiving dreams, visions and visitations from Jesus.

Take Abdul, for example. He was an Egyptian Muslim, and like many of his peers, he hated "Christians" for what he saw them doing to his Muslim brothers around the world. But he was curious about what Jesus taught, and one of his friends had given him a Bible. So he began to read the Gospel of Luke. As he came across the words, "This is my son in whom I am well pleased," a strong wind

Eternal Vision

began to blow in his room and he heard a voice saying, "I am Jesus Christ, whom you hate. I am the Lord whom you are looking for." As these words were being spoken, the Holy Spirit came upon him, and Abdul just wept and wept before the presence of God. Today, he is now a follower of Jesus and an unstoppable witness for Christ in his country.

Abdul's story is not an isolated incident. All across the Muslim world, people are responding to the call of Christ, even though they know it may cost them their lives. This has definitely been the case for Omar, a Saudi Muslim who has been hunted down, arrested and even sentenced to death because of his miraculous conversion. The judge looked at Omar and said, "Deny your new found faith and you will walk out of here a free man. If not you will be beheaded." But Omar couldn't do it. He had met the Lord, face to face! One night he awoke from a terrible dream, trembling and filled with fear. In his dream he had been surrounded by the fire and terror of hell. Having no assurance of his salvation, he cried out for help. Then a brilliant light lit up his room and he heard a voice saying, "I am Jesus, come to me, I am the way to heaven. Follow me and you shall be saved from hell." Omar fell to his knees and cried, "Please help me to find you!" Then the assurance of Christ filled his heart and for the first time in his life he experienced the peace of God.

When Omar's friends found out about his conversion, they immediately had him arrested. According to Muslim law, anyone who leaves Islam must be killed. But Omar refused to turn away from his new faith in Christ. He said to the court, "I will never deny the name of Jesus. If you kill me I will go to heaven, but my blood will be on your hands." The judge was outraged at his response and sentenced him to be executed in three days time. But amazingly, Omar was never killed. The day of his beheading came and went. Two days later the guards removed his chains and told him, "Run, you demon, we do not want to see you again." Later, Omar found out what had happened. On the day he was to be executed, the judge's son suddenly died. The fear of God gripped his heart and he reversed his decision. Today, Omar is fearlessly preaching the gospel all over Saudi Arabia.

True stories like these could be told by the thousands all over the world, and not just in Muslim lands, but among Hindus, Buddhists and Jews as well. As in the days of the first century, Christ is appearing to people and saying, "Come, follow me." In these final moments before his coming, he's saying get ready, because time is quickly running out for this world. To be sure, some people will need brighter light than others because of the darkness they are in and the hardships they will face. But that's okay. It's not how you're called that's important, it's how you respond to the call you've been given. When Jesus calls, his voice is loud and clear. His purpose is not a mystery to any who would sincerely seek him. He says, "Follow me, and I will set you free. Then go tell everyone you know about what I've done." No doubt that second part is getting Abdul and Omar into a whole lot of trouble! But when Jesus sets you free, you can't help but tell everyone you meet about his wonderful power. It becomes your whole purpose for being and your entire passion for living.

WHO IS SAFER?

When Christians were dragged into the Roman arena to be devoured by lions, in the first two centuries after Christ, the world's first "sports evangelism" took place. Whole families were rounded up and told to renounce their faith. Moms and dads, even kids and grandparents were systematically arrested, condemned and executed for the amusement of the public. We have no idea what cruelty and hardness of heart must have been present in Roman society to enjoy such an event. But according to eyewitness accounts there was something different about Christian executions—something visibly noticeable, something that would leave entire audiences haunted for a lifetime. Christians praised the Lord down there. They prayed for their persecutors. They forgave their enemies. People who came to be entertained walked away evangelized. What could have been ignored as a minor sect in a very multi-religious world soon became the talk of the whole empire. These Christians were not afraid to die! Why? What did they believe in?

To be sure, the courage to give your life for something doesn't prove what you believe, only that you *do* believe it. Jesus said, "If anyone would come after me, he *must* deny himself and take up his cross and follow me" (Matt. 16:24). Being willing to give your life for the gospel is a requirement for carrying its message. Signing up to follow Jesus is signing your life away—all of it. And that is why the most dangerous place to be a Christian is not in Sudan (where 2 million Christians have been martyred in our lifetime), or China (where persecution of Christian leaders is on the rise), or Saudi Arabia (where conversion to Christianity is a capital offense). Having seen the fervor and zeal of Christians in these places, I have come to believe that the true danger lies someplace else. Perhaps it is right where Jesus said it would be—a place where the "worries of this life, the deceitfulness of wealth and the desires for other things come in and choke the word, making it unfruitful" (Mark 4:19). The real danger to Christianity is any place where the eternal perspective is hardest to see.

Recently, we met with a church leader in Sudan. We asked him why the gospel was spreading so fast in his country despite the se-

The Real Danger

vere persecution. Immediately he replied, "You know, something amazing has happened to us. We are no longer afraid to die." To look in this man's eyes and hear these words is a life-changing experience.

So I can't help but wonder, "Who is safer? A comfortable Christian in the American suburbs or this guy on Christian death row?" If this world is the most dangerous place in the universe, not because of what can happen to you physically, but because of what can destroy your soul for eternity, I would have to go with Sudan as the safest place you could possibly be as a Christian.

In this Satanic controlled world, the real dangers to enduring faith are not persecution or martyrdom, but the subtleties of comfortable Christianity that keep our eyes focused on temporal concerns and fleeting desires. No doubt that is why Jesus declared these haunting words:

> But woe to you who are rich,
> for you have already received your comfort.
> Woe to you who are well fed now,
> for you will go hungry.
> Woe to you who laugh now,
> for you will mourn and weep.
> (Luke 6:24-25)

It isn't that being rich, or eating well, or "enjoying life" is wrong. But pursuing these things as the goal of your life, and living for them at the expense of Christ's mission, is the most dangerous thing you can do at the present time. This is the worst time in eternal history to make bad judgment calls about how to live your life. We need to tread very carefully. We need to understand where we are on heaven's timetable and adjust our lifestyles accordingly. We are rapidly closing in on the final remnants of Satan's kingdom: the last ethnic groups to be reached will soon be fully evangelized. If there ever was a generation that had reason to believe our Lord's coming was near, this would be it.

Jesus designed Christianity for such a time as this. He organized it for a war. He fashioned it for an end-time army where Christianity is outlawed and considered a dangerous threat. He didn't come here to create an institution where people vie for prestige and power and maximize their comfort. He came here to bring about an "end" to history as we know it. And he said, "I am coming soon." Meaning, *this is the only thing on the agenda!* It's the only thing that matters for eternity at the present time. For as we are following him, and obeying his last command given to every disciple, we will accelerate the day of his return and the conditions associated with it. Therefore, Scripture exhorts us, "Since everything will be destroyed in this way, what kind of people ought you to be? You ought to live holy and godly lives as you look forward to the day of God and *speed* its coming" (2 Pet. 3:11-12).

This is what *true Christianity* is all about. One focus. One passion. One driving determination: to see Jesus glorified in all the earth and returning to his rightful place as ruler of the nations. That's why we're here and it's the only thing that matters at the present time. All who know Jesus as Lord know this passion. The two are never want for company. When you say yes to Jesus, you are saying yes to his mission. You are signing up to follow him—*wherever* he leads. And that journey will take you to the cross. It will take you to the prisons, to the camps, to the war zones of this world—to any place where Christ needs gentle hands and courageous feet. It will take you with Jesus and you will never be the same.

The Real Danger

WELCOME TO KADESH BARNEA

The Lord wants each of us to understand clearly what's up ahead and how we should get ready for it. Today, in over 20 countries it is illegal to preach the gospel, and in quite a few the penalty is death. According to the Bible, it's only going to get worse. We have much work to do, and the Bible says we need to get it done quickly—"as long as it is day." Jesus warned us that the "Night is coming, when no man can work" (John 9:4).

If only we could see this future as heaven sees it. They see the night approaching and they see how rapidly the darkness is advancing. They sense the urgency. We are living in the twilight hours of what Jesus called the "day," and we are in the midst of the greatest harvest the world has ever known. But how many harvesters are still sleeping? How many have lamps with a short supply of oil? How many have turned away to worship other gods? How sad to miss out at the last minute! How many think they are following but have chosen the wrong Christ to follow?

So let's ask ourselves: What comes to our minds today when we think about Jesus? Who is Jesus to me? Is my Jesus the one who was stripped of all dignity, beaten black and blue, lashed to the bone, and left to suffocate on a splintered cross? Do I really know this Jesus? Is he the one who said, "As the Father has sent me, so send I you"? Is that the Jesus I'm following? I can promise you this much: this was not the Jesus of those who called him "Lord, Lord" in this lifetime, but would not stay for an answer.

How easy it is to sign up, but how hard to follow! Do you remember the story of Kadesh Barnea? It is one of the saddest stories in the Bible. Kadesh Barnea was the final encampment of God's people before they were to enter the Promised Land. Twelve spies were sent ahead to scout the land and see how best to take it as the

Lord had commanded. But only two returned with a favorable report. Joshua and Caleb said, "We should by all means go up and take possession of it, for we shall surely overcome it" (Num. 13:30). They saw the giants through the eyes of heaven and said to themselves, "We'll cream those guys for sure." But the others would have no part of it and they turned all Israel with them. So the Lord led them back into the wilderness for forty years, taking them in circles from one place to the next.

One evangelical leader recently remarked, "It seems that most believers have come to a Kadesh Barnea experience at least once in their lives, and they are still living with the consequences of that moment."[2] Today, our generation faces an *eternal* Kadesh Barnea like no other generation has ever faced. The choice is ours, to take up God's promise and believe it, or turn away in fear and reject it. The Lord has given us the ability and capacity to present the gospel to every person in this generation. But it doesn't mean we will, or that everyone will get involved. Satan isn't giving up and there is still a long journey ahead of us. There are over 550 million evangelicals in the world today with more wealth, technology and political power than ever before in history. Yet 2.7 billion people are still waiting and 2,000 ethnic groups remain completely unevangelized.

Certainly the way before us is narrow and hazardous. The way is blocked by civil wars, malaria, visa restrictions, and parents who want their grandkids close to home (the latter may be the most formidable challenge). So many turn back. We meet them all the time as we preach on the Great Commission and our Lord's Second Coming. People often come up to us in tears after the message and say, "You know, Pastor, the Lord called me to the mission field, but I resisted and never went. I have been miserable ever since." Of course, it is tempting to smooth things over and say, "Well, don't worry about it, everything is going to be okay." But everything is not okay. Jesus doesn't call people without a reason. It's a very comfortable theology that says my rebellion affects only me. But nothing could be further from the truth. Consider this letter we received:

> From the first month of my conversion, I had strongly sensed the calling of God to the nations to preach the gospel to those who had not heard. But being married and having a young child, I was gripped by financial insecurity. No excuse. When it comes down to it, I trusted in my own ability to provide for my family rather than the Lord. I rationalized, but I did not follow God's priority. Have I prospered? No. Rather, it seems that I became a Jonah to every ship I boarded. The prophetic word which you have shared is true, and unfortunately I am its bad example. The process of repentance has been difficult. The promise of provision was given by Jesus to those who would seek the interests of His kingdom—to put aside their own business interests and give priority to His purposes in a world mission advance.

The person who wrote this letter is not alone. There are thousands of others like him. But very few people have the courage to speak prophetically into their lives. That's too bad because Scripture tells us that disobedience has disastrous consequences—read it from the Garden of Eden, to the forty years of wandering in the wilderness, to the destruction of Jerusalem in 70 AD. Examine the Bible from cover to cover and you will see that rebellion against God affects not only the transgressor but the entire community as well. We are not islands unto ourselves. We are connected in God's global effort and when we disobey we negatively affect his perfect plan.

Of course, we don't like to believe that. We would like to live in a no-consequence universe. But such isn't the case. Consider what God said to Ezekiel on two separate occasions:

> "When I say to a wicked man,
> 'You will surely die,'
> and *you do not warn him*
> or speak out to dissuade him from his evil ways
> *in order to save his life*,
> that man will die for his sin,
> and *I will hold you accountable* for his blood."
> (Ezek. 3:18)

Can this be possible? Can our disobedience actually have an effect on someone else? Surely if Ezekiel disobeyed God, someone else would be raised up to take his place? But that's not what God said. He warned, "that man will die for his sin." Ezekiel needed to understand the seriousness of the calling he had been given. And so do we. This is not a game where you reload and start over and the past suddenly vaporizes. These are real people and real consequences.

People who fail to grasp this reality are doomed to live a life without eternal purpose—they will wander in circles, being manipulated by one shallow desire after the next. It's a miserable existence and it doesn't end in this life. Before it is too late, we need to pray for our generation and cry out:

> "Lord, please help us!
> Deliver us from the treachery of lukewarm Christianity;
> from the deception of false discipleship;
> and from bowing to the world's perverted agenda for our lives."

The Real Danger

We need to be awakened to the very real danger of pursuing comfortable Christianity as an acceptable alternative to taking up the cross and following the Master. The truth is, my heart goes out to the person who has been miserable his whole life for not going where God has called him. But what can we say, what *ought* we to say to such a person? For the sake of the next generation we can only say one thing: "I hope you *are* miserable! It's nothing compared to the misery of those who are perishing without Christ."

It may sound harsh, but trust me, it is the *nicest* thing you can possibly say. Better we hear it now, and repent, than later when we can no longer do anything about it. We *must* obey, and we must take it seriously that we have been called to proclaim a message of eternal significance. The apostle Paul put it well when he said, "Woe unto me if I don't preach the gospel!" (1 Cor. 9:16). And I'm sure if he were here today he would say it again: Woe unto this generation if you let 2.7 billion people in the 10/40 Window perish without any concern or effort on your part.

There is no other option for followers of Jesus. We have been directed to rescue the lost from "darkness to light and from the power of Satan to God" (Acts 26:18). It really is that black and white. There are no gray areas in God's program of salvation. If you don't know Jesus as your savior, then you are in darkness and under the power of Satan. If you do know Jesus, then you've been rescued. You're on board the ship. But it's not a cruise line. It's a rescue ship and a battleship, and the moment you're on board you are called to service. That's the picture Jesus wants on your mind every moment of every day until he returns. Ask yourself, what am I doing *today* to rescue as many lost people as possible? How many people did I share the gospel with last week, last month, last year? How many people did I pray for to receive Christ as their Savior?

Eternal Vision

KEEPING THE VISION

Those of us who have grown up in modern democratic countries don't really have a concept of Lordship. This is a great handicap. We have never seen kings wield their authority with unstoppable will power. We have never trembled in the presence of someone who holds the power of life and death. Perhaps the closest we come to true "lordship" is being drafted for military service in a wartime situation. For this we can be thankful, because military service is precisely what Christianity is all about.

Biblically speaking, Jesus is the commander of God's army in both heaven and earth. But to any outside observer, it would seem that most of his army down here ought to be court-martialed for rank insubordination. Most believers walk around with a very underdeveloped, Sunday school version of Jesus—which may be helpful at the age of six, but later on has little influence on our behavior. I think we all need to have our lenses checked on this one. When the apostle John was on the island of Patmos, he saw Jesus in a much different light. There was no joking around, or high-fives, or friendly greetings on that day. Not a word was spoken. John did the first thing that came into his mind: he fell flat.

The "disciple Jesus loved" saw his friend as King of Kings and Lord of Lords. He saw Jesus for who he really was, in his exalted position as ruler of the universe. His hair was now a brilliant white and his eyes were a blazing fire. His feet were like molten bronze and his voice was like the sound of rushing waters. In his right hand he held seven stars and in his mouth a double-edged sword. His face shown like the sun. And he said, "I was dead and behold I am alive for ever and ever! And I hold the keys of death and Hades" (Rev. 1:12-18).

To be sure, this is not the Jesus you were introduced to in Sunday school. But it's the one John needed to see. And I think we need to be reminded as well. Who is this person we have signed up to follow? Could it be that many people have conjured up their own idea of who Jesus really is? Have we painted a wrong picture for people? What really comes to our minds when we think of him?

Whatever may be in our minds, here is the reality of the matter: If Jesus is my commander-in-chief, maker of heaven and earth, and he has given everything for me, who am I to deny him the right to lead me wherever he wants me to go? If he were to appear before me today, as he did to John, and if he were to entrust me with a set of instructions, might I possibly try my favorite excuse on him—"Well, you know, I'm actually very busy at the moment." Or if he were to get down on his knees and plead with me, "Please be faithful in this assignment until I return . . ." Could I possibly refuse him? If he got back up, looked me in the eyes and said, "My reward is with me, I am coming again, and I will give to everyone according to what he has done" (Rev. 22:12)—might I possibly forget these words?

But how easy it is, when our lives are full of so many distractions, entanglements, and fruitless endeavors. We have forgotten what it really *means* that Jesus is coming again. It seems that many people have a wrong idea about the Second Coming of Christ. Many are under the false impression that this is a happy time for all those who claim to be his disciples. Indeed, for some it will be. But for others, even those who called him "Lord, Lord," Jesus described his coming like this:

> "Then he will say to those on his left, 'Depart from me.'"
> *I don't know you, we don't have a relationship.*

Eternal Vision

"For I was hungry and you gave me nothing to eat,"
I was in Sudan, chained like an animal.

"I was thirsty and you gave me nothing to drink,"
They beat me mercilessly and left me to die.

"I was a stranger and you did not invite me in,"
Some people heard about me . . .

"I needed clothes and you did not clothe me,"
But they never came, they turned away.

"I was sick and in prison and you did not look after me."
All alone, I lay there, crying out.

"They also will answer, 'Lord, when did we see you hungry or thirsty or a stranger or needing clothes or sick or in prison, and did not help you?'"
Did you actually expect us to take the initiative and find out what needed to be done?

"He will reply, 'I tell you the truth, whatever you did not do for one of the least of these, you did not do for me.'"
(Matt. 25:41-45)
Taking the initiative is entirely what I'm looking for!

Keep in mind that these people called Jesus their Lord, but Jesus didn't buy it. Whatever Jesus was to these people, he was not their Lord. Perhaps he was a "genie in a bottle" or even just an idea, but definitely not a reality in their lives. A clear view of eternity cannot be acquired without taking into account this fact: we *will be* held responsible for how we lived our lives as "believers" down here. Our actions are a reflection of where our faith is—our lack of action the same. Scripture says, *"Each of us* will give an account of himself to God" (Rom. 14:12). There are no exceptions here. Therefore, "We make it our goal to please him . . . For we *must all appear* before the judgment seat of Christ, that *each one* may receive what is due him for the things done while in the body, whether good or bad" (2 Cor. 5:9-10).

What many people don't realize is that God will judge not only what we do, but what we neglect to do as well. The sins we commit and the good things we *omit* are all the same in God's sight. Consider well what Jesus taught about this. What was the crime of the servant who buried his talent in the ground (Matt. 25:14-30)? He was not a murderer or an adulterer. He was just afraid. He simply did *nothing!* He refused to take the initiative, or put himself at risk, and in the end he just sat around and took the greatest risk of all. His punishment might seem a little out of proportion. He lost his position in the Kingdom. He was called a "worthless servant." Even what he had was taken from him. But what really was his crime? What was the gravity of his treason that merited such a response from the Master? It was no less than the crime of someone entrusted with a matter of eternal significance, who neglected the responsibility of that high calling. Following Jesus is a serious matter because of what will happen to others *for eternity* if you are disobedient.

Jesus is looking for risk-takers who are willing to entrust their lives to someone who promises them only one thing: "The man who *loves* his life will lose it, while the man who *hates* his life in this world will keep it for eternal life. Whoever *loses* his life for me and for the gospel will *save* it" (John 12:25; Mark 8:35). Jesus wants people to understand where the real danger lies. It is not where Christian faith is being outlawed, harassed and persecuted, but where it is being left alone and told it's okay to live a quiet, happy-go-lucky, carefree life, without any concern for the body of Christ or the mission of his kingdom.

The burden is upon us to examine our lives and see who really is lord—who is calling the shots? What drives our behavior? What holds us back? Scripture warns us: "If you live according to the sinful nature, you will die; but if by the Spirit you *put to death* the misdeeds of the body, you will live" (Rom. 8:13). There is a part of us that needs to die. There are parts of us that remain unsurrendered to the lordship of Christ. There are fears and worries, burdens and cares, wrong desires and patterns of thought, false motives and petty grudges—many of which operate behind the scenes. Some of them you may be totally unaware of!

I'm beginning to learn the hard way that following Jesus did not end at the altar. It began there. Christ's lordship did not end when the words of surrender left my heart. The journey was just getting started. I've seen many people come and go through revivals and spiritual spurts, but some of them end up just the same. Jesus knocks on the door and gently inquires, "May I come in?" We let him in, but how easy it is to build another room with a new door! And so he knocks again. Full surrender to Christ is knocking out all the walls. Pulling out all the stops. It's saying, "Come in, Jesus, come in everywhere. Make your home in every part of me."

This issue must be settled if I want to see the vision God has for me. All great men and women of faith, without exception, have come to this same life-changing encounter with God. It might not happen in an instant. But it happens. There is a crossing over that occurs and your life is never the same. It can happen to anyone who wants it. The decision is yours alone. Ask yourself: How much do I

The Real Danger

want of Him? How much do I really love Him?

The apostle Paul said, "I resolved to know *nothing* while I was with you except Jesus Christ and him crucified" (1 Cor. 2:2). It's where all heavenly vision begins—only from the cross can we see the world clearly through the eyes of Jesus. How quickly the world would be evangelized if we all lived this way! For once I am convinced of Christ's presence and power in my life, I will not be afraid to do what Paul did, to walk where he walked, to sit in the dungeons where he sat and lift up praises that rock heaven and earth. So every day I'm asking, "Lord Jesus, show me who you are. Help me give my life to you every moment of every day. Help me this day to live for you. Let my whole life become a prayer of surrender and a demonstration of your love and faithfulness."

CHAPTER FIVE

WHERE YOUR TREASURE IS

*"But store up for yourselves treasures in heaven . . .
For where your treasure is, there your heart will be also." (Mt. 6:20-21)*

I magine it's 1941 and you're on a tour of a Nazi concentration camp with a group of journalists.

As you enter the courtyard, your tour guide explains that the camp has been divided into two halves. "This is an experimental facility," she tells the group. "What you are about to see may be a little disturbing to some." To your left you can hear the faint cries of children and infants. Somewhere over there, out of sight, a woman is weeping uncontrollably.

"People on that side have absolutely nothing to eat," your tour guide continues. "We'll go over there first."

As you enter through another set of gates, your body immediately forces you to stop. The sheer horror of what hits you overwhelms your senses and paralyzes every part of you. Piles of bodies, some stripped of all their clothes, have been stacked five to six feet high. Their skeleton faces and shrunken forms lay frozen in a sea of agony. Small kids lie famished on the floor, some holding their stomachs, others just waiting to die, numbed from the pain. Two women, with evident sorrow in their faces, have begun slowly stripping the clothes from a dead body. With temperatures dropping below freezing, every rag in this place has become a valuable commodity. Thousands of human beings, exposed and huddled for protection, lay stretched out in this vast wasteland of barbwire and frozen dirt, waiting for death to claim them in the very mass graves they have been forced to dig. From the distance, an elderly gentleman lifts his hand to you. His piercing gaze and cry for mercy will forever stain your memory. There is no way he will last the day.

"Why aren't these people being fed?" you inquire of the tour guide.

"They are, actually," she answers. "Their food allotment is quite generous. It just never reaches them."

As you pass through to the other side, you have no idea that what you are about to witness will be far more disturbing. Here on this side, the people have so much food they're playing games with it. They have food fights twice a day—as there is not much else to do here, one prisoner explains. But they're a creative bunch, no doubt about that. A few guys have organized a baseball game with some old French bread and a dinner roll. They have ear muffins to shut out the cries of those on the other side. If that doesn't work they play their music. They dance, they sing, they parade around the campfires—life is good here they tell you, compared to the other side.

"Our experiment is going exactly according to theory," announces your tour guide. "This side can help the other if they like. There are a few here who try, but they aren't usually welcome back. Altogether amusing, isn't it?"

Now I'm sure, such a scene would bring even the mildest of Christians to outrage, and rightly so. But if that is true, then I think we need to wake up. For this scene is exactly how heaven sees our world. In this Satanic controlled death camp, there are the "haves" and the "have-nots." And if you happen to be one of the Haves, then watch out, because yours is not a position of great privilege and honor. It is the opposite—it is a precarious and hazardous position, one meriting great caution and prudent behavior. For Jesus said, "Woe to you who are rich. You have already received your comfort. Sell your possessions and give to the poor. Provide purses for yourself that will not wear out, a treasure in heaven that will not be exhausted" (Luke 6:24; 12:33).

What Jesus had to say about money is perhaps the most frightening warning in Scripture. How you use your money is indeed an ethical issue, but it's more than that—according to Jesus, it's a clear sign of where your heart is. Because there are people suffering for lack of it, and Kingdom priorities yet to be fulfilled for want of it, we can no longer spend money any way we like as followers of Jesus. We are fortunate to be aware of this reality. This issue is so black and white in heaven's sight, it honestly makes me shudder to think about how ignorant we are—not because we have to be, but because we choose to be. To heaven it is all very obvious. This world is in a drought of basic resources. And some of us are sitting on vast reservoirs. Therefore, what we decide to do with it will tell heaven exactly what kind of people we are, despite any protests or clever explanations to the contrary.

More often than not, I think this is what the angels hear: "Friends, we have nothing to drink and our children are dying."

"Actually, I'm not sure we *are* friends and we hardly have a relationship. But in any case, this is my lake and I'm sorry about your situation. I wish I could help you, but I just can't. What if everyone comes here? Why don't you look someplace else . . ."

"But please, we beg of you, can you spare just a little?"

"Well, alright, but don't come back, and don't tell anyone. Here's a glass of water. And don't forget to return the glass!"

Now you may say that's a little exaggerated. No one would actually say such things. But verbalized or not, those of us in wealthy, industrialized countries proclaim these very words every day to billions less fortunate than ourselves. We live as though the rest of the world did not exist. We somehow think we've died and gone to heaven, and so we delude ourselves that this condemned planet is something other than it is. But the truth is no different than it was in the days of Jesus: money will surely bring out the best or the worst in all of us.

Jesus wants his followers to be overcomers in this area. He wants to see Satan impaled on a sword of generosity. He wants to see greed completely demolished in our hearts. He wants to see unholy fear rooted out of our very nature. Jesus said you can't serve both. You've got to choose. In fact, many people refuse the call of God on their lives because they are hung up right here. Satan has one big lie to sell you and it goes like this: "God won't take care of you. So guard what you've got. Stay close to that sure supply. Don't move. The moment you do, you're doomed. I'll come after you and you'll starve to death!"

But Jesus says, "Come follow me. For where your treasure is, there your heart will be also" (Matt. 6:21). The Master had a lot to say about money. In fact, next to prayer, Jesus talked about money more than anything else. He was looking at the eternal part of who we are and he was saying, "I want it all. I love you so much, I won't let anything get in the way."

Where Your Treasure Is

THE LIFESTYLE OF CHRIST

There is a myth floating around out there and it goes something like this: It's all relative you know—what's poor in one country is rich in another. So what difference does it make what lifestyle I choose? By someone else's standard my house is a garbage can.

This is a myth, not because it isn't true, but because heaven doesn't buy it. Heaven will not measure your life on the basis of how you lived compared to others, but on the basis of how you adjusted your lifestyle to help as many people as possible. It is time we wake up and realize where we are. This is not a cruise ship on its way to the Bahamas. It is the doomed remains of the sinking *Titanic*, on its way to the bottom of the ocean, and time is running out to get people into the rescue ships. But how many still don't get it? How many are still dancing and partying on the upper decks, too deluded with themselves to look around?

Jesus came to show us how to live in such a time as this. The Bible says, "Whoever claims to live in him must walk as Jesus did" (1 John 2:6). Notice, Scripture is talking about those who "claim" to live in him. There are 2 billion people who claim to be Christians in today's world. But don't be deceived. Look for the proof! If there is no evidence that someone is following Jesus (ie, walking as Jesus walked), Scripture says such a person "is a liar, and the truth is not in him" (1 John 2:4).

Now you may say, "Is it really that black and white? Surely there must be room somewhere in God's economy for lukewarm, half-hearted, ordinary Christians?" But don't bet eternity on it. The issue here is not earning your way into heaven; the issue is, has Christ transformed your life? Because when he has, there will be evidence. And if there is none, Scripture says you are deluding yourself.

So how did Jesus walk? What characterized his lifestyle? What kind of palatial spread did our heavenly King construct for himself? There was once a guy who came to find out.

> "I want to follow you!" he said. "If you're the guy with the Kingdom, count me in!" Jesus said, "Foxes have holes and birds of the air have nests, but the son of man has no place to rest his head." (Luke 9:58)

Jesus didn't automatically sign up every recruit that came his way. The first thing he confronted people with was lifestyle. When the rich man came to Jesus, hoping to assert his righteousness, the Savior pointed to his bank account. He said, "Sell your possessions and give to the poor . . . Then come follow me" (Matt. 19:21). There is a cost to following Jesus, and the Master never hesitated to tell people what it was.

However, it doesn't stop there. The disciples had signed up. Night and day they were with Jesus. They had more devotional points than all of us combined. But they were still in need of a heart change—big time! Do you remember the scene when Jesus was about to enter Jerusalem? These guys had been with Jesus from the very beginning, and at the end of it all, he pours out his heart to them. He says, "We are going up to Jerusalem and the Son of Man will be betrayed . . . they will condemn him to death . . . to be mocked and flogged and crucified" (Matt. 20:18-19). Now you would expect to hear something like, "Lord, what should we do? How can we best help you?" But Scripture records no such thing. Instead, they get into an argument about which one of them will be the greatest in the coming Kingdom. They had only one thing on their minds: Who is going to get the power? It makes you want to say, "It's the Lord, stupid!" But I wonder if I would be right there with them.

Amazingly, even after Jesus rises from the dead, this question is still on their minds. They ask, "Lord, is it at *this time* (finally, we've waited so long!) that you will restore the Kingdom?" (Acts 1:6). But again, Jesus is very patient with them. He tells them, Don't worry about the times and dates. "You will receive power when the Holy Spirit comes on you" (Acts 1:8). And by the way, it's not the kind of power you're thinking of, but it's the power to be my disciples and to rescue people for eternity.

Honestly, these words of Christ send me to my knees. How blind and selfish we are, and yet he still loves us. Why he tolerates us hypocrites I'll never know. But he's stuck with us by his own design. He bent his knees to wash our feet and show us the way. He came to serve, not to be served. In short, he came to show us how to live. And the truth is, living the lifestyle of Christ is not for the half-hearted, half-committed. You've got to set aside all your pride, all your insecurities, all your fancy pedigree and notions of propriety, and just serve. We would have never made it this far if he had not lowered himself to serve us on that day and simply wash our feet. He walked the talk. He lived the passion. He was right there at the edge where people were falling off. And he was King of Kings and Lord of Lords. So who am I to say I can't go the extra mile? This guy left heaven for earth to save a wretch like me!

When the reality of all this sinks in, the natural response is to say, "Lord, all I have is yours. All my life, all my ambitions, dreams and desires, and yes, even all my wealth, it's all yours." But if it doesn't come naturally, don't force it. Let the Holy Spirit do his work; just ask him. In the early Church, the Spirit's power had so transformed the Body, Scripture records, "All the believers were one in heart and mind. No one claimed that any of his possessions was his own, but they shared everything they had" (Acts 4:32). What a difference the

Holy Spirit makes! From trying to be the greatest, to simply loving and caring for one another, the Holy Spirit's power had so changed the disciple's hearts, they could no longer live for themselves or remain self-absorbed in their own survival.

When Jesus is truly reigning in your heart, you will know it. There will be clear manifestations of it. And according to the Book of Acts, a major one is how you begin to use your God-given resources. You begin to realize they are not your own. They are a trust. You are a steward of them. You have been gifted with a certain measure for a special reason and it has nothing to do with your own comfort.

You alone must make the decision on this one. No one can or should make it for you. The worst thing that could ever happen is for someone to set up a community that forced people to live this way, or a fellowship that administered your possessions. For that would defeat the whole purpose of what Christ seeks to accomplish in your life: generosity guided by his Spirit. As Peter said to Ananias, "Didn't it belong to you before it was sold? And after it was sold, wasn't the money at your disposal?" (Acts 5:4). And that is true. What you do with your possessions is a personal matter—between you and God. But just the same, as a committed disciple of Jesus you *will* feel compelled to appropriate your wealth to the command of Christ for the advancement of his Kingdom. So beware of those who would tell you otherwise. False discipleship occurs when people like Ananias try to masquerade as those completely sold out to Jesus. They want to put up a front of sacrifice, commitment and generosity, when in fact they are carnal, selfish and filled with greed and fear. We must not set up discipleship programs to accommodate people like Ananias. If we do that, we join with them in their hypocrisy—if in fact we are not already given over to it!

Where Your Treasure Is

The reality is, we have a sickness that is endemic to our sinful nature, and if we are not careful it will kill us, just as it did Ananias and Sapphira. I think it's important for us to remember that Jesus didn't come here to create two special orders, one for the committed and another for the not-so-committed. The Bible says, *"Whoever* claims to live in him *must* walk as Jesus walked" (1 John 2:6). If we consider ourselves his followers, we need to be thinking about how our lifestyle measures up to his own. Would Jesus buy this car, that house, would he wear that shirt—where do we draw the line? There is no forbidden list of "brand names" and "designer labels" we can reference. But one thing is for sure: we are to be living our lives in such a way that we can give the very most to fulfilling the mission of Christ. We are to get by with what we can. We are to limit all unnecessary expenses.

We need to remember where we are and where we are not. This is not heaven. I have heard many people say, "Go ahead, spend it! You're a child of God and he wants you to have everything." That's partly true, but it breaks down here: you're not the only child of God. It's time we grow up. We are living in a cursed and condemned world, in a place where greed is the root of incredible evil and the source of unthinkable suffering. So while it is true that you are God's child, and he wants you to have everything, he also wants you to be aware of your other brothers and sisters. Just think of a family of ten at the dinner table. Mom has cooked up a wonderful chicken dinner. You're passing around the plate when the fourth kid pipes up. "Hey Dad, can I have it all?" A little out of place, to say the least, but that's exactly how we sound sometimes in the ears of heaven.

We need to pray and ask the Lord for grace in this area. Many of us need to ask for forgiveness. I know I do. We need to cry out,

"Lord Jesus, set me free! From the power and curse of greed, from the paralyzing fear of not having enough, and from the tyranny of shallow Christianity. Grant me the faith to trust you for my daily bread and the courage to bless others with the bread you've given me."

WELCOME TO THE BANK OF HEAVEN

"Good afternoon, ladies and gentlemen. I would like to welcome you to the Bank of Heaven. Some of you will be eager to check your accounts here. But before you fall in line, we feel it would be best to prepare you for what you may find in these eternal vaults. You see, not all have invested equally in our various offerings and we would like to minimize any trips to the first-aid room."

So may begin your introduction to eternity. When the apostle Paul received a gift from the church in Philippi, he told them something very interesting. He said, "You know guys, this is awesome. But I want to clear something up. I don't need your money. And I'm not seeking what is yours. I have learned to be content in every circumstance."

"Oh, that's wonderful," the church committee might have interrupted, "you see we have this carpet problem in the west wing . . ." But fortunately for them, Paul didn't pause with his introduction. He went on to explain why he would accept the gift. He writes:

> "But I am looking for what may be
> *credited to your account.*
> I have received full payment and even more.
> I am amply supplied."
> (Phil. 4:17-18)

Where Your Treasure Is

The great missionary Paul was an investment broker for the Bank of Heaven. Have you ever thought of our missionaries like that? Well, we better start thinking! Are they amply supplied? We better make sure. I remember a long time ago when my father was having difficulty raising funds for the ministry. He just felt awkward asking people for their hard-earned money. Then an elder missionary prayed for him and gave him some advice that has greatly helped him. He said, "Don't worry about a thing. Ask them to give, it's the nicest thing you can do for them. Ask as many as you can. They will thank you for it! They will come up to you in heaven and shake your hand and say, 'Thank you for asking me!'"

This elder missionary was absolutely right. A day of reckoning is coming. A day of judgment and reward. Jesus foretold us and he warned us, "Although they cannot repay you, you will be repaid at the resurrection of the righteous" (Luke 14:14). I wonder how seriously we take these words? Sometimes I think the angels must look down in complete amazement at our behavior and ask themselves, "Didn't we warn them? Could we have made it any more clear? How dense are these people!" Without any question, we really are blinded in this area, and especially so, if we live in a time of peace and prosperity. Jesus warned us of the "deceitfulness of wealth" and its power to "choke the word, making it unfruitful" (Mark 4:19). Scripture warns us that "People who want to get rich fall into temptation and a trap and into many foolish and harmful desires that plunge men into ruin and destruction" (1 Tim. 6:9).

And yet how many kids, even Christian kids, grow up thinking their number one priority in life is to "get rich"? If a kid says he wants to be a millionaire when he grows up, no one washes his mouth out with soap. Instead, we smile and say, "Oh, how nice." But we should be more careful. What is it about money that is so incredibly dangerous? Or to put it another way, why would someone care more for a few pieces of paper, or tiny trinkets of metal, than for their own eternal destiny? It really is incredible! How many billionaires on the *Forbes* 400 list are on fire for Jesus? I can't think of any. And yet these are some of the "smartest" and most gifted people on the planet—the most praised and exalted.

Something in that ought to make it painfully obvious what is really going on. Satan is the ruler of this world and money is what he uses to control it. There is spiritual energy that surrounds money. Compromise with money is deal-making with the enemy. So Scripture is warning us to be very careful. As believers, we must live in the world and we must use money. But we must exert great caution as we do so. For this reason, God has provided an escape. He says, "Seek first my Kingdom—invest everything you possess in my purposes, and you will be investing for eternity."

Now you may be wondering: Is it wrong to make money, even lots of money? It's not an easy question to answer, and it depends on your calling. I don't suppose I would wish wealth on anyone. But if your motive is to serve the Lord and to advance his Kingdom, you stand a good chance of not only surviving, but thoroughly plundering this world for the glory of God and his mission.

Just the same, here is a danger that not many recover from. Don't think you can outwit the Devil here in his own territory. Not on your own. Stay close to the Lord and stay accountable to others. Jesus says, "From everyone who has been given much, much will be demanded; and from the one who has been entrusted with much, much more will be asked" (Luke 12:48). Everything you have is on loan to you, and you must give an account for it. So invest wisely and remain ever vigilant, for Satan will stop at nothing to keep your heart and soul from the Lord and his Great Commission.

Where Your Treasure Is

In fact, many people are not receiving what God has for them—the joy and the passion of knowing him intimately—because money is getting in the way. They are committing spiritual adultery in the area of their finances—distracted, as it were, by the beautiful girl or the handsome guy sitting at the table across the way. It seems so strange that there would be a connection between something so awesome as knowing the Lord and something so temporal as a few pieces of paper with numbers on them. But Jesus said, "When it comes to me and money, you will either love one or hate the other" (Matt. 6:24).

Our relationship with the Lord and his presence in our life is directly related to this issue. We have to choose. But let's keep in mind and never forget that the Lord wants to bless us for all eternity! He doesn't want us to miss out on what his Father is offering. He says, "Store up for yourself treasure in heaven" (Matt. 6:20). And he's not joking, or exaggerating, or trying to manipulate anyone. He's telling us the way it is. So his presence in our life, or lack thereof, is to be a sign to us of how we're doing. Just as pain and pleasure help our bodies know what is proper and best, the power of his presence keeps our spirit on course with his eternal plan. He wants us to enjoy eternity without any regrets.

For example, can you imagine an investment broker coming over one afternoon and making you the following deal:

> We have two investment plans here—you can live for 70 years spending as much money as you like, but you'll be forever bankrupt after that—and I mean forever as in *forever*. Or you can live very simply while here on earth and give as much money away as possible, and we guarantee you'll be an *eternal billionaire*.

Would it really take you a whole lot of time to make up your mind? But remarkably, many are still pondering the question! Still thinking it over. I can only imagine how the Lord must see it all. Here we have people walking around thinking they are the greatest thing ever to hit this planet because they have a few more green pieces of paper than the others. And at the same time, here is a guy living in a cardboard shack in Bangladesh. He is investing his life in prayer and the Lord's work, ministering to the poorest of the poor. He doesn't have much to eat. His water isn't the cleanest. By the world's standards, he's a loser. But heaven knows better. He's richer than Bill Gates—for all time to come.

That's the eternal perspective. That's the shock of eternity many are in for on the other side. But the truth is, even Bill Gates can live for the Lord 100%. It won't be easy. There is no greater handicap than being wealthy. But it's not impossible either. John Wesley, the great English evangelist of the 18th century, set a good example here. He could have been a very wealthy person from the royalties and gifts he received. But he set a standard for himself. He said, "Earn all you can, save all you can, give all you can." He lived like it, too. He decided early on in his life to only live on what he absolutely needed—29 pounds a year. Though in later years he earned up to 1,500 pounds annually, he never kept more than 29 pounds, and the rest he gave away. Not once in his life did he ever lack God's provision.

So how about us? Are those of us in the wealthy West doomed to be the eternal losers in the Kingdom of Heaven? Not necessarily. The issue is not how much you have, but what you do with what you have. Even so, having a lot of money, according to Jesus, can be a great spiritual handicap.

For example, what advice might an angel give to Bill Gates or

Where Your Treasure Is

Ross Perot, as an investment broker for the Bank of Heaven? Would they accept it? Even coming from an angel? Here's how I imagine the meeting might go (if the angel had a sense of humor):

"Well first, Bill, I would just like to say what an honor it is to meet you. I really enjoy using your software and I'd like to recommend a few changes. But we'll get to that later. Anyway, to get us started, let's examine your portfolio."

"Now, let's see . . . First, I really think you ought to consider selling that house you just built. Or turn it into an orphanage. Whatever . . . just get rid of it."

"But I just finished!"

"I know, I know," the angel says. "Napkins, please, for my friend Bill."

"You can get by with a much smaller place I'm sure and use the money for something more eternally substantial."

Bill starts to rethink and looks at his watch.

"Hey look, buddy, I've got so much money, I'll be investing more than anyone else anyway. So you just think about that."

"Well, that is true," the angel replies. "But the Bank of Heaven doesn't measure it that way. We look at how much you gave, relative to how much you kept, and then calculate the dividends from there."

"Well, that's a real bummer. I'm not sure I like your bank. Are you a monopoly up there? Because if you are, I might have to report this. By the way, what kind of software are you using? Do you have a firewall?"

"I'm afraid we do. It's very effective."

"Ah, but nothing is foolproof!" Bill exclaims. "Anyway, I'll think over your offer, but you've got to do a little better with the dividend program. That's ridiculous."

Now if you're a rich person, or even the average guy who would like to be rich, you may find yourself agreeing with Bill Gates. But that's just how deceptive wealth can be. It makes objectivity so close to impossible. In fact, there is a true story like this in the Bible and to this day we don't know if the rich man choose his money or his soul, because he waffled on the offer. Luke records:

> "When he heard this he became very sad, because he was a man of great wealth. Jesus looked at him and said, 'How hard it is for the rich to enter the Kingdom of God! Indeed, it is easier for a camel to go through the eye of a needle.'" (Luke 18:23-25)

The Lord is a broker for a very big bank. And yes, it does have a monopoly up there. But no matter how little you think you've got, it's important in the eyes of eternity. Jesus said of the poor widow who gave her last coin to the Lord, "She put in *more* than all the others" (Luke 21:3). An investment in eternity is an investment with sacrifice. Heaven is watching and keeping score.

THERE YOUR HEART WILL BE ALSO

There was a certain rich family with six brothers that lived many years ago. They had the very best that life could offer, and they were determined to keep it all in the family. So the angels decided to test them. One day, a sickly and decrepit old man came and camped out at their gate. It was a beautiful gate, carved with elaborate care and made of the best materials. It proclaimed to everyone who passed by, "We've got the money!" So it seemed like a good spot for a beggar to camp out. Now as you can imagine, the owners didn't see it that way. They tried various means to get rid of him. They cursed at him. They kicked him aside. They complained to the mayor. One day they set the dogs on him. But he just lay there, he had little strength left and he knew he would soon be with the Lord. He didn't quite understand why God had allowed this to happen. But the angels knew and they kept it all on record. When he died, they greeted him warmly, dressed him royally with heaven's finest, and seated him with honor at a magnificent banquet table. A friend of the angels was finally home, safe and sound, and thousands had gathered to greet and honor him.

After he died, the rich family had his body thrown into the city's garbage dump, a place named Gehenna, so called in their language for its never ceasing fire and smoke. "Fitting place for him," they laughed, "the eternal refuge of human garbage." Within a few days they had forgotten all about him, though the brothers all agreed it best to put a few big dogs outside the gate.

* * * *

Jesus told this story two thousand years ago and its message is just as powerful and shocking today as it was then (Luke 16:19-31). We have not heeded its message. Most never will. But it's there just the same. Money kept this family out of heaven. Money condemned the hearts of these people to an eternity of darkness. Money so deceived them that even if someone from the dead were to come and warn them, they would not believe him.

It's time we heeded the warning. Money hasn't changed. Satan's methods are still in full force. The enemy showed Jesus the great cities of his day, and perhaps a few in the future: Paris, New York,

Eternal Vision

Rome. He said to Jesus, "I will give you all their authority and splendor, for it has been given to me, and I can give it to anyone I want to" (Luke 4:6). Satan has been given the power to make you wealthy. He has the authority to prosper you and make you great. He has a special deal for every one of us. Something inside you will find it very attractive. It's all you've ever dreamed of, but there's a catch. He wants you to build him a gate—a beautiful, heavy gate, with an iron bolt on the other side. And with this gate he wants you to shut out the cries of those without Jesus—the poor, the wretched, the blind. He wants you to forget all about the 2.7 billion who are least evangelized. He wants you inside, listening to his latest TV program and thinking about those mortgage payments and credit card debts he has helped you acquire. It's his world, his system, and his money.

But most of all, he wants your passion, and especially the best years of your life. He wants your strength, your youth, your wisdom, your talents—whatever might be useful to the Great Commission. He promises every one of us: Just stay out of the action, and I'll give you all the desires of your heart.

There is a great contest going on today over your life. Your Savior is asking you, "What do you treasure? What are you investing in? Watch closely, because there you will find your heart" (Matt. 6:21). When John the Baptist was called to prepare the way of the Lord, he came with a very curious message. He said, "The axe has already been laid to the root of the tree!" (Luke 3:9). He came to announce an impending judgment. The Lord was coming, but these people were not ready. "What should we do then?" the crowd wanted to know. In reply, he said three things and they all had to do with money. He didn't say, "Well, I think we need more prayer meetings, Bible studies and worship services—that should do it." Instead, he said, "The man with two tunics should share with him who has none, and the one with food should do the same" (Luke 3:11).

The Lord is indeed coming again, and he is going to measure our spirituality and concern for him, not by the length of our worship services, but by the depth of our pocketbooks. The message of the Spirit has not changed. He is still saying to us today: "Woe unto you who are rich, for you have already received your comfort. You have hoarded wealth in the last days" (Luke 6:24; Jas. 5:3). So I can't help but wonder: how serious do we think the Lord is about this? Do we actually believe him?

To look at our lifestyles and to examine our spending patterns, I would have to conclude—most people are living like Jesus doesn't matter. In practice, we could really care less. And that's too bad, because about other things we are very careful. If the label on the cover of that bottle says,

WARNING: FATAL IF SWALLOWED
POISON

... we understand this very well. You won't find mom using its contents as a milk substitute for tomorrow morning's cereal. But when it comes to spiritual warnings, we seem to treat them like suggestions. Even if that's all they were, we ought to pay attention, considering the source. But we are so forgetful, and just a little too naïve. According to Scripture there is *no more spiritually dangerous substance in the universe*. Yet nowhere do we find on any of the bills we print, the same ominous warning we put on every other toxic thing:

WARNING: FATAL IF MISUSED

For *"No one* can serve both God and money."
(Matt. 6:24)

CHAPTER SIX

❧

ONLY ONE WAY?

"Salvation is found in no one else, for there is no other name under heaven given to men by which we must be saved." (Acts 4:12)

The law of gravity says that if I drive my car over a cliff, I'm going to plunge to the bottom of the ravine. Now if I do that (and I happen to survive), I can shake my fist at God and say, "Look what you made me do! This is your fault—why did you have to go and make gravity and ruin my whole afternoon!" But of course, I had better not say it too loudly. A passing psychiatrist might overhear me, and that will be the end of my argument with physics. To every thinking person it's just obvious—gravity is necessary for the proper functioning of the universe. I might not like it, I might not understand it, but I better respect it.

In the same way, the Bible tells us that God has spiritual laws of cause and effect that are also necessary for the proper functioning of all things seen and unseen. God's law says, "If you honor your parents, things will go well with you. If you don't, they won't." Whether I'm aware of this principle or not, it's operating just the same. Whether I'm a Buddhist, a Hindu, or an evangelical Christian, if I violate God's spiritual principles I will reap the effects.

I think it's important for us to remember this because we live in an age where social opinion validates truth. If you can get enough people to believe in something, then it must be true. More often than not, this puts us in conflict with God's spiritual laws. Take "hell" for example. Most opinion polls tell us the place no longer exists. Apparently hell actually did freeze over! But if that is so, then someone forgot to inform Jesus, the one who introduced us to the place. Now mind you, we live in a very contradictory age. We like the idea that Jesus was a great teacher and a social revolutionary, but we would rather not accept what he had to say. For Jesus put things in very black and white terms. He said there is only one way and I am that way. I am the door. I am the bread of life. I am the vine and you are the branches. Remain in me and you will live. Apart from me you can do nothing. He told us we were lost, in complete darkness, and under the power of Satan. Our condition apart from him was complete hopelessness.

Scripture says, "The sinful mind is *hostile* to God. It does not submit to God's law, *nor can it do so*. Those under the sinful nature *cannot* please God" (Rom. 8:7-8). Jesus didn't warn us that he was the only way because he wanted to create an intolerant religion or because he wanted to make himself look good. He was God, walking among us, and he was telling us *enter by the narrow way, because it's the only one that will save you.*

But try mentioning this subject to a non-believer in today's pluralistic environment and you had better get ready to duck and run. A friend of mine once found this out the hard way while sharing the gospel at a state university. He was invited to speak to a group of young ladies in their dorm lounge, but no one warned him about what might happen. In the middle of his presentation, one young lady abruptly interrupted. She stood up from her seat in the back and got right to the point:

"Do you mean to tell me that if I don't accept your Jesus I'm going to burn forever in hell?"

"That's what the Bible says," my friend replied.

"Well, you can go to hell," she said, and walked out. So did everyone else.

To be sure, the subject of hell should be handled with care. But it should be handled just the same. Too often we ignore the matter because it's too hard to explain. But while we may find it difficult to comprehend an eternal hell, we need to find out why it's there and live our lives accordingly. A loving God wouldn't allow anyone to suffer endlessly unless he had no other alternative. Neither would a loving God warn us of such a place if it didn't exist. There are no "boogey-man" stories in God's revelation.

Jesus, on good authority to say the least, brought to our attention the reality of hell. He said it's a place—a real place. Many people have tried to soften hell by saying otherwise. But that's not what Jesus said. He warned his disciples, "If your right eye causes you to sin, gouge it out and throw it away. It is better for you to lose one part of your body than for your *whole body* to be *thrown into* hell" (Matt. 5:29-30). According to Jesus, hell is a place where you will go. It's not a state of mind. It's a place where your "body" will be taken. To be sure, there is mental anguish in hell. But just as believers will experience the joy and pleasure of eternity in resurrected bodies, so those in hell will experience the reality of that place with real feelings in a real body.

Jesus said, "Even now the reaper draws his wages, even now he harvests the crop for eternal life" (John 4:36). According to the Author of our salvation, eternity is settled in this lifetime. There is a sifting out that is taking place all over the world. There is no middle ground. You're either in Christ, or under Satan's power. I've heard people say, "Surely a God of so much creativity wouldn't have just one way to find him." One of my friends once remarked, "You know, Christianity is a nice religion, but I can't accept that Jesus is the only way." But the truth is, if there are other ways, then Christ died for nothing. He was the biggest fool in the world and so are we for following him! Furthermore, if Christianity isn't true then it is evil—the worst kind. It is not a nice religion at all. The entire basis of Christianity says that unless you are in Christ you are under the control of sin. You are being manipulated by evil spirits. You are deceived and lost. Now that's not very nice. But that's the essence of Christianity, take it or leave it.

Jesus came to introduce us to a few unchangeable spiritual laws that the world finds very objectionable. But as believers, we might as well get used to it. A watered down gospel never saved anyone. Jesus said I am the way, the truth and the life, and here's why:

First, you can't save yourself. You can't pay for your sins. You can't make things right no matter how hard you try. You cannot set yourself free from the power of Satan.

Second, unless intercession is made on your behalf, you will be forever lost. I am the *only* one who can make that intercession.

Third, I am entrusting those who receive this free gift of eternal life to give it away to others. Unless they go, those in darkness will be forever lost.

Now honestly, I can't explain all of this with my limited human reasoning. But I believe it because I've seen it work just like Jesus said it would. And I've seen it *not* work just the same when we act against it. Millions remain without the life of Christ, simply because they've never heard. And they haven't heard because we remain unconvinced about their plight. We simply can't believe that God would actually do what he has promised. And because we have unanswered questions, we refuse to budge. "That's it," we tell God. "If you can't do a better job explaining yourself, I'm not interested." But it seems to me that we want explanations for things that are a little over our heads at the moment. We have to remember that in the scope of eternity we're just getting started. We have a long way to go and we're all in the "first grade" so to speak. Some of us, myself included, would like answers that require advanced calculus to explain, and of course we want them *right now!* But our Teacher reminds us, "Class, these are excellent questions. And there's nothing wrong with them, but I'm afraid you'll have to wait until the 12th grade to fully understand them." Now we can say, "Well, forget you then, we're going out to the playground." But if we do that, two things will happen. One, we will never make it to the 12th grade. And two, we'll miss out on what we're supposed to be learning and *doing* right now.

REAL PEOPLE

Every Muslim believes four things about Christianity. First, Jesus is *not* the Son of God. Second, Jesus did *not* die on the cross. Third, the Bible has been changed—it is no longer reliable. Fourth, (although no one can be sure they are going to heaven unless they die in a holy war), if you become a Christian you will definitely go to hell.

Now if anyone tries to convince you that all religions are the same, they are either uninformed or mentally unbalanced. Islam is practically the anti-thesis of Christianity. So is Buddhism. Jesus offered the world eternal life. The Buddha offered us self-extinction. The Brahmins of Hinduism tell us they're superior to everyone. And if you're born in the wrong caste, then you're a loser for life. Not only that, you deserve to be one. Christianity teaches us that God made everyone equal and loves us all the same. By his grace we can amount to anything.

When you compare light with darkness, hope against despair, truth with deception—there *is no* comparison. The religions of the world are a testimony to man's perversity and complete ignorance apart from God. But pointing out the differences, while it may give us a confidence boost, does little to help people who are deceived. Through fear and repression, Satan has designed false religions to keep people in perpetual bondage.

Under Islamic law, conversion to Christianity is a capital offense. In a Muslim state it is perfectly legal to kill a Christian convert. No trial, no jury, no judge. Just the verdict of your family and friends. Imagine how difficult it must be for a Muslim to make the decision to follow Christ! All their lives they have been taught to despise Christianity and reject Jesus as their savior. In Islamic states there is zero tolerance for evangelism, and even less for conversion. Anyone who even *listens* to a Christian evangelist places himself at great risk. It is commonly believed that if you kill a new convert soon enough you can save his soul from hell.

Jesus said the days are coming when "a man's enemies will be the members of his own household" (Matt. 10:36). Following Christ in the Muslim world is much like it was in the first century—you have to take up your cross daily and never look back. To be sure, the Muslim challenge reveals how much we really love the lost and how much we're willing to risk in order to reach them. If we really want to help the 1.3 billion people living under the darkness of Islam, we are going to need thousands and thousands of people. You can't reach Saudi Arabia with "crusade" evangelism. You have to reach people one by one in the Muslim world. A young mother in Iran is not going to risk her life by turning away from everything she has always believed to be true, unless she is absolutely sure that *you* are trustworthy. You must become the message. You are the first gospel she will ever read. You've got to be there and you've got to model what following Jesus is all about.

There are no substitutes for the hands and feet of Christ. No electronic devices will ever replace them. And discipleship can't happen unless someone is willing to *be* a disciple-maker. There is no other way. Jesus said *go and make* disciples, teaching them to *obey everything*. We have to be there, and we have to live it, for people to see it and believe it. But are we willing? Are they worth it? Are they really that lost? Apparently these questions still linger in our minds, for so few have ventured out into the deeper waters where millions remain without hope.

Jesus came and lived among us because he believed we were *hopelessly* lost—so lost he had to *seek* us in order that he might *save* us. Seeking and saving go hand in hand, they are inseparable from each other. Jesus had to take the initiative, because if he didn't, we would never have made it out of the darkness we were in.

But that was then. How about now? Are people still lost today, two thousand years after Christ came to seek and to save? Personally, I think we face a crises in our generation about how *lost* the lost really are. Because in actual fact, if we were absolutely convinced that non-believers were utterly hopeless without Christ, would we not be doing more to reach them? It's just basic instinct. If I know that a drowning person is really drowning, I'm going to do everything in my power to save him. But if I'm not sure, I might not want to risk the embarrassment, or the prospect of getting my clothes all wet, or the hassle of adjusting my schedule.

Eternal Vision

Every day 30,000 Muslims die without Christ. Do we really believe they are lost? Forever? Many would rather believe they are going to be okay. But Jesus gave us no such assurance. If Jesus warned us about such a terrible place—with fire, torment and everlasting destruction—it was because he wanted us to be thinking about it. Hell has no redemptive value if it is eternal. The only reason Jesus would warn us about hell is to deter us from going there and to challenge us to rescue people who are on their way.

Hell is the most neglected and forgotten dimension to the Eternal Perspective. It makes sense, because if the understanding of hell was meant to stir our will, the enemy of our souls should be doing everything possible to destroy the idea. To be sure, hell is hard to defend. When my unbelieving grandpa died, the first question our relatives wanted to know of us was, "How can you possibly believe that Grandpa went to hell? He never did anything to hurt anybody." But I worry less that hell is now on the top ten list of "theologically incorrect" ideas and more about us Christians who say we still believe in the place, but don't live like its reality is true.

Jesus didn't warn us about hell to give us something to debate about. We need to find out why he warned us, and then we need to live like its reality really matters. If Jesus said it, he meant it. It will happen. Scripture says it is impossible for God to lie (Heb. 6:18). And that means white lies, and half truths, and scary stories about things that aren't really out there.

So here's the gospel truth: If people are really going to hell without Christ, should I not be doing everything possible in my means to save them? No sacrifice could ever be too great for me to make for someone without salvation. I have all eternity to take it easy. They have a few short years to get it right. If I really understand what Christ has done for me, that he has saved me from an eternity of darkness and suffering, then I can no longer sit back and relax, doing whatever I please while others remain unforgiven. That is why the apostle Paul claimed he was a debtor to all men (Rom. 1:14). He simply could not stop preaching the gospel. He was compelled to throw out the life-line which was thrown out to him. Once his eyes and ears were opened he could no longer sit back and relax. Once on board the ship he couldn't possibly stay below deck while the cries of those perishing in the waves below echoed in his heart and mind.

The message of hell is the most powerful message there is. It puts the urgency back into evangelism. It places the value of a human soul so high, it must be my top priority if there is even one person on this planet in danger of going there. I may never fully understand what the Bible says about hell—I might not even like it—but I'm glad it's there. I need it. Every time I think of giving up on the lost, I need to remember what I'm giving them up *to*. The finality of hell means I can no longer pass my neighbor everyday and say, "Well, maybe tomorrow I'll get around to helping him know Jesus." The reality of hell says, "Now is the day of salvation. Now is the appointed time."

To look at our concern for the 2.7 billion least evangelized of the 10/40 Window, I would say we need to hear the message of hell at least one more time. And we need to really take it in this time. We need to ask, "If hell is really true—if people are really going to perish for eternity without Christ unless someone brings them the gospel—then how should I be living in this day and hour and moment while there is still a chance to save them?" Is there anything more important, more pressing, more urgent than this reality?

If that is so, we need to seriously re-examine our priorities, for most believers are doing precious little to prepare themselves for what is their primary purpose for being here. We are called to *rescue those being led away to death; to hold back those staggering toward slaughter* (Prov. 24:11). The Great Commission is a rescue operation, not only because billions of people remain under the control of Satan and his demons, but also because those under this condition are in real danger of being lost for eternity.

If you could visit hell for just thirty seconds, it would forever change the way you spend your time here on earth. Your life would never be the same. You would make Billy Graham look like a junior evangelist. There would be only one thing on your mind: "Lord, help me rescue as many people as possible with my life. May I never be unfaithful to you in this Great Commission."

UNLESS THEY ARE SENT

In the place where I am staying, people have learned not to take electric light for granted. One moment you've got it, the next you don't, and suddenly all is darkness. Why this is so is anyone's guess, but no one really wonders why. It's pointless. It's just the "way things are" they tell me.

Seeing the hopelessness of the poor in Third World countries drives home a very important spiritual principle. People remain where they are, as they are, in great spiritual darkness, because they feel spiritually powerless to escape. Something has blocked their minds. Someone has possessed their will. Only when we recognize this situation can we even begin to help people. Those in darkness will not follow the light until it comes from the distance and touches their feet. They may see it far off, they may even hear a rumor of it. But it takes great light to save people. They need a clear and steady way, or they will not follow.

Ali was like that. He lived all his life in a Muslim country and he wanted everyone to believe as he did. One day he decided to find a pen pal in the United States so he might convert him to Islam. Amazingly, the person he found was an evangelical Christian named Mark. The Lord put a special burden on Mark's heart for Ali and he began to pray regularly for him. Soon an opportunity came for Mark to visit Ali and stay in his home. For two weeks he shared the love of Christ with his new Muslim friend and spent much of the day just praying for him. Ali was amazed at Mark's love for the Lord and later testified how envious he was of Mark's intimate relationship with God. He didn't let on though. At the end of Mark's stay he tried to discourage him by saying, "I want to thank you for coming. You have made me a stronger and more determined Muslim." But Mark just kept praying. That night after Mark had left, Ali had a dream about Jesus. The Lord appeared to him and said, "Ali, I love you." He replied, "I love you too," and then he just wept and wept. When he woke up, his eyes were filled with tears. He gave his life to Jesus and follows him to this day.

Reaching people like Ali is going to require great sacrifice on our part. Is it really worth it? If you believe it is, then here's the next question: "How far are you willing to go to reach someone without Christ?" Ask Jesus this question and he'll point you to the cross. He would say in no uncertain terms, "If Ali was the only person on this planet, I would come and die for him. I would risk everything to save him." Now what if the only way for Ali to be saved is if someone like Mark takes the initiative to pray for him and authenticate the message of the cross by walking as Jesus walked? Would I be willing to say, "If Ali was the only person on this planet, I would risk everything to point him to Jesus. I would make it the number one priority of my life"?

Jesus came to serve us because Satan had lied to us. Satan said,

"God doesn't love you. You can't trust him." Jesus said, "I'll prove how much I love you. I will leave heaven and its glory behind. I will give my life to save billions of people who presently hate me and want nothing to do with me. I will make myself vulnerable to all the abuse, the hatred, the slander and the violence of those whom I have come to rescue." Now that's love. But am I willing to do the same? Can I really accept the heavenly commission, "As the father has sent me, I am sending you" (John 20:21)? Honestly, if I don't believe the lost are really lost, I'm not going to get very far. It's simply not worth it.

Jesus said, "No one can go into a strong man's house and plunder his goods unless he first binds the strong man" (Mark 3:27). Jesus said this in the context of driving out an evil spirit. He was there—he saw the guy, and he set him free. Nowhere did Jesus drive out evil spirits from a distance. When Jesus loved people, he did it with both arms. Jesus sat at the well and talked with the Samaritan woman when society said, "You can't do that." Jesus let a prostitute wipe his feet with her hair when the religious leaders of the day said, "You shouldn't even come near her." Jesus hung between two thieves on the cross and loved them even though they both insulted him. To the very end he was identifying with people—feeling their pain, their loneliness, their desperation, and saying "I love you" with every breath.

If we're going to be like Jesus we need to get up close and personal. We need to intercede as he did, as if lives depended on it. How many times have I wrestled with flesh and blood before I have wrestled in the heavenly realms? How often have I evangelized before I have served? How easy it is to communicate words but not love! Our message lacks power when it is only heard and not seen. Only when faith and service are working together to model the

'Christ-way' can we fulfill our Lord's command to make disciples. Disciples are followers, not just listeners. There are no shortcuts to fulfilling the Great Commission.

Would Ali have come to know Jesus without someone praying for him, without someone going and sharing the love of Christ, one on one? Only the Lord knows. But this one thing I do know: that's the way it happened. Now this *is* my business. "For how can they believe unless they hear? And how can they hear unless someone is sent?" (Rom. 10:14-15). On this matter I can talk about. There is nothing I can do about those who die having never heard the gospel. Whatever I decide about them will not change their fate. But if, indeed, I have been called to do something about those who are living without Christ *today*, then I had better be thinking about what that means. Because on this reality will I be called into account.

SPIRITUAL GRAVITY

God sent Jonah to Nineveh because he was going to destroy that city in 40 days. Now what if Jonah decided he really didn't have the time? What if he said, "You know, I think I'll go in a couple of months when the weather is a bit nicer"? Or what if he never went at all, even after his three day fishing trip in the Mediterranean? What if he thought, "Come on, God is a nice guy and I really doubt that he's going destroy all these people, children and all. Just a warning, no doubt"? Maybe he did think it over, just like we're thinking it over today. "Will God actually send people to an eternity of darkness if they don't receive Christ in this lifetime? Surely there must be some second chance, some other way?"

The trouble with our wondering about all of this is that it demonstrates we are focused on the wrong problem. We are trying to justify our lack of obedience! In so doing, we are cutting out the very nerve of evangelism, which is the utter hopelessness of those without Christ. If we spent more time focused on reaching the lost, and less time wondering about what might happen if we don't, we wouldn't have to worry about it in the first place!

I measure every idea and difficult issue by this one standard, "What effect will this have on the Great Commission?" Satan didn't call it a day after the cross. He didn't roll over and say to his followers, "Oh well, I goofed. We might as well surrender." To the contrary, he got ready for action. He lost round one, but round two was us. He couldn't change the reality of the cross, but he could still change how we think about it. He couldn't destroy the gift, but he could still keep people from receiving it. Beyond a shadow of a doubt, I know Satan is working overtime to keep the gospel from going out to the least-reached areas of the world. I believe he's working hardest right in our own backyards—in our seminaries, pulpits and publishing houses. Satan is a deceiver, that's his game. He works hard at it. He fights in the realm of ideas. If he can sell you an idea, he can buy your soul. So I think Satan has the best of the best lined up to sell us down the river of indifference. He wants to paralyze our concern for those without Christ by convincing us they're not really that bad off. They can wait. They're going to be okay.

But the Bible begs to differ. The apostle Paul wrote to the Ephesians, "Formerly you were without God and without hope" (Eph. 2:11-12). We don't have to travel very far to prove this one—glimpses of hell can be seen wherever there are people without Jesus. You can find it in Sierra Leone, where 16-year-old kids raped and murdered dozens of people every day like it was a sport during a decade-long civil war. You can find it in India, where parents sell their little girls to become child prostitutes in Hindu temples. You can find it in the allies of Chicago, where runaways have shot themselves up with so much heroin they don't even know who they are anymore. The Bible calls it "death" and it doesn't stop once we leave this earth. It's being without God and without hope.

But are they really without God? Doesn't every religion have God in there somewhere? Tell that to Nicodemus. He came to Jesus one night to talk the matter over. He came by night, because it was a little embarrassing and not a little bit dangerous. Jesus had ruffled a few too many feathers. He told the religious leaders of his day, "You are all whitewashed tombs!" So the conversation went something like this:

> "Jesus, I've seen your work and I believe you must be from God."
>
> (Now coming from Nicodemus this was quite a compliment. After all, he was one of the most respected religious leaders in Israel. But remarkably, Jesus remains unflattered. He gets right to the point and returns the compliment with an insult!)
>
> "Nicodemus, you are not ready to go to heaven," he says. "You have not yet experienced spiritual birth. How is it that you are the teacher of all Israel and you do not understand this?" (John 3:1-15)

Jesus spoke with complete authority and finality. He wasn't afraid to "tell it like it is." His statement to Nicodemus is perhaps the most shocking statement in the Bible. But he knew exactly what was at stake and he was willing to risk the friendship. Nicodemus may have been the best trained and the most experienced religious person in Israel, but spiritually speaking, he was blind as a bat.

Paul said the same thing about himself. He had all the best training, and he knew the Scriptures like the back of his hand. But all of his training, knowledge, and spiritual activity got him no closer to heaven than the thief on the cross was before he met Jesus. Both Paul and Nicodemus did everything possible to obey God's laws. In every respect they were perfect as far as human standards go. But the Bible says they were *completely* lost. The world says, "If you live a good life and try to be nice to everyone, you're going to be okay." But Scripture says, "No one will be declared righteous in his sight by observing the law" (Rom. 3:20). Paul stood condemned. So did Nicodemus. Apart from the cross, apart from the Spirit of God, the most religious people in the day of Jesus stood completely hopeless, bound by the power of Satan.

The power of the enemy is incredible. Most people don't understand what kind of influence he actually has on an unbeliever. What's more, as we get closer to the end, we can expect Satanic activity to increase and deceptions to become even greater (Rev. 12). As time runs out, the enemy will become increasingly desperate and furious. We aren't told all the chronology of what has been taking place in the spiritual dimensions. But what is clear is that demonic activity on this planet has been increasing from the days of the Fall, and it will reach a climax in the final days before our Lord's coming.

Wherever Jesus and the Apostles went they were encountering demonic presence. This is in stark contrast to the Old Testament record where demonic activity is hardly seen. But by the first century something had changed. The whole world stood completely bound by the power of Satan (1 John 5:19; Rev. 12:9-12). As mankind rebelled further against God from the days of the Tower of Babel, Satan's grip on the world increased. Scripture says, "They exchanged the truth of God for a lie" (Rom. 1:25). And, "Since they did not think it worthwhile to retain the knowledge of God, he gave them over to a depraved mind" (Rom. 1:28).

Only One Way?

So in the end, the issue is not how religious you are, or how sincere you may be—the issue is, "Whose kingdom are you in?" It's just like gravity. It only works one way, and you're either working with it or against it. It can help you stay grounded or it can kill you. Spiritual Gravity is just as real and just as dangerous. It says:

> "As for you, you were *dead* in your transgressions and sins, in which you used to live when you followed the ways of this world and of the ruler of the kingdom of the air, the spirit who is *now at work* in those who are disobedient. *All of us* also lived among them at that time." (Eph. 2:1-3)

Paul included himself in this description. He said, "I was lost, bound by the power of Satan, and utterly hopeless before I met Christ." Jesus came to set us free from the power and curse of something so corrosive, only his blood could cleanse it. He said I am the only way, the only truth, the only life, "apart from me you can do nothing" (John 15:5).

At my home church we counsel people every day who have been in bondage for years to everything imaginable. Many of these people have been in churches all their lives, but they're still being manipulated by spirits of fear, anger, bitterness, immorality, deception and depression. They go from counselor to counselor until finally they let Jesus set them free. What amazes me about this is how people can be so close and yet so far away. What amazes me even more is how we can possibly believe that people who have never heard of Jesus might actually be okay.

Having seen with my own eyes what sin has done to people, I can no longer treat the matter lightly. It is as real and heavy as the Bible says it is, "The mind of sinful man is death, but the mind controlled by the Spirit is life and peace" (Rom. 8:6). If this is really true (and it's unlikely that God would be mistaken on the matter), then nothing else should be my priority while I am here on this earth but to save and rescue people by his grace, with the greatest urgency and concern possible in Christ.

The Bible says God has "committed to *us* the message of reconciliation" (2 Cor. 5:19). Notice the word "us." It means God has committed to *you* and to *me* this message of reconciliation. No one is exempted. The message of the gospel is the only thing that can set people free. "We are therefore Christ's *ambassadors,* as though God were making his appeal through *us*" (v. 20). As messengers and representatives of Christ, our responsibility is greater than we will ever know or understand this side of heaven. It's truly a matter of life and death, heaven and hell, light and darkness for those who are perishing. It's as real as the cross, as real as the Second Coming, as real as God, and as real as the day when all of us will be called into account.

When you fully take it in, it's the most sobering reality in the world. As heavenly ambassadors, we *must not* neglect our responsibility. For the message we carry was purchased at a cost so great, it makes every other endeavor on this planet seem trivial, shallow and meaningless. Anything short of a maximum effort to rescue those in darkness is truly a crime against the cross and a mockery of the Blood which has saved us.

> *"For God so loved the world that he gave his one and only son, that whoever believes in him shall not perish but have eternal life."*
> *John 3:16*

CHAPTER SEVEN

SATAN'S FINAL DEFEAT

*"And the devil, who deceived them,
was thrown into the lake of burning sulfur." (Rev. 20:10)*

The Bible says God has prepared hell for the devil and his angels (Matt. 25:41). Many people don't like the idea of hell or even believe in it, but Satan certainly does. Imagine a group of soldiers about to go into battle, when they are told, "Gentlemen, this is it, the last battle. If we lose here, we have lost forever. Any questions?" I'm quite sure if I heard these words, I would fight with everything I possessed. So it is with Satan and his fellow angels. They understand the risks, they know what awaits them, and they are fighting with great intensity and discipline.

Now we are the enemy, from their point of view. We are regular churchgoing folk. We have potluck dinners on Wednesday night and baseball games on Saturday. We like preachers who keep it light and simple, short and sweet. We always give generously to the new building fund, because after all, "It's the house of God, right?"

So that's us. I suppose there's nothing wrong with this kind of Christianity, in and of itself (Lord, forgive me for saying it!). But if that's all there is, then we're a joke, a pushover, a piece of cake on Satan's dinner table. We'll be devoured in no time flat.

Satan is absolutely delighted that most believers walk around in complete ignorance of his plan for their lives. In fact, many live in perfect denial of the war we are engaged in. Not a few would just rather stay out of it. But like it or not, if you are a follower of Jesus, you have signed up to fight in a war that will bring about an *end* to Satan's rebel campaign (Matt. 24:14).

In opposition to this, Satan's forces in the Kingdom of Darkness—"the rulers, the authorities, the powers of this dark world, and the spiritual forces of evil in the heavenly realms"—are engaged in a vicious struggle to delay and prevent the fulfillment of the Great Commission (Eph. 6:12). We have an enemy who fears the believers of this generation more than any other in history. He wants them struck down and neutralized, arrested with fear and content with insignificance. He will stop at nothing to prevent your participation in his undoing.

And most of all, the enemy wants to keep you busy. He wants your time and commitment, your passion and resolve. He wants certain questions kept out of your mind: Why am I here? What should I be doing? What difference does it make if I get involved? I promise you these are the very questions the Devil does not want you to understand. Your Commander-in-Chief is sounding the call to the last battle of the last war that eternal history will ever know. The number one objective of the enemy is to keep you from grasping that reality. Because once you do, once you get it and start living like it matters, everything else begins to fall into place. Then the purpose of this life—our place in this world and our entire reason for being here—begin to take on a meaning we could never have realized or achieved otherwise.

SATAN'S FINAL DEFEAT

WHAT TO EXPECT

Does Satan have a plan for winning? Does he actually think he stands a chance? We don't know all that he is up to, or planning to do, but Scripture gives us a glimpse into his plan for the end-times. In Daniel 7, we read of the final struggle between the forces of darkness and the Kingdom of God. Their plan is summarized for us in Daniel 7:25:

> "He will speak against the Most High
> and oppress his saints
> and *try to change the set times* and the laws."

Despite God's declaration that he will lose in the end, Satan fights on with great passion just the same. His plan of attack is twofold. The first front is a propaganda campaign of deception aimed at controlling the hearts and minds of the nations—"He will speak against the Most High." The second front is aimed at God's people—"He will oppress the saints." He will flood them with distractions, divisions, persecution, even comfort—whatever works to keep them out of the action. And what is the goal? Is there a purpose behind it all? Satan's only hope is to "change the set times and the laws." Our enemy wants nothing less than the total reversal of God's authority and sovereignty in the universe!

Satan understands how God operates. He knows where he and his demons are going once prophecy has been fulfilled. He knows that when certain conditions are met, certain things will happen. He knows that when Jesus returns, he is finished. So his plan is very simple. Every meeting begins and ends with the reality of Matthew 24:14. He says, "Look you guys, this gospel of the kingdom must *not* be preached throughout the whole world as a testimony to all nations! This is end is *our* end! Don't forget!!"

But despite all his rage, his end is sure to come. In this same vision shown to Daniel, we are given a snapshot of the Lamb's ultimate victory. We see Jesus approaching the throne of God and receiving the victor's crown:

> "He was given authority, glory and sovereign power; *all peoples, nations and men of every language worshiped him.* His dominion is an everlasting dominion that will not pass away, and his kingdom is one that will never be destroyed." (Daniel 7:13-14)

If you are a follower of Jesus, this is one of the most exciting visions in Scripture. It tells us there will be a final and complete consummation of human history. And it tells us something more. It says the new dominion coming will never end. It will never be destroyed. You are on the winning side! A new Kingdom is coming that will never be disturbed by evil or darkness again. The hard work of finishing the Great Commission will result in an eternal divide of eternal history that will never be revoked or countered.

Here in this vision we also learn that Christ's dominion of worship will extend over all ethnic groups—into every language under heaven. No language or people will be left out. We will see this picture again in the Book of Revelation (Rev. 5:9). Bringing the good news of the Kingdom to every "people, tribe, language and nation" is the most significant factor weighing on Christ's Second Coming and it remains the single most terrifying prophecy yet to be fulfilled for the enemy.

In short, the Devil has one plan for you: to keep you busy, busy, busy—running here and there, wondering, worrying, hustling and bustling—preoccupied with all manner of nice and cozy, warm and fuzzy, completely insignificant plans and agendas. He wants you useless, ineffective and immobilized. And just in case you're wondering, he would like to keep that a secret (so be sure not to tell anyone!).

We need to understand who we are to the enemy. Our disobedience is imperative to their survival. If we forget this, we will radically underestimate the incredible efforts underway to keep us out of the Great Commission. Those who seek to make an impact must learn to stay close to Jesus and fight back in his power. This is not a game or a hobby or a nice theological topic. This is a life-and-death struggle for billions of hopelessly corrupt spiritual beings that have taken their stand against the King of the Universe. And like it or not, you *must* choose a side or be chosen anyway against your will.

There is only one option for those who wish to follow Jesus in these final moments before his coming. We must become *completely* consumed with his desire to bring salvation to every person in this generation. There is only one program, one agenda, one vision that should occupy our priority concern as a Church and that is the thorough evangelization of the *entire* world as quickly and efficiently as Providence allows. There are many other good things we must do. But let them never distract us from our priority, which is the eternal destiny of billions in our world who have yet to be given an opportunity to follow Jesus as their Lord and Savior.

WHERE THE BATTLE RAGES

Satan is running out of time and the probability is higher now than ever that this next generation will be the last one before our Lord's Second Coming. Everything must now come together in his plan, or he's finished, and all his demons with him. In Revelation we see a picture of Satan's fury against those who follow Jesus:

> "Then the dragon was enraged at the woman
> and went off to *make war* against the rest of her offspring—
> those who obey God's commandments
> and hold to the testimony of Jesus." (Rev. 12:17)

Satan understands that God has connected his fate to the offspring of God's chosen people. Throughout the entire Bible we see Satan's fury at work to prevent messianic prophecy from being fulfilled. He claws and grasps, stammers and resists, fighting over every inch. From the murder of Abel by his brother, to the complete depravity of mankind before the Flood, to Pharaoh's order in Egypt against the Israelite firstborn, to the days of King Herod and his massacre in Bethlehem—in all of this, we can see Satan's determined efforts to keep prophecy from progressing into reality.

Whenever God narrowed down his focus to a particular person or family, Satan came after them in full force. In the same chapter where we find Abraham being called, we find his wife being taken into the house of another man (Genesis 12). His son Isaac made the same mistake. Isaac's grandson Judah, through whom the Messiah was prophesied to come, committed adultery with a prostitute! David committed both murder and adultery. One of his own kids tried to kill him.

In the same way, we need to understand that Satan wants to destroy our descendents and disqualify us from our calling, even more so than those before us. Scripture says, "If you belong to Christ, then you are Abraham's seed, and heirs according to the promise" (Gal. 3:29). And, "Through the gospel, the Gentiles are heirs together with Israel, members together of one body, and sharers together in the promise . . ." (Eph. 3:6). Because of Christ we are now joined together with God's people in the blessing given to Abraham.

We need to understand why this is so significant. The promise given to Abraham was nothing less than the fulfillment of the Great Commission. God said to Abraham: "I will bless you . . . And all peoples on earth *will be* blessed through you" (Gen. 12:1-3). All human history centers around this promise. The entire Bible documents God's purposes in the context of this special plan. It is the determining factor in a heavenly conflict which is rapidly coming to a climax. When this four thousand-year-old prophecy is fulfilled (and it may yet happen in our lifetime!), the end will surely come, and Satan's rebellion will be crushed.

As the enemy sees his time coming to an end, he will become increasingly desperate. Much of his efforts will be on the Church. In the same way that he went after the offspring of Abraham, Judah and David, he is working hard to destroy this next generation of believers.

It is no wonder that Satan has tried to wipe out an entire generation of young people through abortion, birth control and divorce. Most "Christian" nations now have negative birth rates. Muslim nations, on the other hand, are having so many children, Islam will overtake Christianity by the year 2060, simply through biological growth![1]

It is equally no wonder why Satan has tried to create homes without fathers and mothers where his TV programming can raise the next generation. Satan is building a media platform through which he will unify the entire world and he is using this generation of young people to create it. With each new generation he comes closer to his goal, moving the world ever closer toward complete depravity and rebellion.

Though it is true we cannot *ultimately* prevent this from happening, what is frightening is how little resistance "believers" are actually putting up in this struggle! We need to wake up and stay vigilant. Are we being desensitized to things which a generation ago were considered outrageous and unacceptable? Is our conviction of "worldliness" being slowly eroded so that with each successive generation we are becoming more and more sucked up into Satan's program? We need to do our homework and find out!

If only we could see clearly what the enemy is up to. If only we could take a seat at the board meetings and hear the discussion. We might see the very things we are now captivated by sitting on their drawing table! But we might also be surprised at the panic some of God's people are bringing to the highest levels of Satan's empire.

Here is how I imagine the latest update went. Picture, if you will, a room full of the top brass, gathered from all over the world for a special meeting with the head guy himself. Satan takes the floor and quizzes his generals, each one in charge of a special campaign to thwart the Great Commission:

"So tell me, how is everything going with our plans. Are we making progress?"

"Yes, Great One, we are operating on all fronts. Operation Waste The Day is in full force. Christians are now spending more time watching television than praying. We have filled up the Sunday services with everything but fervent intercession."

"How about the other operations?"

"Everything is running perfectly. Operation Let the TV Raise Your Kids is working beautifully. We have made heroes out of every kind of person God hates. Operation Wear Very Seductive Clothes So You Can Cause Others to Fall is progressing on schedule. You should see next year's styles. We use less material and charge twice the price! Operation Do Anything But Lead People To Christ is our best ever. Most Christians now go through life without winning anyone to the other side."

"Well, that's just dandy. Now tell me about my special pet project. How is it working out?"

"Operation Unreached Peoples. Yes, that is still in full force. There are still 3,000 of them."

"What do you mean 3,000? I thought it was 4,000?"

"No sir, the number has gone down."

"Then we have failed! How many times must I tell you that every operation must serve this one! If it is failing then everything else is failing as well. This number must not fall any further or you're finished. Do you understand me!!"

Now, of course, this would never happen. That is, one thousand unreached peoples being reached without Satan knowing about it immediately. Each one of them is a battle, and an intense one at that. But without a doubt, heads are beginning to roll in the corporate headquarters of hell. The tide is turning against them as more and more unreached peoples hear the gospel.

Surrender, however, is not an option. Surrender is eternal defeat. Just as Satan fought to the end to keep the Messiah from coming into this world, he will fight to the end to keep Him from returning. He will do everything possible to keep the remaining unreached peoples in total darkness. And don't forget, he still has a wonderful plan for your life! He has everything ready and lined up to keep you well away from the final frontiers of the Great Commission. You and I are his last, best hope! But we will overcome him by the blood of the Lamb, and by the word of our testimony (Rev. 12:11).

Eternal Vision

Many people have wondered where Satan hangs out. We might easily assume that he would prefer the White House or the Pentagon, or some place of great earthly power. But what really occupies most of his thinking and attention is whether or not the pastor of First Baptist Church is doing anything to fulfill the Great Commission . . . whether or not Dad and Mom are too busy raising issues from the past than to raise a godly family . . . whether or not this generation of believers will place the Kingdom of God before their careers and personal agendas. Do they have the final frontiers on their mind? If not, make sure it stays that way. If so, then shut them down. That's where the battle rages. That's where Satan does his best work. He can't be everywhere, but he might just show up at your church on mission Sunday. Or at your family devotions when you start praying for missionary so-and-so. Keep an eye out for him should the subject come up.

The safest thing your church or family can do is stay away from the Great Commission, but it's also a sure way out of the presence of God. Sounds like a Catch 22, but this is war—who said anything about it being safe? The important thing is that Jesus is in it and that makes it all the worthwhile.

BREAKING OUT

If Satan is to be defeated he must first be defeated in our lives, in our families, and in our churches. The Bible warns us that Satan seeks to disqualify us from our eternal reward through individuals that masquerade as "servants of righteousness" (Col. 2:18; 2 Cor. 11:15). Paul writes of so-called believers whom the evil one has "taken captive to do his will" (2 Tim. 2:26). On seven occasions the Bible warns us of "false disciples" who are agents of Satan's kingdom and apostles of deception.[2] These false disciples seek to become leaders and people of influence in order to destroy the faith and purity of God's people.

As always, we need to be discerning, but especially so as we come nearer to the end. We should not accept everything that comes with a Christian label on it. We shouldn't read every bestseller and say, "Well, if it's sold a million copies, it must be good stuff." We should test everything, because our enemy roams like a lion seeking people to devour.

Satan has one objective for you and your church, one standing order for all of his demons: make them content with shallow Christianity. Make them settle for less. Keep them out of the harvest and get them talking about everything imaginable *except the one thing* they're supposed to be doing. That's his only plan! He has no other chance of survival but to prevent you and your church from participating in the fulfillment of the Great Commission. Our responsibility is to stay awake and remain alert "in order that Satan might not outwit us. For we are not unaware of his schemes" (2 Cor. 2:11).

The enemy is "filled with fury" at this generation of believers (Rev. 12:12). He has only one question on his mind: how much time remains? Every moment is precious to him. His primary objective and only hope is to waste your time and the time of God's people. He has the whole next year lined up with exciting events, special campaigns, lovely parties and "historic" celebrations—anything and everything to keep us perpetually out of the action.

Start thinking in this light and you will begin to see Satan's handiwork all over the place. It's the hundred little things that all add up to nothing. It's the cares and worries which sap your passion and energy. It's the fears and doubts which keep you safely out of range from anything that matters. If we are to be effective against the enemy, we need to find out where he's operating in our lives. We need to ask ourselves, "If Satan has a stranglehold in my life, in this area of obeying the Great Commission, why should I put up with that? I'm a follower of the Lamb!" If you are ready and willing to examine yourself in this light, then ask yourself the following questions, and measure your life very carefully in the following ways:

Area 1: How much time do I spend praying for the lost?

The number one thing Satan wants to do in your life is keep you from praying for the Great Commission. A prayerless life is a defeated life. When I meet people who don't pray, I wonder what planet they think they're on. It's a sure win for the enemy if you decide to write the discipline of prayer out of your lifestyle. Samuel said, "Far be it from me that I should sin against the Lord by failing to pray for you" (1 Sam. 12:23). But how many believers are committing this very crime every day, and they don't even realize it?

Satan would also like to deceive you about the kind of praying you should be involved in. I've met Christians who say, "Yeah, I pray, you know, when I'm driving to work or washing the dishes. But I simply don't have the time to *just* pray." These well-intentioned, busy people simply don't get what kind of an enemy they have. And they don't have a clue what they're missing out on. The truth is, you'll never have the time if you don't have the commitment. Commitment *makes* the time no matter what. There is nothing wrong with praying throughout the day, even while washing the dishes. But I challenge you to pray at least one hour alone with God for thirty days and see if you don't notice such radical change in your life, you will never stop this discipline. Not only that, you will see answers like you've never seen them before.

This was the pattern Jesus left for us. Scripture says, "Jesus *often* withdrew to *lonely places* and prayed" (Luke 5:16). If Jesus needed to pray in this way, who are we to exempt ourselves! He advised us, "When you pray, go into your inner room, close your door, and *pray*" (Matt. 6:6). Learning to pray is the most important thing you will do with your life this side of eternity. God will honor your commitment. If you take him seriously, he will take you ever closer to his throne. You will never be the same.

Scripture says, "You do not have because you do not ask God" (Jas. 4:2). Satan wants you to be a loser for life, but not just for this life! He wants you off your knees, because only there can you hurt him, only there can you invest in eternity, only there can you effect change in the spiritual dimensions. Our preaching is powerless without prayer. Our walk is a limp, our talk is cheap, our efforts are wasted. God has promised us in no uncertain terms: If you're not asking, you're not receiving. If you're not seeking, you're not finding. If you're not knocking, you're not getting in.

If Satan has deceived you in this area, you need to renounce it. Ask the Lord for forgiveness and he will set you free. Pray, "Lord Jesus, help me to honor you in this area of praying faithfully everyday. I want to be faithful to pray for the lost and for the fulfillment of your Great Commission. I ask you to set me free from all hindrances, distractions and lies that have kept me from obeying you."

Area 2: How much time does my church spend praying for the Great Commission?

It seems that prayer for what is closest to God's heart has been written out of the constitution of many local churches. I don't know how it happened, but Satan has sure pulled a fast one here. Last week I was preaching before a gathering of about 1,000 believers. I asked everyone to stand. Then I asked all those who prayed more than ten minutes a day to remain standing. Like an ocean wave, people went down everywhere. More than 90% took their seats, some even chuckling to themselves. They should have been weeping. But it's not unusual. Everywhere I go it's the same. We are not taking prayer seriously in our churches. We aren't taking discipleship seriously. We aren't taking Jesus seriously.

The Master said, "I chose you and appointed you to go and bear fruit—fruit that will last. *Then* the Father will give you whatever you ask in my name" (John 15:16). Now we look at that and say, "Wow, what an amazing promise!" But we should see more than that. We should read, "What an amazing responsibility." Jesus has given us the assignment of asking. He has guaranteed those who are abiding in him, "If two of you on earth agree about *anything* you ask for, it *will be done* for you by my Father in heaven" (Mt. 18:19). If we really lived this way, we would be unstoppable. If every church and every believer began praying only ten minutes a day for the fulfillment of the Great Commission, we would witness so great a harvest all the empty churches and cathedrals in the world could not contain it.

So let's ask ourselves, "Are we being faithful stewards of this amazing trust? Are we prepared to give an account in this area of our lives? Is my church prepared? My family? My cell group? My Sunday school class?" Whatever may be your area of influence, you need to be thinking about this. Don't write off your corporate responsibility before the Lord.

Jesus said, "*Ask* the Lord of the harvest, therefore, to send out workers into his harvest field" (Matt. 9:37-38). Here is something we can ask for and we *know* it is the Father's will! This prayer *will be* answered! There is no surer way to invest in eternity than to pray this prayer. The fulfillment of the Great Commission has come this far only by the faithful and fervent intercession of God's people. It cannot and will not move forward without it.

If your church is not praying for the Great Commission like they ought to, don't be part of the problem! Ask the Lord to help you be part of his solution. Take the initiative and see what you can do. Don't criticize or get hostile. Just start praying for your church. Petition the throne of God with these words: "Heavenly Father, our church has sinned against you. We have not prayed for the fulfillment of your Great Commission as we ought to have. Please forgive us and move powerfully in our hearts that we might fully obey you. May we stand before you with no regrets and may your Holy Spirit guide our intercession from this day forward."

Area 3: How do I spend my idle time?

Everyone has idle time. Some people say they just can't find time to serve the Lord, share the gospel, or pray for the lost. But you would be surprised at how much time these same people have to amuse themselves. I have met Christians who can tell me the batting average of 100 baseball athletes, the number of free throws missed in the last four decades, and the time it takes for a sumo wrestler to get suited up. But they are clueless about how many people in Afghanistan are lost without Christ. They aren't aware that 50,000 precious people died without Christ today in the 10/40 Window. The things that are closest to God's heart are furthest from their minds. They know more about the world's business than their Father's business.

The Bible says, "Whatever you do, work at it with all your heart, as working for the Lord, not for men . . ." (Col. 3:23). I think this is the most important principle for living you can find. Our day belongs to the Lord. Even the smallest things we do are on his time. We are working for him, full time, all the time. And rest assured, the rewards are out of this world. This same verse goes on to say the reason we should do this: "since you know that you will receive an inheritance from the Lord as a reward. It is the Lord you are serving" (v. 24). We can never out-give God with our time. He has all eternity to reward us!

Our Heavenly Father is calling us to live sacrificially by giving what money can't buy. True generosity goes way beyond the balance of your savings account. The stingiest people on this planet are those who have the gift of *eternal* salvation and don't live like it *today*. I honestly don't want to be there when many Christians are called to give an account of their lives. Jesus said, "I tell you that men will have to give an account on the day of judgment for every careless word they have spoken" (Matt. 12:36). How much more then, with every prayer we pray, or don't pray? Of every hour we waste, every day we squander, every year we can't remember, every decade that just passed by? Rest assured, heaven is watching and keeping score!

Scripture says, "He who gathers crops in summer is a wise son, but he who sleeps during harvest is a disgraceful son" (Prov. 10:5). For those who may be unaware, it is indeed harvest time all over the world. Many of our brothers and sisters are out in the fields, laboring hard for the Lord to bring it in. But others are just standing by, wondering what all the commotion is about. Others could care less. They're tuned to ESPN for life. Breaking news is dinnertime and an emergency is using the last drop of barbecue sauce. "Their god is their stomach" (Phil. 3:19). And according to Proverbs, they are utterly disgraceful.

No one would disagree, but this is exactly the way heaven sees the sons of this generation who are still sleeping, dreaming, and frittering away their lives, while the greatest harvest eternity will ever know is being brought in from every village, town and city—in every nation, tribe and language of this world. If there ever was a time to be disciplined and wise, this would be that time. The stakes are higher today than ever before in history. According to the Bible, there will *never* be a time like this for all eternity to come.

We all need to pray, "Lord Jesus, forgive us for the hours we've wasted. Help us get organized and stay disciplined. Begin with me, in my life. May I know your will for every day and pursue it fully and completely. Keep me from distractions and foolish activity. Help me to maximize my effectiveness for you. May you have every moment of every hour of every day I live from this prayer forward."

Area 4: How much time do I spend in the pursuit of money?

When I travel different places speaking, I often get a chance to talk one on one with young people. I ask, "What do you hope to be doing ten years from now? What would you like to accomplish?" Inevitably I hear the exact same things that would come out of the mouth of a non-believer. This never ceases to amaze me. Satan really is good at getting us sucked into his program. I admit, my question is somewhat leading. I'm asking, "What would *you* like to accomplish." To be nice and fair I should ask, "What do you think the Lord wants to do through you?" But I'm not asking the question to be nice. The fact is, most of us are caught up doing what we want to do, what we think will be good for us. No one ever tells us there is something wrong with our plans. Most often adults are just glad that young people have a plan at all!

What is sad is that many starry-eyed young people grow up to be cynical, discouraged old people, because they get stuck on a detour they find hard to change. Satan's program for this next generation is the same as the last one: keep them away from the Great Commission. Get them so busy studying, working, paying off their home, three cars, and five credit cards, they won't even have the time to think about anything else.

Eternal Vision

I have seen many college students with a mission call get trapped in Satan's program one step at a time. It's almost always the same. The story goes something like this:

> Jerry and Lisa receive a call from the Lord to go out as missionaries during a Vision Conference held on their college campus. They prayerfully sign commitment cards and covenant before the Lord to obey his will. Now they long to get out there and reach people in India with the gospel. But they graduate from college with big debt, so they have to wait before they go. They get married, find some employment (just temporary of course), and move into a small apartment.
>
> Soon a couple kids come along and the grandparents say,
>
> "Hey, we should help you guys buy a home. It'll be a good investment."
>
> "Makes sense," Jerry says. "You know we can always sell it and make a profit."
>
> Lisa likes the house. It's a no-brainer. Time passes and wouldn't you know it, Jerry's boss loves his work ethic. So he offers him a better position with good retirement benefits. Sounds great to the both of them, especially with mortgage payments to think about.
>
> The years pass and the kids get older. The mirror starts saying, "You aren't going anywhere." Then one day the doctor says so, too.
>
> "Well, maybe our kids will make it out there to the mission field," Jerry says.
>
> Lisa laughs, "That would be a miracle."

Now of course, I don't want this to sound like there's anything wrong with staying at home and working in a secular job. That's exactly where the Lord needs people to be his witness. But if the Lord has called you to leave your home, family and friends, and go to a place like India, then get out there as soon as you can. Run out there! Run for your life. Let him take care of the details.

Equally, if the Lord has called you to stay and support the work, and fulfill the Great Commission where you are, then remain on high alert. Don't let your guard down. You might think missionaries working on the "frontlines" have a more difficult life, but in my experience they have it easier. Those who stay have to fight daily to remember where they are. We are not home. Not yet.

Keep in mind that money is more than just pieces of paper. It is spiritual currency. Satan is the ruler of this world and he is also its Central Banker. He gives every penny with strings attached. Only Jesus can cut them loose. Only then does it become heavenly currency. But we've got to want the scissors and we've got to ask for his power to keep us focused.

Depending on how much time you spend making money, the hard-earned cash you hold in your hands on payday represents a significant investment of your life. How you invest it will testify, for or against you, where your heart is and what means the most to you.

It has never been easy, but the challenge for all of us is to live according to the standard of Jesus, our Commander-in-Chief, who calls us to a sacrificial, wartime lifestyle. Only by placing his Great Commission before our comfort can we begin to see what investing in eternity is all about. Satan's agenda is to make us all slaves of temporal vision. If God has called you someplace and you're not going because of money, then God is not your master in this area. Money is, and Jesus says you must choose between us.

Not a day goes by where I don't plead for God's grace in this area. I just want to be honest with him and keep my heart pure. So daily I'm asking, "Lord Jesus, I need your wisdom and strength to serve you faithfully, and no other. Keep me free from the deceitfulness of wealth and from the pursuit of false comfort and security. May I fall so much in love with you, the things of this world and its desires will *never* find a place in my heart again."

Area 5: How much time do I waste in sin?

The greatest obstacle to the Great Commission is not a lack of money or missionaries or messages on reaching the lost. The greatest thing that dulls the hearts of believers, weakens our prayers, and makes our witness ineffective is the time we waste in sin. The things *we* nailed to the cross are still alive and many of them are still knocking at the door. Christians are spending more and more time in the counseling room. Pastors are spending more time talking about people's past than their future. Satan would like to convince us that we have to live in his defeat for the rest of our lives.

Many people say, "I'm so messed up, I will never be able to make any contribution to the Great Commission." But heaven sees the exact opposite. Heaven sees people who have something to share with the world. People who have it all together have little to offer those who need the grace of God. We simply need to let God turn our defeat into his victory. That's his business. Scripture tells us of those "whose weakness was turned to strength" (Heb. 11:34). Transforming lives is God's specialty; so don't entrust your heart surgery to a foot doctor! All the psychology in the world cannot solve a spiritual problem. Come to the source of all power and let him set you free.

The secret to living in freedom is no secret at all. You simply have to know the truth, receive it by faith, and abide in it continually. "That's easier said than done!" you may be thinking. And I would agree. It requires something supernatural. People give many good reasons why they struggle with sin, but they rarely give you the real reason. The real reason is a personal one: we are unwilling to confess that Satan has a stronghold in our lives. We know it's there, but we would like to call it something else. The moment we identify the problem for what it is, the Physician can operate on our hearts. Jesus can and will set you free. People in bondage don't believe that. They are deceived. They think it can't be that simple. I have seen people go from counselor to counselor for years and in one day be set free because they finally entrusted Jesus to do it. They saw the truth of God's Word, they believed that Christ could set them free, and they asked him to do it.

The Lord is willing, the problem is us. So if you will, I would like you to try this in one area of your life. Will you ask the Father, in Jesus name, to set you free from all distractions, hindrances and patterns of thinking which might keep you from fully obeying the Great Commission? If you are willing, then get ready for the ride of eternity. Because missionaries are not saints and heroes who got a call; missionaries are fallen, wretched creatures, with a sinful past, who heard the voice of God and said, "Here am I, send me."

Many people wrongly think they must become a saint before they can go. In fact, it is the opposite. By going, you *become* saintly! Once you understand what Christ wants to do through you, sin will come into its proper perspective. You simply won't have time to sin. Temptation will lose its power. You will become so preoccupied with serving Jesus and living for him, you won't even bother with sin. It will become repulsive to you, because you know it will hinder your effectiveness.

The great evangelist John Wesley said, "Give me one hundred preachers who fear nothing but God and hate nothing but sin, and such alone will shake the gates of hell!" If that is so, may the Lord give us 100,000! And we will surely finish the Great Commission in this generation and see Satan defeated before our very eyes. May it be so, and may you and I be counted worthy of such company in these final moments before our Lord's coming.

CHAPTER EIGHT

☙

BRINGING BACK THE KING

*"You are my brothers, my own flesh and blood.
So why should you be the last to bring back the king?" (2 Sam. 19:12)*

On June 5, 1967, Israel was faced with the greatest invasion of its history. An estimated 465,000 Arab troops, 2,880 tanks and 810 aircraft were poised to begin a simultaneous attack from Egypt, Jordan and Syria. Contingents from Iraq, Algeria, Kuwait and Russia combined to form the most incredible army ever assembled since World War II. The U.N. Emergency Force had already withdrawn a month earlier from the Egypt-Israeli border. The whole world stood back expecting the worst. No one lifted a finger to help them.[1]

It seemed that there was no possible way for Israel to survive with such resources marshaled against them. But in six days they defeated all their enemies and gained possession of new territory, including the Sinai Peninsula in Egypt, the whole of Jerusalem, the strategic Golan Heights of Syria and the West Bank of Jordan.

The Middle East has never forgotten this humiliating defeat. Just as Germany longed for a rematch after the First World War, much of the Arab world now awaits the slightest opportunity for round two. According to Scripture, their day will come, and this time only the Messiah will save Israel (Zech. 14).

For evangelicals alive during the Sixties, it seemed that the world was on its way to meltdown. Not just because of Israel's renewed status as a nation, and Bible prophecy about its neighbors joining together in alliance against her, but because all over the world, social upheaval seemed to be gathering momentum. Atheistic Communism was at its height, spreading like wildfire in almost every developing country. Scientists predicted that oil would run out by the end of the century. Industrial pollution was reaching suicide proportions. Society in traditionally Christian countries was becoming increasingly humanistic, secular and even anti-Christian.

But the "end" was still decades away. There was still more to come on God's timetable. For the last thirty years, global society has been on a collision course with its final destiny: a world controlled by one government with one global dictator. It doesn't take a genius to see what Satan is up to. The world is becoming smaller with every passing day. For the first time in human history there is a central place where representatives from all the world's nations have come together to seek and establish peace—just like the Bible said they would in the final days before His coming (1 Thess. 5:3; Rev. 6:4). What was delayed at the Tower of Babel has now come full circle, with the English language fast becoming today's undisputed *lingua franca* of science, commerce and industry. What the Lord said over 4,000 years ago has proven to be exactly true:

> "If as one people speaking one language they have
> begun to do this, then nothing they plan
> will be impossible for them."
> (Genesis 11:6)

No one can be sure what kind of world that might be, but Satan has an idea and he knows God doesn't like it. If this last century was known for its advances in computers and communication technology, this next one will surely be known for its advances in genetic engineering and bio-technology. Satan wants to destroy those made in the image of God by distorting the very genetic make-up of their being. It's a world we can hardly even imagine. But we will never get there. God is going to bring it all to an end. Satan's counterfeit kingdom will collapse and be completely destroyed.

In the meantime we have some solemn warnings from the Scriptures about the days up ahead. They are going to be very appealing and exciting to the world. But very dangerous for believers. How might "Christians" respond when science offers the world its own version of "eternal life"? Those who oppose it will be laughed at and scorned, branded as followers of "death cults" and mocked as superstitious fanatics. Their children will be taken from them as wards of the state, "rescued" in the eyes of the world from people obsessed with "going to heaven." Only the Lord knows what may come and how difficult it will be for those who hold faithfully to his name. But one thing we do know, it won't be easy and so we need to be ready.

The Bible says, the "Saints will be handed over to him for a time. . . ." (Dan. 7:25). As we come closer to the end, Satan will make a final stand to stop the fulfillment of God's plan. All of history is progressing toward this moment. Satan is not interested in creating an alternative utopian society because of his love for humanity. He is concerned about the saints and he wants to stop them. This world is designed to be a force that overcomes and conquers us, not necessarily by violence, but always by carefully organized deception. Satan is not free to do whatever he pleases. As with the trials of Job, he must ask permission for everything he does. His plan for Job was simply to alienate him from God by inflicting emotional, mental and physical suffering upon him. But he couldn't kill him. Only Job could make that decision by cursing God and ending it all. Satan's plan for the Church in the end-times is much the same. We have a choice. We don't have to suffer. All we have to do is bow down to his world and worship it. And he promises to leave you be.

Our enemy comes as an angel of light—a compassionate, merciful, heart-warming messiah. You can be sure he will pay you a visit in a form that is least expected. He is a crafty deceiver and a brilliant manipulator. But fortunately for us, Jesus has warned us about everything we need to know to keep us standing firm. He has told us *exactly* what Satan will do in the end-times, because the enemy can only do what God allows.

It is imperative that we understand the warnings we have been given and keep them on the forefront of our thinking. We have been warned for a reason! As the hours grow darker, and the night steadily approaches, only the truth of God's Word will keep us in the light. We need to get serious about where we are in history, and we need to get organized. I would encourage you to ask yourself, "If I knew Jesus was coming back in the next ten years, how should I be living? What should be my top priority?"

There are four things in particular I would start doing immediately if I knew for certain I was living in the last days. And just in case you're wondering, among them is not stocking up on canned tuna and sardines! Or building an underground bunker. Or buying a shotgun. In fact, people who do such things are the first to fall away! They have lost connection with "the Head" and have forgotten their purpose and calling. But here is what I would do if I were living in the end-times, and what I am doing with great earnest:

1st: I would search the Scriptures with great diligence.

The first thing I would do is find out what the Bible says about those days. What is amazing to me is that God allows people to remain in ignorance, not only if they choose to, but even if others have chosen for them, such as parents, religious leaders or society in general. What is terribly frightening to me is that many people think they are doing the right thing and have brilliant justifications for their behavior, but they are dead wrong in the sight of heaven.

Only the Word of God can save us from the curse of ignorance. So we need to ask ourselves, "What exactly did Jesus say about those final days? How did he describe them and what warnings did he leave us?" One of the first things that comes to mind is this startling statement Jesus made to his disciples. He said, "Because of the increase of wickedness, the *love of most* will grow cold" (Matt. 24:12). Without a doubt, I would take this seriously if I knew I was living in the end-times. How is my love doing? Scripture says in the last days people will be "Lovers of themselves, lovers of money, boastful, proud, disobedient to their parents, ungrateful" (2 Tim. 3:2). I can think of no better summary of our society today. The question is, how much has my society molded my heart, my desires, my ideas?

We need to have a deeper understanding of our corporate responsibility before God. The Bible says of Sodom, "She and her daughters were arrogant, overfed and unconcerned; they did not help the poor and needy. . . . Therefore I did away with *them* as you have seen" (Eze. 16:49-50). I think us rich Christians should take this a little more seriously if we are living close to the end. We should take it seriously anytime, but especially so as we hear the hoofs of God's chariot beating a pathway to our city. Are we arrogant, overfed and unconcerned? Here was the root of all Sodom's sin before the Lord. It came from prosperity and resulted in an unconcern for fellow human beings, culminating in a hardness of heart toward the Lord. We cannot turn our back on those fashioned in the image of God and hope that our relationship with the Lord will continue much longer. We can't excuse ourselves with ignorance. God requires us to know.

Jesus also said there will be an *increase* in wickedness before his coming. Now here is an amazing statement. There has always been wickedness. But is there something different about today that I should be aware of? There is no need to justify through statistics and graphic stories that we live in an evil age, but what kind of evil do I need to be most worried about in my life? The worst kind of evil is the subtlest, the kind that infects even the "best of us." When Jesus came here he didn't rail against homosexuality, prostitution or gambling. His harshest criticism was reserved for those he called "unmarked graves" (Luke 11:44). They were the guardians of correct theology, the respected religious leaders of his day. There is good reason for this. Scripture prophesies that in the last days, people will "gather around them a great number of teachers to say what their itching ears want to hear" (2 Tim. 4:3). It just may be that the increase of wickedness Jesus is referring to is happening right in our own backyards. We the holy, we the conservatives, we the pious are the unmarked graves if we live according to a false gospel. If we choose our lifestyle and then choose our gospel to cushion it, we are the most depraved of all. We have the message of eternal life and we have turned it into a license to tell the world, "Go to hell! We're going to be comfortable and religious."

Jesus came here to start a revolution of love and compassion, a movement of outward concern for the lost, for the oppressed, for the hurting. He came down hard against those who shut the doors of his chapel on people who needed the love of God so desperately they were dying to get in. There is nothing more wicked in the sight of heaven than coldhearted religious piety. Is this happening today? Is it on the increase? I would find out if I were living near the end.

2nd: I would examine my life very carefully.

Jesus warned us about two kinds of believers who would be alive in the last days. He told a parable about ten virgins who were eagerly awaiting the coming of the bridegroom (Matt. 25). But five of them never made it into the hall. You know the story. What was it that caused these five believers—these followers, these disciples, these invited guests—to run out of oil and lose their place in the Kingdom? Could it happen today? To us?

Is it possible that some believers will still *not* be ready despite reading book after book on the Second Coming of Christ? Let's admit it. We love to read about it. But how many are getting ready? How many are fueling up on the oil of the Holy Spirit and preparing themselves for those final days? Jesus said to his disciples (a group of end-time fanatics) when they asked about his coming,

> "Be careful, or your hearts will be weighed down
> with dissipation, drunkenness, and the anxieties of life,
> and *that day will close on you unexpectedly* like a trap." (Luke 21:34)

Did you catch that tongue-twister-of-a-word in the middle? I'm afraid I missed it the first few times. How many times have you said, "You know, I really feel weighed down with *dissipation* this morning"? I'm sure I've never used it, but it captures a whole lot (I had to look it up in Webster's). It simply means the pursuit of pleasure and what results from it—the wasteful expenditure of our limited time and energy. Jesus is telling us, "Watch out, because those who live this way are going to be surprised by my coming."

We live in an age where the pursuit of pleasure is the most important thing on the agenda. There may have been ages where this wasn't the case, but I doubt it. What makes us different is that we are masters of comfort. We live better today than kings only a century ago. But we're still not happy. And we're still not satisfied. I would keep a lookout for this one if I were living in the end-times. I would ask myself: What am I living for? What gets the priority of my time and money? Is it all about me? My comfort, my fun, my *life*?

The second thing Jesus warned his disciples about was "drunkenness." Now this can refer to literally getting drunk on alcohol, or to anything that affects your mental faculties. Millions today are so doped-up on medication they can hardly function in any normal capacity. What's worse, many people in the last days will simply shut down their brains and refuse to think things through. They are as good as drunk. Have you ever tried to reason with a drunken man? Certainly you can persuade him to do almost anything, whether it's good for him or not. But try getting him to stop!

As Christians, we need to stay awake and keep our minds sharp. Every verse written about the end-times is for us and we need to take it seriously. Scripture tells us exactly what our priority should be: "The end of all things is near, *therefore* be alert and self-controlled so that you can pray" (1 Pet. 4:7). Our only priority is Jesus! We need to stay close to him and follow his lead. He has a message for each of us. We need to study what's happening, examine what's being said, know God's Word intimately, and learn how to preach. That's right, the Lord needs you to preach! You're being asked to flex those neurons and start communicating. That's your job. So break out the reading glasses, start studying, start writing, start talking. Get used to it. Everyone is needed and you are no exception.

The third warning Jesus gave about the last days to his disciples was to watch out for the "anxieties of life." It's no secret that stress can wreck your health, but can it destroy you spiritually as well? Jesus warned us of believers who would have the Word choked out of them by the "worries of this life and the deceitfulness of wealth" (Matt. 13:22). Here is a powerful combination. The enemy wants you distracted from your priority and focused instead on mere survival. He wants you beaten down, driven back, and running the other way until you collapse. He wants you sucked into his trap.

But the Lord wants you on top of His mountain! He wants your life filled with joy in the midst of hardship and your spirit filled with praise and thanksgiving through every trial and adversity. He wants you lifted up, high above every circumstance. He wants your soul to overflow with his power. He wants your entire being to delight in his goodness, grace and mercy, no matter what should come.

Yet if we can't learn this now when things are difficult, why should we expect our reaction to be any different when the Day comes to an end, and the Night descends? So we need to examine ourselves: Are we still abiding? Are we growing in faith? Are we pursuing heaven with reckless abandon? If you're in Christ, even the sky is no limit. Let no one hold you back from sky-rocketing with Jesus.

Scripture says there is nothing you can't do when God is going before you. You can do *all things* through Christ. You will overcome *all the power* of the enemy. *Nothing* can stand against you![2] Jesus gave us these promises for a good reason. We're going to need them. He has scattered them out on the soil of his Church, and he is saying, "Here is my word, my promise, my guarantee." It's out there, available to us all. So Scripture says, "Examine yourselves to see whether you are in the faith; test yourselves" (2 Cor. 13:5). Keep yourself in check: Are these things in my heart? Are they deep and secure? Have I kept them well watered and protected, sunlit and shielded, rooted and anchored—against the "worries of this life, the deceitfulness of wealth and the desires for other things" (Mark 4:19)? I need to find out, and the sooner I do the better. Now is the time to be "sure and certain!" (Heb. 11:1).

3rd: I would find out what God's program is and get with it.

One of the most amazing statements in Scripture is when Jesus calls one of his own, "You wicked, lazy servant," upon his return to this earth (Matt. 25:26). The Bible says judgment will begin with the house of God (1 Pet. 4:17). Imagine for a moment that you are a servant in a great house. You have been given your assignments and responsibilities. You are one of the harvesters, and your master has given you a map of his harvest field. He says he will be away on a journey, and while he's gone the harvest will be coming in. He draws a circle around part of his field and says, "Here is where I need you. Make sure everything goes according to plan."

Now perhaps you aren't feeling terribly motivated about this particular assignment and you let it go. You go fishing instead. The master returns and finds his harvest ruined. Of course he's not too happy, but what has he really lost? Only some income and one less servant. With the Lord it is much different. Failing in his harvest has eternal consequence. Those words, "You wicked and lazy servant," can only be properly understood in this context.

So what is God up to today? What is his program for this generation? If only more people understood this, there would be a lot less confusion about how to use our precious resources. I don't want to condemn anyone or any particular church, but what if every decision we made was done with this one thing in mind: Is this expense going to "hasten his coming" (2 Pet. 3:12)? I know of a church that recently installed a million dollar organ. Now I'm not mad at this church, but I'd like to present what I believe to be heaven's point of view on their purchase. No doubt this expense was made with the greatest of motivations. A million dollar organ will make beautiful music, and this music is for the Lord. We should stop at no expense, right? After all, isn't it being legalistic to say how much is too much to spend on such things? Didn't Judas Iscariot do that when he complained about the expensive perfume being "wasted" on the feet of Jesus?

Well, that is certainly one way of looking at it. But I believe it's the wrong argument for the wrong cause. The Bible tells us God has a program—a mission and agenda that he wants to get done. He wants representatives from every nation, tribe and tongue to sing his praises. Now that's heavenly music! To be sure, Jesus doesn't care if your music is made by a million dollar organ or a hand-made guitar. He is looking at the heart. He is watching us to see what we care about most. He knows exactly why we spend our money the way we do and who is really getting blessed. Suppose we knew what was closest to his heart? Suppose we knew that Jesus was deeply concerned that 2.7 billion people were without access to the gospel? Then could we spend money any way we want?

May we never think it is justifiable to misuse the tithes of God's people under the covering of "blessing the Lord" when in fact what he desires is "obedience," not sacrifice (1 Sam. 15:22). He once said to Israel, "When you spread out your hands in prayer, I will hide my eyes from you; even if you offer many prayers, I will not listen. Your hands are full of blood" (Isa. 1:15). God is not honored with our worship if our hands are full of injustice. If we have let millions perish because of our thoughtless "sacrifices," which are really designed to bless us anyway in most cases, then what good is our worship?

There is one reason, and one reason only, why Jesus will call one of his own *You wicked and lazy servant* upon his return to this earth. This servant was entrusted with a certain measure. He had a responsibility to multiply it and put it to good use for the Master. Simply put, what Jesus is saying to His church is this: I want you to be industrious in the Great Commission. I want you to take it seriously. I want you to get it done.

Jesus used "business" examples to describe his Kingdom because the world is so much more serious about its business than we are about ours. We are supposed to be like those traders on Wall Street who are busy making deals—only more so. Or those executives up in first class talking eagerly about their last meeting—only more so. Or those salesmen who go door to door with so much enthusiasm they practically bust the door down with their smile—only more so. Jesus said the people of this world are so much wiser than the children of the Kingdom (Luke 16:8). It's absolutely true, although rightly it should be the exact opposite, and for some it is.

What if we took the loss of souls as seriously as corporate America takes its loss of profits? They take great risks for perishable green pieces of paper. They expend all their emotional and mental energies for a little bit more. We too have been caught up in the frenzy! Might it be said of us that we have more risk-takers for gold than for God in our churches today? Oh, that we would have the same passion for souls as the world has for its profit margins! What if we seriously looked at the balance sheet and said, "We have a serious problem here! Fifty thousand souls are perishing every day in the 10/40 Window and we have not done *even half* of what we ought to reach them"? What if every church had a board meeting about this problem and asked, "What are *we* going to do about it"?

Or what if everyone said, "Well, it's not really my problem. If God wants to reach them, I'm sure he'll find a way"? To these wicked and lazy servants there is a special statement in reserve, and it should come as no surprise to them. But amazingly, they *will be* surprised and that is only fitting. For the people they condemned to an eternity of darkness are also in for a big surprise.

In the end, the issue is not whether we have concern for others that counts, the issue is whether our concern for others is greater than our concern for ourselves. That's what matters, and that's why Jesus will be justified to say what he will upon his return.

4th: I would get organized.

Jesus told a story about the end-times that I find very interesting. He talked about a servant who was made responsible to give other servants "their food at the proper time" (Luke 12:42). He was a "faithful and wise servant" in the beginning. But this servant became lazy and neglected his responsibility, spending the resources entrusted to him for his own pleasure while the Master was away. Now who might Jesus be talking about in this parable? Could it be us? The Church? Those entrusted with the Master's business? Seems to fit. What have we done with the resources entrusted to us to "bless the nations"? Have we kept them, misused them, withheld them? Have we "hoarded wealth in the last days" (Jas. 5:3)?

He told another story about two brothers who had responsibilities in the vineyard. One started out well, but in the end he turned away. The other rebelled at first, but later returned to take his brother's place.

What I find interesting about these two parables is that Jesus is interested in people who finish well: not people with good intentions, not people who get all excited at a mission conference, not people who rush to sign commitment cards. He's interested in finishers. It's the common denominator in every parable Jesus told about the end-times. The virgins who ran out of oil, the servant who buried his talent, the unfaithful manager who mistreated the servants—each fell victim to the same trap. They failed to discipline their lives when it mattered most.

So how do you get organized to ensure that you will maximize your potential? I can think of no more important question for us to ask today. We *will be* called into strict account before the Lord, so we might as well get it together *now*. Until we grasp that reality we are doomed to misprioritize our lives. Jesus made it clear to his disciples that he is no way interested in people who look back, or have second thoughts, or complain through every difficulty. Perhaps it sounds a little harsh to some, but it's exactly what we need to hear. Our enemy is not a nice guy. He's just waiting to do us in. Our Lord is like a coach trying to get his young football recruits ready for the big game. He's letting us have it square on the chin. He's saying, "Get it together, guys. Your mama isn't going to save you out there."

If we're going to do more than just survive, if we hope to overcome and win, we need to organize our lives around a central plan. Every good plan has three important factors that we should keep in mind: time, capacity and measurable goals. Your plan should take all three into account. For example, let's say you knew for sure there were only ten years left before the Lord would return. How might you use them? What can be done in ten years? It's not a whole lot of time. Ten years for most people vanishes like the setting sun. But ten years can be the time of your life if you learn to live them one day at a time in the Lord's power.

The next thing to look at is your capacity. This is a faith issue from beginning to end. Only the Lord knows what you and he can achieve together. Your job is to give him the chance. Your capacity is as great as the promises of God and as wide and deep as his love for you. So begin with what you know. Ask yourself: What do I know I can do for God *right now?* The first step in any good plan is to accurately assess where you are. And then build from there.

Wherever you are, or whatever you are doing, there is one thing you can learn to do now which will be of use to you in any and every circumstance. Get connected to Jesus in as real and powerful a way as is supernaturally possible. Just start spending time with him. You can pray. Don't believe the lies. You *must* pray! Learn to pray longer and more passionately with every day. You can sing. Yes, you can! Just start praising the Lord and watch what happens. You can learn his Word. Soak it up. Start teaching others around you who are eager to learn. Jesus said, "The night is coming . . ." (John 9:4). So start investing while it is Day. When the darkness falls, you'll be ready. If they take your Bible, that's okay, you will *be* the Bible.

Our calling is to make disciples, no matter where you are or what you are doing, make disciples. Maybe you aren't sure where the Lord will send you, but without a doubt, you *are* somewhere on this planet. Are there people around? Then make disciples. When you're not teaching, you're learning. When you're not being challenged, you're challenging others. The *cause* must become your consuming passion. Organize your life around it.

People who are really into something fill their lives with it. I have friends who think skateboarding is God's gift to humanity. They have posters, T-shirts, bumper stickers, and wacky haircuts to let the whole world know what's the coolest thing to be doing on this planet. They might not seem organized, but they are very determined. They practice for hours to get that jump just right, that flip just perfect. They get together to show off their moves and they bring a fresh supply of stickers with them: Skateboarding Is Not A Crime! They put it on all the signs that would tell them otherwise. They have their way of keeping the passion alive. So you must also.

Your capacity is much bigger than you think or know. Give God the chance to use you powerfully. Don't limit yourself with small thinking. Surround yourself with the right people. I know people who want to get into the movies so bad, they become waitresses at Denny's on the off-chance they might serve lunch to a movie producer. "Hey, it could happen," they tell you. "This is Hollywood." So what about us? What do we want to be? What are we desperate about? Reaching the lost? Well, let's take the initiative. Where is that going on? Who is reaching the lost in a big-time way? Go help them. Learn what you can.

Finally, the next thing you must have in your plan is measurable goals. A fellow named John Hyde started praying that God would allow him to reach one soul a day. He prayed like it, too. He would spend hours on his knees before God every day. The Lord honored his prayer and granted his request. The next year he asked God for two souls a day, and the next one after that he asked for four! Each time the Lord granted his request. It wasn't long before a great revival broke out in the area of India where he was ministering. The Lord honored his faith and he will do the same for you and me, and for anyone who will seek to do great things in his great harvest.

Another fellow like John Hyde was George Müller. He came to London from Prussia when he was in his twenties. As a follower of Jesus he was shocked by the unconcern for the thousands of orphans living on the streets. Although he had little money, he prayed, "Lord, use my life as a demonstration of faith. If it is your will, use me to provide a home for every one of these kids." The first thing he did was rent a house. And then gathering as many kids as would come, he started his first orphanage. One morning he had absolutely no food to feed them, but in typical George Müller fashion he gathered the kids together and said, "Children, let's thank the Lord for our breakfast!" While he was praying, there was a knock on the door. It was the local baker. He said, "Sir, the strangest thing happened. Last night the Lord woke me up and told me to bake this bread and bring it to this house." George returned to the children and began thanking the Lord. Soon there was another knock at the door. This time it was the milkman. His horse had gone lame right outside and he offered George all the milk he could take!

This was only the first of many miracles George Müller would see in his life. In the decades that followed, the Lord answered every prayer he prayed (quite literally) and honored the goal he set in faith. He was able to provide a home for every orphan in London. Not only that, he had more than enough for his own ministry. Never once did he ask anyone for money. Even so, he was able to support hundreds of missionaries all over the world with the excess.

As you are faithful like George Müller, the Lord will use you to ignite fires everywhere you go. One of those inspired by George Müller's faith (and there are many) was a guy named Hudson Taylor. He left for China when he was only twenty-two years old. He was just one guy, all alone, with few resources. He witnessed the vast interior of China with over 200 million people and no missionary work. So he asked God, "Will you give me two missionaries for each of the twelve interior provinces of China?"

It wasn't long before the Lord sent him back to England to share about this great need. Upon his return to China, exactly twenty-four missionaries had signed up to join him! On the day he departed from England, sixteen new candidates were sailing with him, and another eight had already arrived in China ahead of him. But that was only the beginning. Hudson kept asking. The next time he returned he asked for 30, and then 70, and then 100! Each time the Lord granted Hudson's request. His faith was building, his goals expanding. And the Lord was smiling on it all.

Successful people in God's Kingdom are those who learn what God wants done and in faith rise up and say, "Lord, use me to do it!" By the end of Hudson Taylor's life, thousands had been sent to China and tens of thousands had come to know Jesus. One of Hudson's biggest financial supporters was George Müller. Today, there are over 100 million believers in China!

Eternal history has been irrevocably altered because these men were determined to set *measurable goals by faith*. They took them seriously and organized their lives for action. They saw the need and they had the faith to believe, "My God is able to meet it!" The ripples of their obedience extend deep into our time. It can happen for you and for me just the same. It only takes three things: the vision, the passion, and the strength. Rest assured, you have none of these things! But you know Someone who does, and he stands ready to give them at anytime. Just ask Him. Then buckle up and get ready for the ride of your life. You will never regret it. The only ones with regret in heaven are the ones who never tried.

CHAPTER NINE

THE BLESSING

*"I do all this for the sake of the gospel,
that I may share in its blessings." (1 Cor. 9:23)*

*H*ave you ever wondered why some people are successful and others are not? Books about people who have made it to the top are eagerly bought up by those on the bottom. Everyone wants to know the big secret about how to get there. Theories and principles abound, many of which contradict each other. But one thing is sure, success in this world ultimately comes down to something you can't control: the favor you are given or not given by other people. You can do all the right things, be the most disciplined person in the world, have all the right talent, and still get nowhere fast. Such is life we say, and there is a very good reason behind it.

The Bible says the god of this age is at work in *all those* who are disobedient (Eph. 2:2). We live in a world that is masterminded and controlled by "powers and principalities" that are far beyond our manipulation. Want to make it in Hollywood? Want to become a millionaire? Want to be president? You would be a fool to think you can just walk in on power, wealth and success without the aid of, and indeed, the permission of, the "powers that be." The question is, whose power is at work in your life?

God is not opposed to making his servants wealthy, powerful and successful. But he *is* opposed to anything that might hurt his children. Satan wants to turn good into evil, a blessing into a curse, worldly success into eternal failure. But though we live in a system designed to overcome us, through God's power we have the capacity to plunder it for his Kingdom. We can hit the enemy at the root of his strength, for all "power and wealth" were purchased by the blood of the Lamb (Rev. 5:12).

There is one businessman I know of who decided not to let the Devil have any room in his business. So he gave it to God—quite literally. He manages the only business in America, and perhaps the world, that is legally owned by God. His name is Stanley Tam and he operates one of the world's largest plastic manufacturing and distribution companies. He started out in something totally different and with few resources. But from day one he determined that the profits of the company would go to advancing the Lord's work around the world. And so from day one the Lord began to prosper Stanley's efforts and multiply his capacity for business.

Stanley Tam came to understand the principle of The Blessing. Though it is the greatest secret of success in the world today, it is nonetheless an open secret, available to any seeker who would earnestly desire it. So it's more like a mystery. The clues are all there, but few people put them all together to see the big picture.

THE COVENANT OF BLESSING

The Blessing is the theme of the entire Bible, but most people miss it because they read their Bible in a somewhat haphazard way—almost like digging through a mountain of gold looking for silver.

The Blessing

They don't realize the Bible is actually a very organized document. If you want to see the big picture, you have to begin where the Bible begins, in the first few chapters of an amazing story.

The Blessing was first given by God to the son of an idol worshiping Mesopotamian tribesman. God appeared to him and said, "Abraham, I have a promise for you, a special deal to offer you that will change your life and the course of history." This promise, or covenant, would bring prosperity and success to those who followed its precepts, but failure and disaster to those who misused or opposed it.

Moses referred to this covenant when he said to God's people, "Now remember the Lord your God, for it is he who gives you the *ability to make wealth* and so confirms his covenant, which he swore to your forefathers" (Deut. 8:18). The Covenant of Blessing is referenced all throughout the Bible. It has often been called "The Golden Thread" of Scripture. It reveals something very fascinating. The Bible is not a scatterbrain collection of unrelated documents. It has an introduction regarding its theme, then a massive unfolding of that theme, and then a conclusion regarding the outcome. In other words, the Bible *begins* with a thesis statement and then like any good book sets out to prove it.

This reality is so compelling it is one of the clearest demonstrations of the Bible's authenticity and one of the best defenses of its authorship by the Holy Spirit. Not only that, the thesis statement of the Bible is the guiding force behind all of history. The amazing weight of this realization will change your life more than any other perspective. It is the key to both temporal *and* eternal success in a world where prosperity can cost you more than you will ever gain. It's available to anyone who will say, "Lord, I want it," and it's fully realized in all those who have been willing to live it. From Abraham to the present, all those who have followed the principles of this covenant have seen success beyond anything they could ever have imagined possible.

There are four basic principles of The Blessing and they are outlined for us in Genesis 12:1-3, as part of a covenant God made with Abraham. As you will see, these same promises also belong to us through Christ. Here in these few verses we find the "open secret" of success and the thesis statement of the entire Bible:

The Covenant of Blessing

> "Abraham, leave your country,
> your people and your father's household
> and go to the land I will show you.
> I will make you into a great nation
> and I will bless you;
> I will make your name great,
> and you will be a blessing.
> I will bless those who bless you,
> and whoever curses you I will curse;
> and all peoples on earth
> will be blessed *through you*."

Did you notice that last statement? And the last two words of that statement? It is the key within the key to this special promise. Here we find one of the first and most important prophecies in Scripture. No other ancient prophecy in Scripture is so clearly defined and readily documented. This is an important fact about the Bible itself. God designed his Word to be self-authenticating. He doesn't want you to have groundless faith. He wants it anchored in his promises. Now think about this. God promised a Mesopotamian

The Blessing

nomad, over 4,000 years ago, that through him and his descendants all peoples on earth would be blessed. So either this prophecy is true or it's not true. Either God said it and meant it, or it's a lie and nothing at all will come of it.

From this point on, the Bible sets out to *prove* this statement—to demonstrate the faithfulness of God and the authenticity of his Word. If you skip to the end of the book, you'll get a sneak preview of how it all turns out. In Revelation we witness the final fulfillment of the Covenant of Blessing. We see people from every nation, tribe and tongue standing before the throne, worshiping the Lamb (Rev. 5:9). Everything else in between, the entire story of the Bible, reveals step by step how this promise would be fulfilled. All other prophecy in the Bible and all of God's activity on this planet centers on the fulfillment of this central promise: through Abraham and his offspring, all peoples on earth will be blessed.

To fulfill this promise, God covenanted with Abraham to provide all the power necessary, both material and spiritual, to get the job done. God said, "I will make your name great and you *will be* a blessing." Now here is something amazing. The undisputable fact is, we know more about Abraham than any other person from this period of history. Today, over three billion people (Christians, Muslims and Jews) consider Abraham to be a very important person.

But how did it happen? How did an ordinary guy, who lived four thousand years ago as a nomadic sheep herder and tent dweller, become so famous? He never built a city. There are no monuments to him in the ancient world. But of all ancient people his name is the most well known in all the world today. Now why is that? What made him so special? You can search the story of his life from beginning to end, and you will only find one thing: He simply said *Yes* to God and his mission. By faith he became a recipient of God's power and grace when he made a decision to participate in His Covenant of Blessing. This one guy changed the world, not because he was any different than you or I, but because he believed a promise that guaranteed him success if he would live by its principles.

This is so fascinating it merits far more study than this short chapter. In fact, our organization has designed a special seminar called *The Blessing* to explain this in more depth. If you haven't taken this course yet, I highly recommend it. But in the meantime, here is a brief overview of the four key principles from the Covenant of Blessing that are important for us to understand if we seek its power to be activated in our lives.

Principle One: You've got to give something up.

The first thing God asked Abraham to do was leave his father's household and country. Now put yourself in Abraham's sandals for a moment. The world was not a safe place. What's more, people living in these times had little way of determining fact from fiction in the rumors they heard. Many people ventured no further from their small village for fear of the dragon that lived on the other side of the mountain. There was no CNN with video cameras to monitor human rights. No United Nations, no War Criminals Court, no judicial system. There were no ATMs to make withdrawals if you got in a jam. Law and order was basically a matter of might makes right.

So here was Abraham, all by his lonesome, being asked to give up the comfort and security of his family and homeland and go to a land which God had not yet shown him, but promised to reveal on the way! I can just imagine the reaction Abraham got from his dad when he tried to explain all this over a cup of coffee. And I have no idea what Sarah was thinking when she agreed to go along! But she must have been quite a woman of faith.

The Blessing

Now God promised Abraham that if he obeyed him, The Blessing would be activated in his life (Gen. 18:19). That Blessing, or heavenly anointing, was the spiritual power required to do all that God had promised. The vision was incredible and far-reaching: *all peoples* on earth would be blessed through Abraham and his descendents. If Abraham was willing to give up his secure future and venture out, God promised to lead him to a special place where He would use him very powerfully.

Now the same is true today. God wants to do something in your life, but like Abraham, you have to put yourself in a position where he can use you. He wants to empower you to be a blessing, to be a participant in his covenant, and to see prophecy fulfilled through *you*. But there's the catch: you have to do your part. Many people are missing out because they refuse to give up their "homeland"—their comfort zone, their place of security, their pleasant dreams of earthly heaven. The hardest thing in the world is to venture out into the unknown and put your family at risk and your future on the line. But that's what the Covenant of Blessing is all about. God has made a promise. He has spoken. And that means as you step out in faith, God will give you the impossible, to the amazement of all those you encounter and all those you leave behind.

Most people miss out because they are unwilling to have an exchange with God. They never see the abundance just waiting to be activated in their lives. They never see it because they only focus on the risk instead of the reward. For example, Jesus promised us several incredible blessings or *sources* of spiritual power. But very few people ever see these blessings come into their life, because when the moment comes to seize them, they shrink back.

Jesus said, "*Blessed* are you when men hate you, when they exclude and insult you and reject your name as evil, *because of the son of*

Eternal Vision

man" (Luke 6:22). Now here is something not many of us look forward to, and rightly so. But following Jesus in this world is going to get you into trouble. Jesus says when that happens, get ready, because I'm going to bless you. God has reserved great spiritual authority and power to *anyone* who is willing to take risks for the Kingdom. With this promise in hand you can look at any difficulty and say, "Go ahead and bring it on! You only make me more like Jesus! You only increase my power in him."

Imagine how such a blessing, such a heavenly perspective, would change your life and your world. You would see the power of suffering—that wherever there is sacrifice on behalf of the Kingdom, heavenly grace and strength are administered in direct proportion. For as you come to know the "fellowship of his sufferings," God's power will begin to flow through you and make you more and more like his Son. So Jesus goes on to say, *"Blessed* are you who weep now; *Blessed* are you who are poor; *Blessed* are the peacemakers" (Luke 6:20-22; Matt. 5:3-11). Again, these are not easy things. But to those who weep, to those who sacrifice, to those who step out into the cross-fires of this world and bring His love and peace—to those who are out there where the action is—our Lord is promising an eternal Blessing that will fill your life and rock your world.

It's an exchange that will take you into the unknown—into the high-risk zones and the unchartered territory on the map. Out there you'll find the unimaginable, but you won't be alone. It's a well worn path. Abraham, Joshua and Daniel all walked it. William Carey, Hudson Taylor and C.T. Studd have all left their tracks. You'll meet a special breed of people out there who have learned what eternal success is all about. They all came to know the same secret: On your own you can do nothing. But when you get plugged into God's purposes you can do *anything*. God's power is reserved for the execution of his will. So whoever would seek it, whoever would desire to do great things here on this earth, must find out what God wants done and then get with the program. To be sure, these guys were all forceful men. The Kingdom is not for the timid at heart. William Carey said, "Attempt great things *for* God, expect great things *from* God!" They were risk-takers and builders, gold miners and entrepreneurs. But the gold they found never faded, the wells they dug never ran out, and the songs they sang filled the whole earth.

They were hungry and thirsty for a righteousness that came by faith. They set out to claim the promise and on the way they changed the course of eternal history. There was nothing particularly special about them; they weren't actually that brave to begin with. But they learned bravery. They acquired an adventurous spirit. And they became forever changed when they met the source of all true courage. They simply learned to trust and obey a God who would do the impossible through *anyone* who would follow his lead and get out there.

So here's the bottom line: the Covenant of Blessing requires us to do something. We have to take the initiative as God leads us. Then, *and only then*, will we see his power activated in our lives. You've got to find out where God wants to meet you and come on his terms. He has a special place for you—so find it! He has people for you to encounter—so venture out! He has miracles to perform through you—just embrace them! Don't shrink back from hardship and trial. That's where God is going to meet you. Let him do his work. For it is through sacrifice that God gets the glory. It's all about him and his promises—his plan that he promised 4,000 years ago to an ordinary guy who changed the world by simply saying "Yes, I'll go." And then he did it.

Eternal Vision

**Principle Two: God will lead you to a place
where you will prosper.**

After Abraham obeyed God and ventured out, the Lord began to show him more of His plan for him. As Abraham was faithful with what he knew he *must* do, God took him to the next level and revealed a little more. This is a very important principle. Many times God doesn't give us all the details at once. Such was the case with Abraham. He had no idea where God would take him, but he knew there was a definite destination—a special *place* where God wanted him to be. It was the place of blessing, the perfect setup where God's plan for Abraham and his family would be fully realized.

That place for Abraham was the land of Canaan. Upon his arrival, God showed up once again and promised him the humanly impossible. He said, "Abraham, to your descendants I will give this land" (Gen. 15:18). Now it just so happened that Canaan was the most hotly contested piece of property in the Middle East. The three largest kingdoms of Abraham's day—the Hittites, Babylonians and Egyptians—all converged on this strategic area. It was the center of trade and influence, and anyone who could hold it would be greatly prospered. God said, "Abraham, it's all yours." And the amazing thing is, Abraham actually believes it! No questions asked. I don't know about you, but I would be thinking, "Lord, am I really hearing you right? How can this be?" But Abraham had come to understand how serious God was about his covenant. No expense was too great, no problem too big. God wanted Abraham to be a blessing to all nations on earth and here was the best place to get that going. So God said, "Abraham, this is where it's going to happen. This is where my glory will be made known throughout all the earth."

The same is true today. Finding the place where God can best use you is the most important thing you will do with your life. But keep in mind the lesson Abraham learned: When God makes a promise, when he gives a vision, it is *always* so big and so impossible that only his divine intervention can make it come to pass. If we forget this, we end up in big trouble. I have seen many people abandon the place where God has sent them on the first encounter with a serious problem. I could tell the story of at least a dozen people I know personally who left the place where God had put them, and as a result, they accomplished little for the Kingdom in the "foreign places" where they wandered. This is the same thing that happened to Israel when they refused to defend the promised land they had been given, or when they stopped using it for the purpose it was intended, or when they just gave up and went down to Egypt for help, instead of going to the Lord.

Of course, there were exceptions, and with every one of them God showed himself mighty. There is no record of God ever letting his people down. From a human point of view it made perfect sense for Hezekiah to surrender Jerusalem to Sennachrib. There was no escape. There was nothing they could do. In a matter of time, they were all going to starve to death. I'm sure Hezekiah's critics had a field day. "Give it up," they probably argued. "God isn't in this one."

But Hezekiah knew better. He remembered the promise. He embraced the covenant. And he saw 185,000 soldiers slain in one night by one angel (2 Kings 19:35). When we humble ourselves before the Lord and simply ask him to do the impossible on the basis of his promise to us, we are beginning to learn what the Covenant of Blessing is all about. God designed his promises to be used when they're needed. His promises don't guarantee we won't have problems. It's the opposite. They were designed to help us because we *will* have problems.

Eternal Vision

The God we serve means serious business with his covenant. So invoke it! Depend on it! That's the whole idea. Get passionate about it. He means to bless you in the sight of all the world. He fully intends to fulfill his covenant, and that is precisely the reason *why* he has surrounded you with the impossible. That's where the glory is! Never retreat before evil. Never surrender to Satan's agenda. Defend what God has given you and called you to do. Then the glory of the impossible will be yours, because you *can* do all things through Christ who *will* give you strength.

During World War II, it was said that Winston Churchill was defeating Hitler with his words. In many ways that was true. He refused to let his spirit be defeated. He said to the brave people of England before the Battle of Britain, "We will fight them on the beaches, we will fight them on the landing docks, in the streets and in the countryside. We *will* defend our island!" The place God has given you could be your home, your ministry, your business, or any good thing God has called you to defend. It's the place where God has called you to be a blessing. But rest assured, that place *will* be contested for. So stay alert, keep awake, and never surrender even one inch of that place where God has put you. Remember: *no one* in history has *ever* been let down who stood with God in the midst of the storm and refused to let go or give up.

There are many risks to be taken today and there are more to come. Where are the pioneers, the fearless warriors, the revolutionaries? The Kingdom has need of them. The pages of the Bible drip with blood. Jesus said you will be hated, hunted down, arrested and martyred. It *will* happen, and in some countries it *is* happening. But we know how it all turns out in the end. God's Kingdom *will* prevail. Every nation, tribe, people and language will be reached with the gospel and our Lord shall return, just as he promised.

The Blessing

In the darkest hours of WWII, when Hitler had conquered France and was preparing to bomb England into the stone ages, the question of surrender never came before the English parliament. Churchill said, "I promise you only blood, sweat and tears." No one said, "Hey, wait a minute, let's talk this over!" There was complete resolve to do whatever it took to defeat the enemy. The same must be true today. The hour is going to get dark and the sun is setting even as we speak. Every believer is needed, without exception. There are missions to be dared, heroic acts to be accomplished, lives to be sacrificed. But who will volunteer? Who will sign up? Who will step forward and say, "Here am I, send me!"

Now if you don't think you're the courageous type, you're in good company here. Neither was Abraham. He made Sarah promise on an oath of love that wherever they went she would tell everyone she was his sister. Not much bravery in that! Can you just imagine how it must have been for Sarah to be "taken" into Pharaoh's household as his wife? Sarah must have been thinking twice about the fellow she married on that day. But that's the kind of world Abraham and Sarah were venturing into. Abraham had no physical power to protect his own wife.

Yet he should have known better. Later, God would use Abraham to conquer an entire army, perhaps the greatest army of his day. This violent coalition had just defeated five kings, but Abraham knew God would give him the victory with just a handful of men. Abraham *learned* courage, he learned to be adventurous, he learned to step out in faith. And I'm glad he did, because if he could do it then so can I, and so can you. But we have to stay close to Jesus and fight back in his power. He has the courage, he has the strength, he has the authority. And he stands ready to give it to *anyone* who will simply ask for it.

Eternal Vision

Principle Three: Spiritual power is required.

One of the most amazing promises in the Covenant of Blessing is God's guarantee of spiritual authority and protection. He said to Abraham, "Whoever curses you I will curse." Curses are not a thing of the past. They are used all over the world to bring sickness, death and financial ruin. When a person enters into a covenant with Satan to bring harm on another, the powers of darkness have been given the authority to carry out that curse.

Not too long ago, a friend of mine noticed how his neighbor's rose bushes never had any roses. He asked her about it and she explained that they had been cursed. "What do you mean?" he asked in amazement. Then she told him about a powerful cult which used to occupy the college campus across the street. My friend knew the cult. This group used to pray against our organization night and day after the Lord gave us a vision to purchase that campus for a world mission center. (At that particular time, when this lady's roses were cursed, the cult occupied 90% of the campus. We had the rest, but the Lord had promised us all of it.) One day this cult had a national gathering. During that time, one of the cult members came over to the house of my friend's neighbor and said, "We need these roses for our celebration." Then she proceeded to take them! The owner was shocked at her behavior and told her to stop. The cult member became angry and, pointing her finger at the rose garden, she declared, "Then may your rose bushes never produce roses again." And they never did from that day on.

Words are very powerful in Scripture and they are just as spiritually potent today. The opposite of a curse is a blessing, and a blessing pronounced in the name of Jesus is the most powerful force in the world. God can and will empower your words with a special anointing. Through them he will demolish the forces of the evil one.

The Blessing

The cult on our campus was determined to curse us into oblivion. Night and day they would chant their mantras against us. What they didn't know was that another prayer had been prayed—a much more powerful one. Before our organization ever thought of occupying that campus, a missionary named Erik Staddell got on his knees in the old college chapel on that campus and began to pray. He recalls, "I went in and a burden of prayer came over me. I prayed all day and into the night. My wife sent my children looking for me, but I told them I couldn't leave—not yet. I prayed there for a week before the Lord let me leave." While he was praying, the Holy Spirit revealed to him the purpose of this intense intercession and he cried out in faith, praying in the Spirit's power: "Before the face of the Lord our God we both speak and confess that the campus of Pasadena College is consecrated for world missions, and can never belong to any other purpose."

The words had been spoken—the blessing of God released! There was no turning back. And in much the same way, Abraham was promised that *he* would be a blessing, meaning God would use Abraham's very presence in a situation to bring about his eternal purposes. The first recorded instance of healing in Scripture comes through the intercession of Abraham. God said to King Abimelech in a dream, "You are as good as dead because of the woman you have taken. Now return the man's wife, for he is a prophet, and he will pray for you and you will live" (Gen. 20:7).

Now of course, God could have healed Abimelech the moment he returned Sarah. But he had a special reason for doing it this way. He wanted Abraham to speak the words and proclaim the blessing. God wants us to participate with him and to use his blessing to bring him glory. When God places his hand upon you, it is because he wants your life itself to be a demonstration of his power. He wants the whole world to know what he has promised you. That's why he will always give you the opportunity to exercise your faith. He will set it up, just as he did with Moses in Egypt and Elijah on Mount Carmel. He will announce through your life, "This is the way; walk in it" (Isa. 30:21).

God so desires to bless the nations through his people, and he will do so in the most remarkable ways if we are willing to take the initiative and pursue his will. In the 1930s, Everett and Garnet Howard received a call from God to preach the gospel in the Cape Verde Islands. There was a great famine in the land. They witnessed the deaths of thousands of people soon after their arrival. On the Island of Fogo the famine was particularly severe. So they journeyed there and began to pray. Despite opposition from the local religious leaders, they began sharing the gospel. A few responded, and together with these new believers they gathered to ask God for a miracle. Not too long afterwards the unexplainable happened. Ten thousand feet above sea level, at the highest point of the island, a spring of water burst forth which runs to this day.

The whole island knew that the new believers were praying for a miracle. A great revival began and thousands came to know Jesus. In the midst of that revival, a young boy with leprosy came up to them. No one would come near him. But Everett just loved him and told him all about Jesus, the one who healed the lepers and died on the cross to pay for his sin. The boy received Christ and asked if Jesus might heal *him*. Everett smiled and said, "Of course. Just ask him." So the boy did. Then he went home. Three days later he walked into the church beaming a great smile. There was no trace of leprosy anywhere on his body! His healing was a testimony to the whole island of God's power. Everett and Garnet became famous throughout those islands for saying, "Always attempt enough to need God in your program!" That, in a nutshell, is what the Covenant of Blessing is all about: attempting the impossible for the glory of God.

The same power that produced a spring on that mountain and healed the leper is available to you today. Often we feel overwhelmed by evil and the increasing darkness we see in our world. We need not be. True, things are going to get worse. Satan's forces are gearing up for a final showdown like the world has never seen. Never forget this reality. But don't let it worry you just the same. You have The Blessing. You have the power, bought and paid for by the blood of the Lamb. Bank on it. Cover yourself under its authority.

Many people don't understand the significance of this. Some people think spiritual warfare is a recent thing. It is not, it existed all the way back in the time of Abraham. God said, "*Whoever* curses you *I* will curse." No spiritual force could prevail against him. The same is true today, only more so. Yet many are not operating under the protection of the Blood, and so they stand defeated even before the battle begins.

Ask an occultist priest (don't really) and he will tell you exactly what he uses blood for, and he's not kidding you. Call him superstitious if you like, but he can bring the most ardent atheist to his knees with just a few drops. It's sounds so foreign to our ears. Why would blood have anything to do with anything? But for whatever reason, God has chosen to use certain physical elements to help us understand spiritual realities. Under the right conditions he has allowed these physical properties to connect with spiritual authority and power.

Jesus said, "This is my *blood* of the covenant" (Matt. 26:28). It is a stumbling block to many, but to those who overcome, it is the power of God unto salvation. This blood opened up the gateway between the physical and the spiritual. The promise given to Abraham came to a climax with the shedding of this blood. It brought greater power to the Covenant of Blessing than had ever been there before. But just the same, many are too proud or sophisticated to say, "There is power in the blood!" There certainly is and Satan knows it. He is well aware of what that blood can do to him and his kingdom. It is the only thing he fears. And it is the only thing that can save us. If we are to be effective against the enemy we need to humble ourselves and invoke its power in our lives. How many times have I felt the cleansing, healing power of God when singing that great hymn: "There is power, power, wonder working power in the blood of the Lamb"? We do have power, but we have to use it. We do have authority, but we must understand it. We do have The Blessing, but we must live like it.

Principle Four: The Blessing will have eternal significance.

The word "blessing" has very special meaning in the Bible. When Jacob wanted to receive his inheritance from Isaac, he asked his father to *bless* him. Even though he was pretending to be Esau, the blessing was given and could not be taken back. Isaac said to Esau, "I have blessed him and indeed he *will* be blessed" (Gen. 27:33). In a similar way, when God promised to bless Abraham he was saying, "I am adopting you into my family and making you my son. I am giving you access to everything that is mine. I have blessed you and you *will* be blessed."

Now this has great significance for us today. The Bible says, "If you belong to Christ, then you are Abraham's seed, and heirs according to the promise" (Gal. 3:29). The same Covenant of Blessing that made Abraham a success is available to anyone at anytime through the blood of the Lamb. It is a covenant of sacrifice, a costly blessing. It comes with great responsibility. The Blessing cannot be used any way you please. Jesus said, "You may ask me for anything in my name, and I will do it" (John 14:14). Now this does not mean you can ask for a 50 million dollar mansion with an Olympic swimming pool and a twenty-car garage, and it will be yours, guaranteed or your money back. It means you can ask for anything under the *authority* of His name.

A king's name in the Roman Empire only had authority under the jurisdiction given him. In the same way, the kingdom Jesus rules is a heavenly one, and he promises you all the authority and power required to carry out its mandate: *Go make disciples of all nations.*

Now ask God to bless your business so you can bless the nations, and you're talking his language. Ask him to help you play better basketball so you can be his witness in your school, and heaven is listening. Ask him to increase your capacity, anoint your gifts, and fill your life with his presence so you might be a blessing to those around you, and the answer is sure to come. A life of blessing begins with finding out what God wants done and making yourself available to do it. It begins by asking, "Lord, I want to *be* a blessing to those *you* seek to bless. Please show me the way."

Today there are 2.7 billion people with little or no access to the gospel. Two thousand ethnic groups are still waiting. Are we going to be a blessing to them? Heaven is watching and waiting for *anyone* who will rise up and say, "Here am I, Lord, use *me* to do it!" The Bank of Heaven is ready to bankroll you. The angels stand ready to back you up. All the power, grace and authority of the Lamb are available in full measure.

This hour is the most exciting moment of eternal history. You can be sure Abraham is getting ready to celebrate. The promise given to him so many years ago will soon be completed. We are the ones who must cross the finish line. The baton has been passed to our generation. But who among us will have the honor of carrying it to the end? We're not far off, but how many will recognize the time in which they live and get with the program? It's time to dust off those running shoes! And it's time to start sprinting. We're so close, so *very* close to the end. The unshakeable, unstoppable tidal wave of history is with us. We have all the authority in heaven and on earth to get it done. We have an eternal promise, a guarantee of success from the King of Kings and Lord of Lords. All authority has been given!

All we have to do is say, "Lord, I want to bless *you!* I want to see all nations worship you—every tribe, people and language singing your praises." Here is a prayer that rings louder in heaven than any other. Start living like it matters and you will witness a life transformed by the same power that made Abraham the most well known person of his generation. God said, "I will make your name great," and he wasn't exaggerating. He will do the same for you and for me. If we're willing to give up those things that will hinder his purposes, and just head out in faith, God promises us the glory of the impossible. That's where The Blessing is and that's where I want to be. By faith let's get out there and never look back.

CHAPTER TEN

≈

COURAGE UNDER FIRE

*"So do not be ashamed to testify about our Lord . . .
But join me in suffering for the gospel, by the power of God." (2 Tim. 1:8)*

*H*ave you ever wondered where the early Christians might decide to worship if they were here today? Where would they feel most comfortable? Imagine Peter, Paul, Silas and Timothy visiting the 21st century on a survey trip for the Board of Heaven. What might they think of some of our churches? How would they rate our worship? Our commitment? Our giving? Might they see two kinds of "believers"? Two kinds of churches? How might they describe us comfortable Christians living in an age of persecution and sacrifice?

> While others toiled, they slept away
> While others hungered, they drank and ate
> While others cried, they laughed and sang
> While others struggled, they danced and played
> While others died, they lived in vain

There is a great contrast in Christianity today. Many don't ever get to see it and I honestly feel sorry for them, because heaven sees it every moment of every day. It's a wonder how they have the patience and discipline to keep silent. Perhaps they are like the martyrs in Revelation crying out "How long, O Sovereign Lord?" They are told to wait a little longer, for his justice is soon at hand.

We need to have our eyes opened to the reality of who and what the Church is today. Many of our fellow believers live in lands where Christianity is outlawed and considered a dangerous threat. This is not going to get any better. According to the Bible, it can only get worse. As we come closer to the end, and as the gospel penetrates every final frontier, the enemy is going to unleash far greater persecution than the world has ever seen. The war against the Church is just getting started, and no matter where you are, you will feel the effects.

One of the best ways to get ready for those days is to join with our fellow brothers and sisters who are presently being persecuted and standing by their side in the faith. We need to live according to the same standard, the same lifestyle, and the same heavenly outlook as those in the persecuted Church. The attack of the enemy against believers in the end-times may come in many forms. For some it may not be imprisonment, confiscation of property, or martyrdom, but in actual fact may be something worse. It may be the temptation of indifference, the lure of decadence, and the deceitfulness of riches, which "choke the word, making it unfruitful" (Mark 4:19).

Jesus said the love of many would grow cold before the end, and he directly related this to our response to his suffering Church (Matt. 24:10-12). The Bible commands us to bear one another's suffering "as if you yourselves were suffering" (Heb. 13:3). It's an obligation, not a recommendation. When John wrote to the seven churches of Revelation, he called himself a "companion in the suffering" (Rev. 1:9). There was a special communion between the churches of those days. To be a Christian was to risk everything, and to live for Jesus was to be willing to die for his sake. The author of Hebrews wrote, "You joyfully accepted the confiscation of your property, because you knew that you yourselves had better and lasting possessions" (Heb. 10:34).

There is something authentic about Christianity that is being persecuted. Scripture tells us it's *impossible* to live a godly life without being persecuted (2 Tim. 3:12). There's something wrong when the Devil isn't bothered by what you're doing. *True Christianity* will always be contested because it refuses to soft-sell the gospel. Comfortable Christianity, on the other hand, is nowhere to be found in Scripture, but with one exception: in the lukewarm water that Jesus spews out of his mouth!

Our Lord utterly despises half-hearted followers. The reverse is also true—shallow Christians have no great love for the real Jesus. These lukewarm believers create their own little bubble world to cushion them from reality. But real Christians take a stand for what is right, no matter what the cost. Of the first twelve apostles, ten were martyred for their witness. You had to kill these guys to shut them up. But even then, Scripture says "they still speak."[1] Their message took on a life of its own and reached down into our generation. The seeds that died are still filling the whole earth.

So let's ask ourselves: How many of us today would feel comfortable around these loud-mouths? How many of us would stand by them if it meant being shamed and ridiculed? I know some believers from China who would feel right at home. And I know another person who considers them closer than family. He's someone we call Lord and Savior, but to others he's something more. They can call him friend. For he said, "Greater love has no one than this, that he lay down his life for his friends" (John 15:3).

To be counted worthy of such company is the greatest honor life can ever hold. Jesus said whoever helps one of these "will certainly not lose his reward" (Matt. 10:42). In fact, he promises the same reward will be given both to prophets *and* to those who aid them! But how many are missing out on this eternal offering simply because they refuse to take the initiative and find out where Christ is suffering today?

Without exception, we will all be measured by this same standard: *How did we live in light of our Body's suffering?* The reason we are strong is to help those who are weak. The reason we have freedom is to work hard for those who do not. The reason we have wealth, influence and power is to reach those whom no one else can. We have no excuse, and there is no reason why we too can't join the fellowship of His suffering. Wherever you are, whatever you are doing, if you are living a godly life, *you will be persecuted.* Living for Jesus is dying to yourself. And when you are living for him, he will lead you to that place where you can speak the loudest for his glory.

WHERE IS YOUR HEART?

The Lord is testing the hearts of this generation of believers through their concern for what is closest to *his* heart. A great sifting out is taking place all over the world. Recently, an advocate for the persecuted Church wrote about her experience while watching a Voice of the Martyr's booth at a Christian conference. Her account is like a living parable of the Church today. She writes:

> One lady came up to the table, and after hearing about Christians being persecuted for their faith (the same faith she shared) responded by saying, "I just don't have time to read about stuff like that." Unmoved, she walked

away. Then, a girl (maybe 10 years old) walked up to the table. Her response is forever burned in my memory. She took a step back, put her hand on her heart and with the most precious and concerned expression on her face told me, "I just heard someone talk about this . . . his message touched me so much." And then she said, "I never knew . . . I never knew . . ." She looked over everything on the table, came back five or six times, and even brought her mother over. I showed her some of the ways that persecuted Christians were being helped. When I told her about the Action Pack program, she suddenly and excitedly said, "I can do that . . . I can do that!" Later, she convinced her mom to let her buy one with all of her spending money.

I think the Lord allowed this encounter to happen for a special reason. Sometimes the more sophisticated we become, the less room remains for what really matters. We let the cares and worries of this world choke the life out of us and render us useless for God's purposes. Many people have become so shallow they are incapable of carrying around another's burdens. They can hardly think past the small world that occupies their short attention span.

But Christians are called to be much different. Paul said, "I face daily the pressure of my concern for all the churches" (2 Cor. 11:28). Can you just imagine someone saying that today? There are some who actually do. Brother Andrew, founder of Open Doors and former Bible smuggler, is one of them. He just won't change the subject. Talk with him for five minutes and you'll be talking about the persecuted Church—from Cuba to India to China. He once said, "It's easier to cool down a fanatic than to warm up a corpse." When asked to choose a quote for my senior yearbook in high school, I choose this one. I figured every true Christian was a fanatic. But now that I've seen more of the Church I'm beginning to get worried. Let's hope Brother Andrew was wrong about the corpses, because we've got plenty that need warming up!

Paul wrote to the praying churches of his day, "We do not want you to be uninformed about the hardships we suffered in the province of Asia" (2 Cor. 1:8). What an honor to be a part of the apostle Paul's ministry team. He urged them, "Join with me in my struggle by praying to God for me" (Rom 15:30). Paul wanted the Church to know what he knew, to feel what he felt, to believe as he had come to believe. He said, "I want to *know* the fellowship of his suffering" (Phil. 3:10).

So how about us today? Is this our passion? Where and when do we put on the brakes that keep us from *this kind* of fellowship? Have we stopped to ask ourselves, "Where is Christ suffering today?" Where is he being chained and beaten, starved and ridiculed? He said people like these are the "least of my brethren," but he said something else that ought to give us pause. He said whatever you do to one of these (and whatever you don't do) "you do unto me" (Matt. 25:40).

Do we desire a deeper fellowship with Christ? Do we really want to *know* the fellowship of his suffering? Where might we discover it? My father was once imprisoned for his faith. Locked up in solitary confinement to break his spirit, he testifies that he has never felt closer to the Lord than he did during that time. There really is nothing that compares with this kind of fellowship. How often I have experienced the transforming power and presence of God when praying and worshiping with those suffering for their faith. They are unforgettable experiences.

Many people want to grow in faith, but they are not doing anything that requires it. Try visiting some of our brethren in China who are being tortured in labor camps and see your faith grow in quantum leaps. One of my best friends from Nepal was mobbed by a large group of Hindus soon after he became a Christian. His body was broken and bleeding, but all he felt was the presence of God all over him. After he recovered, he returned to that same community and forgave them. He showed them the love of Christ. Today, those who formerly tried to kill him are serving the Lord right alongside him. Now that's the power of Christ! Authenticate Christianity in action. Would you like to see it? Come visit my friend's church.

Jesus came to build a body, interconnected and interdependent. Scripture says one part of the body cannot say to another, "I have no need of you" (1 Cor. 12:21). But we do this very thing when we live as though there were no hardships, no trials, no sacrifices to bear. We need to wake up. People who stay out of harms way and hide under a rock their whole Christian life miss out on all the joy of being in Christ. Jesus came to give us power so the world might believe, but we can't experience that power if we aren't using it. Rest assured, all those who seek to follow Jesus in this world will encounter conflict and resistance. There are no exceptions.

That is why all of us, no matter where we are, can be "companions in the suffering." We can join with our brothers and sisters around the world with one heart and voice. We can follow their lead by living holy lives and radically proclaiming the truth of the gospel. We can join their fellowship by faith. We can pray for them, encourage them, take care of their families, and even influence legislation that might help them. But most importantly, we can identify with them. We can learn from their example, and take a stand right where we are.

THE FELLOWSHIP OF SHAME

"This person believes in Jesus" read the sign above the dunce cap. In China, criminals are paraded in towns and villages to be mocked and abused by those who wear them. Though intended to humiliate them, Christians in China have come to wear them with honor. On one particular "parade" the police ran out of dunce caps for a group of Christians. One of those left out, a believer named Brother Shui, prayed, "O Lord, why did you forget me!" On the second day of the parade the police found an extra dunce cap for him with the appropriate sign. After the ceremony and his release from prison, Brother Shui asked if he could keep the hat as a reminder of his crimes. The police thought it strange but they consented. Back in his village he wore it every day as a witness to everyone!

Christians in places like China have learned what it means to "bear the reproach" of Christ with joy and thanksgiving. Jesus said, "Blessed are you when men hate you, when they exclude you and insult you and reject your name as evil, because of the Son of Man" (Luke 6:22). You don't have to visit China or Sudan for this to be true in your life. To know the fellowship of his suffering you only need to take a stand right where you are. Much of the persecution Paul received came from within the Church itself. Jesus said the time is coming when a man's worst enemies will be the members of his own household (Matt. 10:36). When people fear the world more than Christ, you can be sure those who rock the boat will be asked to leave, or will ultimately be tossed overboard, because prophets seldom run or hide.

The world shames those it seeks to control. To be laughed at and ridiculed for the sake of Christ is the highest honor any believer can receive in this lifetime. Here is one area we can find immediate fellowship with the Body of Christ around the world. Ask yourself:

What pressures do we face today to give in and compromise? I can think of many. You don't have to search very hard to see that wealth, comfort and ease are far more effective weapons for neutralizing the Church than imprisonment, labor camps and torture.

The world has a whole agenda lined up for us. Psychologists tell us how to raise our kids (and how many is good to have). The media tells us that we need more stuff, so Mom needs to work (so we can buy a bigger TV for the "family" room). Only a few real families remain. America has become a nation of broken homes. When all is said and done, evangelical families may be the only ones left standing. But even in our churches, the pressure to conform to the standards of this world keeps a stranglehold on many.

I remember the afternoon my mom was crying in the kitchen after church on Sunday. Her friends had ridiculed her for having a fourth child. "How sad," they thought. "She'll be stuck at home for the rest of her life." But the Lord reassured my mom that day, "Children are a blessing from me." So she went on to have six more! She has never regretted it. She's the happiest person I know. Most of her old friends are now depressed and divorced. No kidding.

The world has a lot to say to us. Don't be surprised. This whole world is designed to overcome and destroy true followers of Jesus by whatever means possible. The world says to us, "Go ahead, be a Christian. That's great. Just keep it to yourself." Quiet and Christian are a contradiction of terms, but how many of us have tried to make them compatible? We say, "Well, they have had enough opportunities to hear the gospel, so why should I bother?" But have they really heard? True, many have heard bits and pieces of the message, but how many have yet to see a witness! How few have observed the living testimony of the love of Christ. If I were a non-Christian

Eternal Vision

looking at us quiet Christians, who claim to believe people are on their way to hell without Christ, I would be thinking one of two things: Either these people are the most selfish people in the world, or they don't really believe what they say they believe.

I remember one Indian brother in the United Kingdom who came to know the Lord and immediately began sharing the gospel with as many people as possible. An elder Christian approached him and said, "Sir, why are you behaving like this?" In amazement he replied, "But I thought it was part of the deal?" What a testimony about our churches today! Sometimes I wonder who the mature Christians really are—the new ones who can't be stopped, or the old ones who can't be started.

The world says, "Fanatics are those psycho people who blow up high-rises and U.S. embassies. You don't want to be one of those." No denying it, fanatics are people who will do whatever it takes to get their message across. But our calling is no different, with one slight modification: we are to do so in love!

When I was in high school, people labeled me a fanatic. I was determined that everyone on my campus would hear and "see" the gospel before I graduated. For better or for worse (mostly better I hope) everyone knew who I was and what I represented. I defended Creation in Biology class. My history professor was an atheist who got my hand up with almost every lecture. My principal was a New Age enthusiast trying to convert the whole school through evangelistic assemblies and daily doses of Buddhism over the school's intercom. There was plenty to talk about if you were a Christian on my campus. I'm sure I made a lot of mistakes, but it goes with the territory. It wasn't very diplomatic for Peter to say to the Jewish leaders, "You guys are murderers!" But that was the truth, and what counted in the end was Peter's boldness to proclaim it. The world is watching us to see if we really believe what we so confidently assert to be true. I remember one Buddhist girl who wrote in my senior yearbook, "Thank you for introducing me to Him." This was one girl I had never shared the gospel with. But she was watching me. She became a Christian because of what she saw—a Christian fanatic, so called, who meant what he said and lived like it mattered.

A recent poll by the AARP revealed that the number one thing kids talk with their grandparents about in America is religion. Next in line is cigarettes, drugs and sex.[2] It doesn't surprise me. We have secularized our society to such a degree, and mocked Christian values with such persistence, that a great spiritual vacuum is emerging in the new generation. The time for bold witness is at hand. I'm glad the grandparents of America aren't afraid to pray for the salvation of their grandkids and leave a witness. They know of a world we will probably never see again. As America becomes increasingly secular and humanistic, you can believe that *all* those who seek to live a godly life in Christ Jesus *will* be persecuted. Are we willing to be a companion in this fellowship of shame? Time will tell.

If we're going to reach the remaining 2.7 billion least evangelized in the 10/40 Window, we're going to need an army of Christians who are not afraid of anything that might hold them back, whether they be at home or abroad. Regardless of what friends may say, what family may think, or what the world may do, the Kingdom needs people who will say, "I'm going to live for Jesus, and you'll have to kill me to stop me!"

The gospel can only advance as far as fearless feet and unashamed hearts will take it. Paul said he was not ashamed of the gospel for one simple reason: it was and *is* the power of God unto salvation. Jesus endured more shame than we could ever possibly imagine so we might be able to say these words.

So let's think about it. Are we ready and determined to focus our lives around this one central vision: "Christ and him crucified"? Paul said this is all I want to know (1 Cor. 2:2). He wanted to experience only one thing: the "fellowship of sharing in his sufferings, becoming like him in his death" (Phil. 3:10). I can only begin to imagine the depth of this commitment! But I know there is nothing more powerful. Jesus was King of Kings and Lord of Lords. And yet he let himself be taken by the enemy. He gave himself up. He said here I am, you can do whatever you want, I will never stop loving you. He was the first to say it, the first to live it. And he said, "As the father has sent me, so send I you" (John 20:21).

Are we ready to take up his challenge? Are we willing to say, "I'm not ashamed of the gospel, because it is the power of God unto salvation"? *Are we willing to live it?* Without a doubt, it's a message worth dying for. But are we willing to make it a message worth living for? A message that will not be denied a hearing and one that can't be shamed into back corners and whispers? Will we shout it from the mountaintops, though it be from a cross, "Father, forgive them, for they know not what they do"? That's the hope we have, the love we share, and the life we possess. Can we possibly keep it to ourselves?

THE FELLOWSHIP OF COURAGE

"Stand here," the guards said to Mark as they brought in his father, tied hand and foot. Just a young boy, Mark stood there in horror as they beat and tortured his father before his very eyes. Covered in blood, and with many bones broken, they tossed him in a wheelbarrow and commanded Mark to push it out of the prison. They led him out in the city square, and gathering a crowd of witnesses for a mock trial, they propped Mark's father up on a stage. Then, after hundreds had gathered, they demanded that Mark's father publicly renounce Christianity. "We offer you this precious chance for life," they said. "Choose wisely." With all the remaining strength Mark's dad could pull together, he composed himself and said in a loud, clear voice so everyone present might hear:

"You can cut off my head and you can spill my blood, but I will never forsake Jesus Christ! He has been faithful to me and has blessed me for many years and nothing you can do can ever make me renounce my loving Friend and Savior."

At that moment he was violently yanked off the stage and thrown into the mud. Before Mark's eyes and all those gathered he was beaten continuously until he died. But what happened next was exactly the opposite of what the guards intended. Mark says, "When I saw the faith and courage of my father, it made a deep impact on my life. I decided to be fully committed to the Lord for the rest of my life. Many other Christians in the crowd were strengthened in their commitment by my father's example. The Church in the area was emboldened to stand against the hardships that were to come our way later."

Thousands of leaders in China have been tortured to the point of complete physical breakdown. Many are still alive today and you can meet them and hear their courageous stories. They refused to deny their faith in Christ and the Chinese government has made a living example of them. They are living epistles of faith. Their bodies have been crippled, paralyzed and mutilated. But their spirits are full of joy and thanksgiving. They have one message for us: What are you doing with the strength God has given you? How are you using your freedom?

We can go just about anywhere today and be living witnesses for Christ. It wasn't always so, but for the first time in history, world conditions have made even the most remote village accessible within 48 hours of any point on this planet. We have no excuse to leave the world unevangelized. There are over 100 million evangelicals between the ages of 18 to 30. Properly mobilized and equipped we could evangelize every person in our generation in a few years.

But why are so few responding? What has happened to us that we have become so unconcerned? Like the invited guests in the parable Jesus gave, we have so many excuses. I hear them all the time. They say, "Well, I'm just not sure it's for me." Or, "If I can just get this one thing done, I'll finally have the time . . ." And then there's my absolute favorite, "You know, brother, it's really not my gift."

How nice that our government didn't wait for volunteers to defeat Nazi Germany and Japan in World War II! No doubt these tyrants would have conquered the whole world had we left it up to the whims and fancies of volunteers to stop them. And yet here we are today with the worst peril humanity has ever faced looming overhead and we can only get a handful of people to take seriously the final words of our Heavenly Commander. In the next twenty years, close to 400 million people will perish without Christ in the 10/40 Window. Perhaps the Lord will bypass us altogether and set loose a million Chinese evangelists to the frontier regions of the world! In fact, such a movement is happening even now and gaining momentum. But just the same I don't want to be left out. I want to be where the Spirit of God directs me so I might dwell daily in his presence.

We need people to boldly and persuasively challenge others to get involved in finishing the Great Commission. Two of my heroes are George Verwer and Greg Livingstone. Greg Livingstone has a burden for the Muslim world. He is quite well known for his challenging messages and unique advertisements in Christian magazines.

One of his advertisements reads as follows:

> **Wanted: Missionaries to Muslims**
> Bitter cold. Scorching heat.
> Long hours. Sickness almost certain.
> Possible imprisonment.
> Safe return not guaranteed.
> Honor and recognition from peers doubtful.
> Eternal Rewards.
> Interested parties apply.

Amazingly, Greg's courage to go anywhere and do anything for the Lord has inspired over 800 people to join with him in reaching Muslims through the agency he founded called Frontiers. Thousands have come to know Jesus through their faithful witness. Greg himself is a missionary on the frontlines even though he is well past retirement. He remains an unstoppable advocate for the needs of over 1.3 billion Muslims and he is determined to reach all of them!

But it wasn't always so . . . Greg used to be a normal, happy-go-lucky, mind-your-own-business Christian until he met George Verwer. Greg was invited to a prayer meeting at Wheaton College, and since he had nothing else to do that night, he decided he might try it out. He recalls, "I remember thinking at least there might be some pretty girls hanging out there." But the moment he walked in he was hit with the surprise of his life. George Verwer walked up to him and said boldly, "We're all praying for the nations of the world here. What nation have you taken!"

Not wanting to be outdone, Greg answered back, "What's left!"

"Libya!" answered George. And so began Greg's journey into the heart of the Muslim world.

We need more people like George and Greg. Want to be one?

Eternal Vision

Start hanging out with these guys for a few minutes and you'll be infected for life. A Christian on fire for God is more contagious than anything on this planet. That's what God wants you to be. He wants to give you a virus without a cure. He wants to fill you with so much passion and enthusiasm for his global cause, no one can think about your life without making a decision where they stand.

You may not think of yourself as the provocative type. You may be the quietest person in the world. It doesn't matter. When Jesus ignites your life with his holy fire, you're going to be unstoppable. When you come to understand spiritual realities, no one will be able to shut you up or turn you down without a fight. Even the shyest, quietest, most polite Victorian lady will be screaming at the top of her lungs if her baby happens to be drowning. That's the way you're going to be when the Spirit of God hits you with Great Commission fever. You'll be an unquenchable fire on that day, and your fears will disappear.

Martin Luther King Jr., a man who could hold the world's record for the most death threats received in a lifetime, once thought about giving up the struggle for civil rights. After organizing a bus boycott in Montgomery, his phone began to ring non-stop off the hook. The callers were merciless and filled with rage:

"We're gonna burn your church, boy..."

"You've got a pretty little wife there, preacher..."

"We're gonna light your house up, *tonight*..."

On and on the hate calls went. His courage and will to go on were shaken. He felt like running. Finally after a particular call, he decided to get out of town. What was the point of putting his family at risk? Surely someone else could take up the cause. But as he left the phone and turned away, trembling in fear, something happened. God showed up and changed his life forever. He says, "At that moment I experienced the presence of the Divine as I had never experienced Him before. It seemed as though I could hear the reassurance of an inner voice saying: 'Stand up for righteousness, stand up for truth, and God will be at your side forever.' Almost at once my fears left me and they have never come back."

God promises you the same strength today. The same courage that took Jesus to the cross is available to anyone who wants it. The same strength that led Daniel's three friends into the fiery furnace is present with us now. The same power that anointed David as he ran out to meet Goliath is ready to fill anyone who will pick up a sling and head out. From beginning to end, the Bible sends the same message: The courage will come, the strength will be there, the power and grace will flow in and through you. Just step out in faith and watch the fire fall.

THE FELLOWSHIP OF SACRIFICE

Rev. Meeks is a pastor in Chicago whom the Lord has used to reach thousands with the gospel. In a recent campaign, two thousand people were saved and joined the church as members. His spiritual secret is something he willingly shares. Every day at six in the morning, without exception—including weekends and holidays, he gets up and calls a friend of his. And then he prays. An hour later, his friend calls him back. He says, "And you know, I'd feel real bad if I went back to sleep while he was up all that time praying!"[3]

Rev. Meeks has set a great example for the rest of us. I know my life has been blessed by following his lead on this one. In fact, I think we all need a phone call each day to wake us up. We need the Holy Spirit to ask us: Are you still on fire? Are you still with us? Have you fallen asleep spiritually while your brethren in the suffering Church are up seeking His face? Are you taking it easy while

Eternal Vision

they toil in His harvest, winning souls for eternity?

I would recommend everyone reading the life story of Chinese house church leader, Brother Yun (*The Heavenly Man*). It will change your life. If it doesn't . . . well, what can I say, just give up—you're hopeless (just kidding!). But I know it will, without a doubt. When Brother Yun became a believer, the first thing he did was try to find a Bible. He went to his pastor and asked where he could find one. The pastor shook his head and said, "If you want a Bible, you'll have to pray for one." So he did. For one hundred days, Brother Yun fasted and prayed. He ate only a bowl of soup each day. At the end of this time, the Lord gave him a vision of where he could find a Bible. He followed the instructions and found a man who gave him the greatest treasure of his life.

Later, after he became a house church leader, he was thrown into prison. Tortured without mercy, one day after the next, he refused to deny the faith or tell the authorities about his fellow believers. His legs were so severely damaged he could no longer walk—he would likely be a cripple for life. But one day the Lord spoke to him that he was to escape from the prison. Without even thinking about it, in faith he rose to his feet. He walked down the hall unnoticed in China's number-one maximum security prison. He passed through three gates on three floors and into the courtyard of the jail, in full view of all the guards. No one paid any attention to him. When he came to the large gates leading to the outside, usually locked down tight, they were wide open. Brother Yun walked right out into the street, and immediately a taxi cab pulled up and he got inside. He was taken to the home of believers who had been praying for his release. The Lord had spoken to one of the ladies in a dream that Brother Yun would be released the next day. They believed the Lord and were expecting his arrival!

The whole Chinese army was alerted, but miraculously he was able to escape the country. Today he is free, but what do you suppose he is doing with his freedom? Has he become like so many of us in the free world, consumed with materialism and content with shallow Christianity?

If you have any doubts, read the book! Recently, Brother Yun came to speak at our church (somewhere in SE Asia). We are helping him set up a training center for equipping cross-cultural church planting teams. His vision is to send out 100,000 missionaries from the house churches in China over the next twenty years. Before he left the country, the house church leaders commissioned him with these words: *March forward towards the Muslims, the Hindus and the Buddhists in Europe, America, Africa, and Asia! May you accomplish the holy mission God has given you, to take the gospel back to Jerusalem, until the last holy disciple is added to the Church!*

Already, over 400 missionaries have been sent. As I sat listening to Brother Yun speak, I couldn't help but think: If the apostle Paul were here today, would he be doing any differently? If Jesus were walking among us, would he not have the same vision? Would he not be preaching the same sermon I am hearing? Well, don't look now, but Jesus is still Lord of his Church! Which brings up an interesting question: Where is that Church? And *who* is that Church?

Have we missed out? Is it too late? Have we put down the cross and picked up the TV remote instead? Have we decided there are no more sacrifices to make, no more tears to be shed, no more souls to save? I suppose it could be too late, but I hope not. I hope those of us in the free world will rise up and join with our brethren who are working hard for the Lord despite the difficulties and hardships they face each day of their lives. There is still a great harvest to be brought in, and all hands are needed!

Eternal Vision

So let's join their fellowship by faith, and together we will literally see millions rescued from darkness to light and from the power of Satan to God in this generation. We can give of our time in prayer, our wealth to further the cause, and our sons and daughters for His service. There is still much to be done and God wants us all to be a part. But how many are asking, "What sacrifices can *I* make to join with you, Lord? How much can *I* give?" If there's any doubt in your mind about its worth, let the souls of the harvest be the first to tell you. Let their cries for joy fill your heart and ignite a fire within you. Let all the angels rejoicing in heaven convince you. It's all for his glory, his worship, his honor—the Lamb is worthy of it all! As you stand before his throne in worship, you will cherish every moment of earthly sacrifice for all eternity to come.

ARE WE LISTENING?

The believers who are judged by Jesus for not sharing the concerns of the persecuted Church all have one thing in common. They were unwilling to give of their precious time and resources for those in need. They had other concerns and more urgent agendas. Jesus says he was hungry, thirsty, naked, sick and in prison. But these people never knew it. Perhaps they didn't want to know. He says, "I was a stranger" (Matt. 25:43). The person they ignored was not someone they knew real well. Perhaps he was a brother in China. Or a sister in Sudan. Maybe he was a lonely pastor in Turkmenistan, tossed out of his home and told to leave the country, or else.

The issue here is one that deserves more attention and careful study, not to mention concern, on our part. Though they have the capacity to clothe, to feed, to care for and encourage, there are going to be many believers in the last days who will fail in their responsibility to care for the suffering Church. They are the ones whose oil will run out. They are those who started out, but turned back. They let the cares, the worries, and the deceitfulness of wealth come in and choke the Word. If they really knew the command of Christ, if they really understood his warning, if they really discerned the signs of the times, could they possibly ignore what was happening in their generation? Did they know about the need and make a conscious decision to turn away? Or were they ignorant by default, because they made no effort, took no initiative, sought no burden to carry? Either way, Jesus holds them accountable. It makes no difference.

If this sounds a little harsh, let's keep in mind that the words Jesus used were the harshest. He said, "Depart from me, you who are cursed." Imagine hearing those words! To the ones who ran out of oil, he said, "I don't know you." To the servant who misused his talent, Jesus said, "Throw that worthless servant outside into the darkness."4 Jesus warned us about all of this for a reason. He wants you and I to understand that the judgments of God are real and they *will* happen. How much more *must* they happen since he has warned us! God is merciful as well as just. He has given us plenty of warning. He is telling us, "Take this seriously. Do not live for yourself in those final days (or at any time). Find out what needs to be done. Find out who is suffering. Find out who is in prison. Find out who is hungry, naked, sick and homeless for my sake and the gospel's sake. Find out, and there you will find my presence, my power, my strength—and an oil that will never fade or burn away."

It is of utmost importance that we understand and appreciate where we are on God's timeline. We happen to live in an age where sacrifice is the most powerful weapon in the Kingdom of God. Satan wants to keep you away from sacrifice more than anything else. Only in the cross will you find the power to defeat him.

Eternal Vision

Jesus told us to pray for our enemies because all who follow him *will* have enemies. He said bless those who persecute you because you *will* be persecuted. And he said blessed are you who mourn because you *must* mourn. Only a heart that is broken for the lost will be able to pray for and bless those who are deceived and controlled by the enemy. The greatest thing we can do for the persecuted Church is join with them in *their* prayers for the salvation of their persecutors. The Church in China doesn't ask the Lord to change their government. They ask for souls to be saved. And so should we. Light dispels darkness, just as a broken and contrite spirit dispels the power of Satan.

One night before a Billy Graham crusade, members of Graham's staff went out on the balcony of their hotel room. To their surprise they looked over and saw Billy weeping over the city and crying out to God for souls to be saved. He was weeping for the enemies of God, and crying out for mercy. The next day, thousands from that city received Christ as their savior. Is it any wonder? A heart in touch with God, a heart that will be used to win souls, is a heart that is deeply grieved for those in the grip of darkness. That's the way we need to be if we are to know the fellowship of *His* sacrifice. There is no other way. The path to winning souls is a pathway to the cross.

The Lord is asking something of you today. He's asking you to give all your heart, soul, mind—and yes, even all the strength of your body to his mission. He needs *you!* He needs willing hands and courageous feet. Like Winston Churchill, he promises you "blood, sweat and tears." But unlike Churchill, he promises you something else: a joy and a love that will never leave you or forsake you.

It's the offer of eternity, but how many actually want it? How many have conveniently purged sacrifice from the very constitution of their lives? How many of us are more concerned about saving our decaying bodies than saving souls for eternity? Evangelicals spend more money on weight-loss programs than they do on missions. We spend even more money putting the weight back on! We love to eat, we love to fellowship, we love to watch our televisions and buy more things. But do we love what Jesus loves? Do we share his passion? His concern? His brokenness?

Keep in mind how heaven sees all of this. They see the contrast. They see all of us, side by side—the believers in China and Sudan, imprisoned and harassed, and the believers wandering around in spiritual Disneyland, wondering which ride to get on next.

We would do well to broaden our vision. There are certain kinds of behavior that are inappropriate when the circumstances call for a change in attitude and focus. As a child we learn a lot about what is appropriate behavior in various contexts. We learn when to be quiet, when to be polite, when to dress up, when to play, and when to be still. In the same way, some of us need to grow up and mature a little in the reality of our Body's suffering. It's simply inappropriate, if not immoral and disgraceful, to live at ease in such a time as this.

If you think I'm way off here, I'll make a deal with you. When we get to heaven, you can come up to me and throw a cream pie right in my face and say, "Ha-ha, look who goofed. The joke's on you, silly man." But I really wonder if you'll get the chance. Nobody likes a party pooper and I'm not saying all of this to turn off the music. I couldn't if I tried. I'm asking us to listen. For there are other voices, there are other cries, there are other questions, and we need to hear them. We need to answer them before it's too late.

CHAPTER ELEVEN

Radical Discipleship

"If anyone would come after me, he must deny himself and take up his cross daily and follow me." (Luke 9:23)

*M*y dad was in college, studying at UCLA, when he got a very personal letter signed by the President of the United States. It was the letter most everyone his age hoped they would never get. "Your country needs you!" it said. Actually it was a French colony named Vietnam that needed him and tens of thousands more like him. He thought for sure the letter must be a mistake, so he went down to tell them so. The next thing he knew he was placed on board a U.S. Army transport plane headed for Texas. Upon arrival he was handed an empty box and a postcard. "Put your civilian clothes in the box," they said. "Then write a note to your parents telling them where you are and what's happened to you."

Just like that, my dad's life was to be changed forever. And there was nothing he could do about it. Like most people my dad's age, he had no intention of volunteering for the war in Vietnam. One semester he unwittingly dropped a class that put him below full-time status. Within a week his school had reported him to the government. A week later he was training for jungle warfare in the Texas desert. Such is life.

Now Christianity also needs recruits. But unlike the U.S. Army during times of full-scale war, only those ready and willing need apply. The letter has been sent out and the commission given. To every adventurer and opportunist, it's an open invitation to join in the greatest campaign of eternal history. The recruitment ad reads something like this:

Wanted: Followers of Jesus

MUST BE WILLING TO
Give up marriage
Be martyred
Be imprisoned
Go hungry
Love your enemies
Pray all night occasionally
Get up early and intercede before the throne
Be ready in season and out of season
Be joyful always!

Now I suppose it's not a very clever ad. It would probably get a D-minus in an Advertising 101 class. But when Jesus called people he made it clear what following him was all about. He never hid the truth from those who came to follow him. When the apostle Paul was recruited, the Master didn't hesitate to tell him what he was getting himself into. The Lord said, "I will show him how much he must suffer for me" (Acts 9:16).

Paul's assignment was to rescue people "from darkness to light and from the power of Satan to God" (Acts 26:17). It was the first part of his re-education as a disciple of Jesus and it completely ruined his life for the ordinary. On the first day of his conversion he learned something that some of us have successfully avoided learning for years! But like it or not, following Jesus is signing up to fight in a heavenly invasion of Satan's kingdom. Becoming a Christian is not a matter of signing up for goodies in heaven. If we tell people that's all there is to it, we cripple their understanding of God's Kingdom. When Jesus called people, he put everything in the perspective of heaven's costly and urgent rescue operation.

He told his disciples in no uncertain terms, "Time is going to be different from now on. The Kingdom of God is at hand and this age will soon be coming to an end. You will not be able to carry on business as usual. We're at war and you're either with me or against me."

Though he was signing up volunteers, he didn't make any apologies for the Kingdom's priority agenda. No one ever heard him say, "Sorry fellas, I know you're really busy, but I was wondering if you might spare a few moments to help me out. I've got a few ideas about how you might like to use your time." Instead, he simply said, "I'm here, and this is my agenda, folks. Take it or leave it. I'll be back soon and I will give to everyone according to what they have done. Sign up sheets can be found at the foot of the cross."

REAL DISCIPLES

What does it mean to be a disciple of Jesus? Are we ready to find out no matter what the cost? Are we willing to live up to the standard set by the Master? Do we measure up, make the cut, pass the bar? I'm afraid we have let many people sign up without reading the fine print in the heavenly contract (the "red letters" in some Bibles). How many have volunteered without asking, "Hey, by the way,

Eternal Vision

what exactly is a disciple? What do they do and how do they think?"

For those who have been wondering this very thing, I came across the following definition in the Encyclopedia Britannica (from a very old, unpublished version):

> **Disciple of Jesus** \dis-ī-pəl əv jē-zəs\ *n.* (ca. 25 AD): Someone who does what Jesus does and lives like he lived. They go places no one else wants to go and they get things done like Jesus did. They're rocking the boat on Sunday and by Monday they're leading the charge. They're on a mission with God. They have a purpose that can't be delayed or hindered. They're headed somewhere off the maps and they have a plan to turn the world upside down.
>
> Disciples are people who are looking for good things to do. They take the initiative. They don't sit around and complain about how messed up things are. They look for solutions, they're creative. They do a lot of praying, a lot of heavenly asking, but they're seekers too. They look for and find the answers God is sending. Disciples are people who water hardened soil, and while they're waiting for the harvest, they're in the forest picking raspberries. They're busy people. They're always looking for better ways to help as many people as possible.
>
> Disciples are ready to defend the helpless: they seek out injustice and stomp on it. They're pro-active and they work together. They know that two are better than one. But they never forget that one person *can* make a difference. They're willing to go it alone if no one else will go with them. But they know the One who is stand-

ing by them all the way, and in the end, He's all that really matters. His energy drives them forward and ignites their passion.

But disciples get discouraged every now and then. That's why they stay connected to each other, because disciples are natural encouragers. They look for the downcast, the tired and the oppressed, and they go out of their way to lend a helping hand. They're just ordinary people who have been asked to do the extra-ordinary and have found that nothing is impossible for those who trust in the Lord.

They're people like George Müller, who found a home for every street kid in London. They're people like the Rev. Martin Luther King Jr., who dared to stand in the face of injustice and say to those with brandished sticks and fire hoses, "We've already gone too far to turn back!" They're people who can't sit still when the world has been set ablaze.

They're conspirators. They have plans and agendas for their city, for their nation and for the world. They're political lobbyists for the Kingdom. They just can't get off the subject. They're on the front lines preparing the way for a heavenly invasion. They're building a highway where the tanks will come rolling down.

When one thing doesn't work they try another. They don't give up. They sign up for the jobs no one else will. They don't seek recognition or credit. They're quiet about the things they've seen accomplished. But ask them a question about what God has done and you can hardly shut them up.

I suppose that must be the best entry ever left out of the Encyclopedia Britannica! The published definition in Webster's is a little more concise. It reads, "A disciple is one who accepts and assists in *spreading* the doctrines of another." A disciple is an activist and an advocate. Anything less and discipleship isn't taking place—just an exercise in pew-warming and fence-sitting.

BAND OF BROTHERS

America lost the war in Vietnam, not because we lacked the personnel, or the right technology, or the money. What we lacked was the will and the national motivation. We inflicted far more casualties on the enemy, but they still won. We turned on ourselves and became our own enemy. In the end, we just simply walked away.

The same thing can happen today in Christianity. We have enough people to finish the task of world evangelization. There is plenty of money and personnel, and the world has never been more conditioned for the rapid spread of the gospel. But we could fail to seize the day if we lack the will, the motivation, and the proper perspective which will see us through to victory.

What we need today are churches who are committed to Great Commission Discipleship. The Lord would rather your church be five committed people than 5,000 draft-dodging, comfort loving, overstuffed rabbits who want nothing better than to stay caged up for the rest of their lives. The U.S. Marines say, "We're just looking for a few good men." Jesus is looking, too. He's watching every one of us, and he stands ready to show himself mighty in the midst of all those who are fully consecrated to him.

I hope with all my heart that your church will be one of the few good discipleship programs the Kingdom needs to get the Job done.

Radical Discipleship

There is only one assignment we have been given, and the purpose of your church is to be about the central business of that mission. Discipleship happens when people learn to obey the commands of Christ. Disciples are *made* when teaching bears its fruit. Anything short of bearing fruit is not discipleship. Jesus said, "Teach them to *obey everything* I have commanded" (Matt. 28:19-20). Discipleship can't happen without obedience, and teaching people to obey goes way beyond a twenty-minute pep-talk each Sunday. Just ask any basketball coach and he'll tell you the same. Talk is cheap without the walk. If I want to teach someone how to follow the Master, I need to help them make the connection between what they hear and what they actually do—morning, noon and night, seven days a week.

The heart of discipleship is not what you know, but *who* you're becoming. It's about mentoring, coaching and modeling. I have seen people more effectively "discipled" in one hour of counseling than in fifty hours of just listening to sermons. Don't get me wrong, there is nothing wrong with sermons—we need them. But disciples can't be *made* from the pulpit alone. It takes much more than a Sunday morning service to *make* disciples.

As with everything in Christianity—faith and action, mind and body, soul and spirit must work together. A person's soul may be saved and cleansed, but their spirit may be discouraged. A person's mind may be in the right place, but their body is chained down to addictions. A person's faith may be jumbo-sized, but if they never pray the prayer and speak the words, the mountain before them remains unmoved. Effective discipleship helps us make the connection between what we know we ought to do and actually doing it. If I only teach someone what they're supposed to do and never show them how, I have just guaranteed that person will get discouraged and give up.

If I want to teach someone to be a car mechanic, I need to get under the hood with him and get my hands greasy. If I want to teach someone to play baseball, I need to suit up, head for the nearest field, and kick up some dirt. In the same way, discipleship takes practice, hard work, and dedicated coaching. Discipleship is messy. It's not perfect, because people aren't perfect. Jesus went over the same things again and again with his disciples, and he was God! Discipleship requires lifelong commitment. And it takes leadership. That's what disciple-making is all about: showing the way, modeling the teaching, painting unforgettable pictures with your life.

One of the most effective disciple-makers I know is Bill Bright. He is discipling over 10,000 people and will continue to do so even though he is now with the Lord. He once told his secret to a group of leaders: "Invest your life in a few good people. Pour your energies into them." He simply followed the strategy of Jesus. The Master Discipler took 12 men and said, "Come live with me." The apostle Paul did the same. He wrote to the Church in Corinth, "I urge you to imitate me" (1 Cor. 4:16). And then in the very next breath he could say of his disciple Timothy, "For this reason I am sending him to you . . . he will remind you of my *way of life*" (v. 17). That's when you know discipleship has taken place: when people start living out what they are being taught, and so become reliable examples for others to follow. Paul summed it up this way, "Teach these things to reliable men who will be *qualified* to teach others" (2 Tim. 2:2).

Jesus and Paul knew what they were doing. The most powerful force on this planet is a group of believers so in love with Christ and so committed to one another, they would rather die than be disloyal to their mission and purpose. Disciple-making is about *becoming* that kind of fellowship—forming a band of brothers (or sisters as the case may be!). Jesus prayed for his discipleship band, "May they be brought to *complete unity* to let the world know that you have sent me" (John 17:23). Joining a discipleship band is almost like getting married. There are no secrets. There are no problems too big or small. The group stands ready to defend its members no matter what—through the good times, the bad times, and everything in between. And through Christ, they are closer than blood. They are united in soul and spirit by the Spirit of God.

Being a band of brothers is sort of like a football team. People come from all different backgrounds. They're all shapes and sizes. Some people come from broken homes, shameful pasts, and abusive relationships. But football is their sanctuary. It's a place to leave all that behind. When game time rolls around there is only one thing on everyone's mind: how to move that ball down the field and score the winning touchdown. There must be absolute focus and determination to work as a unit, with one mind and will. If one lineman goes down, the team goes down. The quarterback gets sacked and yards are lost. The team gives each lineman a reason to stay his ground and push forward to victory.

Deep inside all of us, we long for friendship so real and so strong we could depend on it with our very lives. Jesus came for this purpose, to make this kind of friendship possible. Apart from Christ, true friendship cannot exist. Real discipleship is all about building and strengthening the kind of lasting relationships that help people fulfill the command of Christ: love one another as I have loved you. You can't love people if you don't know them, and no one can love you in return if they never get to know the real you behind the mask.

This isn't automatic and it doesn't happen overnight. We have to do our part. If we're going to help others, we ourselves must become vulnerable, transparent, and ready to listen—willing to take correction at any time. Mentoring is all about letting someone *read* your life, *study* your behavior, and *scrutinize* your motives. Paul said to his disciples, "*Whatever* you have seen in me, put into practice" (Phil. 4:9). We must be willing to say the same if disciples are to be made and "equipped for every good work." And before you can make disciples, you must become one!

CONSECRATE YOURSELF

Some of the most effective discipleship I have ever seen has taken place on the mission field. Sad to say, this has not been in the churches we have set up, but in the mission societies we have formed to set up the churches. The churches are the ordinary kind where people are taught to know what Jesus commanded, but not necessarily helped to obey. Basically they are exact copies of the churches we grew up in. No one stops to think: does this really work? Are we making disciples?

However, the mission societies are much different. Here you have a group of people who have signed up for a greater commitment. We have agreed to work together and in submission to one another. We're willing to be assigned and we let ourselves be trained for the job. Our training is hands-on, it's real life, and it's working with other experienced followers of Christ and learning from their lives.

When I began to see the contrast between discipled missionaries and undiscipled believers, the lights began to go on. What if every local church were as committed as these mission societies—as organized and focused? Suddenly a small church of 120 people isn't so small. Only a few mission agencies have that many people! Jesus started out with 12 ordinary people and changed the world. And if

I'm not mistaken, he's still the head of his Church! He's still the Master Discipler and he longs to get a hold of every one of us.

Now most people will say such a transformation is impossible. But that's because they've never visited a place like China. One of the fastest growing house church movements in China has the following requirements for their disciples:

1. At least 4 hours a day must be spent in prayer and Bible reading, starting with 2 hours of prayer from 5 to 7 am.
2. Wherever they are sent, disciples must be ready to suffer or even die for Christ.
3. Every disciple must be ready and active in witnessing for Christ.

Now perhaps these Chinese believers are just crazy. Or perhaps they're more in tune with the Holy Spirit. I'll let you make the call. But imagine if every church encouraged their members to such commitment! Would they not have the same results as this house church movement in China? Is it really so great a tragedy that millions have come to Christ in China because a few committed believers have been willing to make sacrifices in order to reach them?

Many people secretly long for the power of God to fill their lives. Most pastors would greatly appreciate it if revival would finally come to their Church. They love to read about such things and hear the stories told. But they will *never* see the glory of the Lord fall until they consecrate themselves accordingly. And yet it seems we have it all backwards today in our discipleship. We tell people to work hard in their jobs—to consecrate themselves in the pursuit of money. They work 8 to 10 hours a day for a few pieces of paper with numbers on them. But will we challenge them to work hard for souls? At least as hard as they work for money? To pray and fast and weep before the Lord so the lost may be saved? To make winning people for Jesus the absolute priority of their lives? Absolutely never! But to the believers in China this is a no-brainer.

Consecration means getting your house in order so the Lord can use you. It means doing whatever it takes, persevering until the answer comes, and sweeping out all the dirt. Jesus told the disciples to wait in Jerusalem until they received power from on high. Now what if they didn't wait? What if they prayed for a while and said, "Well, I guess that's enough. Let's go take care of business." Had this been their attitude they would have completely failed.

Being used mightily of the Lord begins with a corporate commitment to prayer and fasting for souls to be saved. The first disciples would not be distracted by anything else. They said we "will give our attention to prayer and the ministry of the word" (Acts 6:4). And what was the result? "The Lord added to their number *daily* those who were being saved" (Acts 2:47). Notice, Scripture does not say, "And the Lord added to their number every Sunday morning those who responded to the altar call." That's because Acts tells us, "Day after day in the temple courts and from *house to house*, they *never* stopped teaching and proclaiming the good news that Jesus is the Christ" (Acts 5:42).

One of the most powerful revivals in India came about because believers banded together in a special prayer union. They committed themselves to praying half an hour every day at noontime for a spiritual awakening to come into their lives and into their communities. They asked the following questions of their members:

> 1. Are you longing for greater power of the Holy Spirit in your own life and work, and are you convinced that you cannot go on without this power?

2. Will you pray that you may not be ashamed of Jesus?

3. Do you believe that prayer is the great means for securing this spiritual awakening?

4. Are you willing to pray until the awakening comes?

Every day without fail they would cry out to the Lord to send his power into their witness. It wasn't long before the Holy Spirit descended upon the towns and villages in their area just as he did at Pentecost. Tens of thousands came to know Christ and the Church became well established in that part of India.

Groups like this get things done for the Kingdom because they are functioning the way Jesus intended his Church to operate. He called his disciples to a higher standard. He didn't call them to know a bunch of facts about theology. He called them to *live his theology*—to be ready and fitted for *action* in his Great Commission. If we're going to make disciples we need to find out what the Master wants done. Disciples aren't made for discipleship's sake, just as the army doesn't make soldiers for military parades on Broadway. There is something we're supposed to be doing. We have an assignment from the Master: to rescue people from darkness to light and from the power of Satan to God (Acts 26:18). It's the only thing on his agenda. If we're not rescuing people then we're not following, because that's where the Master is and that's why he came—to seek and to save the lost.

We can do many things and train people with all kinds of programs, but at the end of the day we must ask ourselves, "Have we enhanced this person's effectiveness in winning souls for the Kingdom?" If not, we have missed the whole point. In the U.S. Army's basic training, one of the main objectives is to prepare a soldier to return fire. The fact is, many people naturally freeze up in the heat of battle and never fire their weapons at all. They're just dead weight (sometimes literally) on the battlefield. Many Christians are the same. They testify how inadequate they feel to evangelize. Their lips are sealed tight with Super Glue whenever the Holy Spirit prompts them to witness. The main thing they're supposed to be doing is the main thing they feel least equipped to do. These same Christians will tell you their prayer life is non-existent. Something is amiss in their education. Discipleship isn't taking place.

Our Lord's only assignment to his church is strictly about fulfilling the Great Commission: winning people, serving people, building people and sending people. It's about people—period. It's not about programs, institutions and traditions. Becoming a Great Commission Christian is becoming a people person. You might be the biggest lone ranger, anti-social, hide-in-a-corner, stick-to-the-wall-like-a-flower person there ever was, but if you want to be used by God to fulfill his mission, you need to die to yourself and change your perspective. When it comes to the Kingdom, being shy is a crime. You need to get discipled and you need to get ready, because God has other ideas for your life.

BEWARE OF FALSE DISCIPLESHIP

When Paul wrote to Philemon he said, "I pray you may be active in sharing your faith *so that* you will have a full understanding of every good thing we have in Christ" (v. 6). Notice he didn't say it the other way around. That is, wait until you have a full understanding, and then go share the gospel. The fact is, if you're not using what you know, you're not benefiting from it. Most disciples are actually regressing in their faith because they're not sharing it. Eternal life is a gift—to be used carefully. Heavenly wisdom is a trust, to be employed faithfully. You grow in Christ as you are a faithful steward of what he has given you. As in physical training, if you don't use it, you'll lose it (not the muscles, of course, but the ability to use them).

False discipleship seeks to shortchange people. It says, "Let's lower the standards and make things as easy as possible." But Paul wanted believers to be *active*. So did Peter. He said, "Prepare your minds for action" (1 Pet. 1:13). He wanted disciples to be initiative-takers and Kingdom opportunists—always prepared to give an answer for Christ. In other words, stay *conditioned* for action. If you're an athlete, you know that taking a break for over 30 days is disaster—you have to start your conditioning all over again. In the same way, following Christ is a lifelong discipline. Discipleship is the *discipline* of following Christ "in season and out of season" (2 Tim. 4:2).

So let's think it over: Why does discipleship have to be such a radical commitment? What's wrong with taking it easy and just hoping everything sort of works out? What's the big deal anyway? To find the answer, simply visit any NFL or NBA locker room during halftime and listen to the pep talk: It's because we're a team. And to the extent you're a lazy bum, one of your team members has to pick up the slack. For example:

> *Am I praying like I should be?*
> If not, somebody, somewhere has to make up
> the difference.
>
> *Is my life being used to the maximum to reach the unreached?*
> If not, some other disciple will have to reach
> the people I'm not reaching.
>
> *Am I discipling others to live 100% for Jesus?*
> If not, there will be even fewer people, including
> myself, who are fulfilling the Great Commission.

Eternal Vision

The Bible says the purpose of discipleship is to "prepare God's people for works of service." That's why we're here: to be fully occupied in the Lord's work. And this same verse goes on to tell us the reason, "*so that* the Body of Christ may be built up until we *all reach unity* in the faith" (Eph. 4:12-13). God wants to bring you into maturity. His method of doing this is through discipleship—and this can only happen as you are faithfully serving in his Kingdom. If you're not serving, you're not being discipled—period. If you're not involved in the Great Commission, you're not growing in Christ. If you're not plugged into God's purposes for this generation, you're life isn't going anywhere.

Satan wants to cut you down as an infant in Christ. He has his own discipleship program all cut out for you. He wants you "tossed back and forth by the waves and blown here and there by every wind of teaching and by the cunning and craftiness of men in their deceitful scheming" (Eph 4:14). He has people ready and waiting to lead you into the lukewarm waters of shallow Christianity. He has his best servants trained and equipped to send you down the spiral of defeated Christian living.

The Bible warns of such people because they are incredibly destructive, like cancer cells spreading from place to place. They are active in our churches, Sunday schools and small groups, and from heaven's point of view they are the most dangerous people on this planet. But beware! They're the nicest, too. They've got the biggest smiles and the coziest lifestyles.

It's easy to fall victim to their teaching because they appeal to the part of you that is not yet consecrated to the Lord. They aim for the unsurrendered area of your heart. There is only one way you can avoid their cunning scheme for your life. You need to know the truth. You need to understand what God wants to do in you and through you and what he expects from his disciples. You need to know his standard and refuse to forget it.

I have never seen a person of prayer and fasting led astray into false discipleship. Most false teaching feeds the sinful nature and encourages it. The Bible warns us of people who will "change the grace of our God into a license for immorality" (Jude 1:4). These people preach freedom in Christ, but they themselves are in bondage. They are deceived by Satan, and "having lost all sensitivity, they have given themselves over to sensuality . . . with a continual lust for more" (Eph. 4:19).

We need to take our stand against them, not in anger or provocation, but by being an example. Sure they will mock us, scorn our commitment, condemn us even. But we will love them. We will pray for them. We will refuse to be infected with their disease.

If you're committed to being a radical follower of Jesus, you can be sure Satan will try to stop you. But if you band together with other like-minded followers, you stand a good chance of not only overcoming, but winning a few from the other side. Jesus said, "By this *all men will know* that you are my disciples, if you love one another" (John 13:35). Jesus wants us so close together, even those who oppose us will be secretly dying to get in on what we've got. Most people haven't a clue what it means to really love someone. They haven't even the capacity. But you will learn and the Holy Spirit will be your teacher. Just give him the chance by taking the initiative to build up those around you and encourage their walk.

John Wesley and his brother formed a small group on their campus that literally changed the world. They were known as the "holy club." They regularly asked each other very personal questions so they might walk in holiness. Now that's love! The world will say,

"How rigid, how legalistic, how sad!" And of course they did say all those things to Wesley and his friends. But nonetheless, this small band changed all of England. Even secular historians can't deny it. Through the influence of the Wesleys, slavery was abolished, corruption was curtailed, and civil war was averted.

But John and Charles never took credit for any of it. They knew it was the power of Christ that enabled them to preach to so many. It was the Holy Spirit who inspired tens of thousands to consecrate themselves in similar small groups. From these societies came hundreds of missionaries who planted over 100,000 churches around the world. Even today, their example continues to touch people through the cell church movement, which has brought renewal to thousands of churches on every continent.

So what was it that made these two brothers different—what distinguished them from those in their generation? It was simply a willingness to get organized, to do something about holiness, and to help others find the way. What the Lord did through these two brothers he will do again through anyone. If you will desire to do great things for him and to live a holy life, you will accomplish more for the Kingdom in one year than the hundreds of people who ridicule your commitment will ever accomplish in a thousand years. It's entirely up to you, but entirely possible in Christ. It's the only thing that really matters. It's living life the way he lived and walking where he walks today. It's taking up your cross daily and refusing to put it down. It's radical discipleship, step by step with the Master.

CHAPTER TWELVE

※

JUST ASK

"For everyone who asks receives; he who seeks finds; and to him who knocks, the door will be opened." (Matthew 7:8)

*O*ver 100 years ago, Turkish soldiers entered the Armenian community where my great grandmother lived. Going from home to home they burned each one to the ground with the victims tied up inside. As they were approaching my great grandmother's home, she gathered everyone in the family for prayer. When the soldiers came to the front of her house, preparing to knock down the door, they suddenly paused, turned around and went away.

After the family immigrated to America, the Lord continued to work many miracles in my great grandmother's family. Once, my grandpa (her eldest son) injured his hand while he was at work. Since he was a diabetic the situation became very dangerous. The infection turned into gangrene and spread throughout his body. In a last attempt to save his life, the doctors amputated his arm. Even so, the surgeon, who also happened to be an atheist, shook his head and said, "He won't last the night." But my great grandma refused to be shaken in her faith. She declared to the doctors and to everyone present, "My God is able to raise him up!" That evening, she went out and gathered the small Armenian church together and they prayed all night.

The next morning the surgeon went into my grandpa's room. "Hello, doc!" said my grandpa with a smile, sitting up in bed. Surprised to find him alive, he removed the bandages and received another surprise. The skin had totally healed over. Running down the hall, he began shouting to everyone, "It's a miracle, it's a miracle!"

Later, my grandpa testified that he actually did die that night. He was taken to heaven and was with the Lord (he had just given his life to Jesus a month earlier). He was told many things of which he was only able to share a few. He asked the Lord if he could stay, but the Lord said, "No, I'm sending you back." He became a great man of faith and was used by the Lord to help many people receive physical healing as well as salvation in Christ.

Another person like my grandpa was my great grandfather (from the maternal side of my dad's family). After he escaped to America, he settled with his family in Philadelphia. There was no Armenian church he could attend and he didn't know English very well. But every Sunday he would attend the nearest local church and pray aloud in the Armenian language before the service began. One of his special requests, which he asked God every week, was that his descendants might serve the Lord to the fifth generation.

Years later, my dad was stationed in Philadelphia while in the army. He was not walking with the Lord, but as he passed a particular church he suddenly felt drawn to go inside. He had no idea about his grandpa's prayer or that his grandparents had ever attended church there. But once inside he felt the powerful presence of God. He sat down and opened one of the Bibles right to the prodigal son story. It was the beginning of a spiritual breakthrough

Just Ask

for my dad and full surrender a few days later. When he told all of this to his mom, she smiled in amazement and told my dad of his grandpa's persistent prayer in that very church.

Not too long after my dad's conversion, he fell in love with a beautiful young lady who had also become a Christian through the persistent prayers of the most unlikely person. My mom was raised in an atheistic home. Her parents taught her to despise Christianity and even to harass others who believed in Jesus. But one day she met a believing Jewish lady in the park who began praying regularly for her. They became friends, and when the opportunity presented itself, she shared her testimony with my mom. This lady and her husband had traveled everywhere with Elvis Presley and were leaders in the occult. But during one of their meetings, as they were in meditation, she had a forty-foot vision of Jesus. He said, "I am the one you are seeking." From that moment on she started following him! She became a powerful witness for the Lord and a great intercessor for his Kingdom. She led many to Christ, including my mom.

Without a doubt, I have come to believe that God takes prayer very seriously. He means what he says, and he will do all that he has promised. He will answer your prayers for your children, and your children's children, and their children as well. Prayer transcends decades, reaches across vast oceans, and alters the course of eternal history. To be prayed for by another is the greatest honor there is or ever will be. I can only say thank you to the Lord for the unmerited privilege of praying parents, grandparents, and great grandparents.

According to the Bible, prayer is the most powerful force in the world. Jesus said, "If you believe, you shall receive whatever you ask for in prayer" (Matt. 21:22). Jesus made this statement six different times.[1] He emphasized it again and again. He talked about prayer more than any other single topic. His disciples remembered him as someone who "often withdrew to lonely places and prayed" (Luke 5:16). Jesus prayed, not only to set an example for us, but also because he *needed* to pray. Prayer is no mere ritual. When Jesus shed tears of blood in the garden of Gethsemane, he was really crying out. When he prayed for himself and his disciples in the upper room, he was really interceding (John 17). When he stayed up all night to pray, and the next day chose the 12 Apostles, it wasn't because he couldn't fall asleep and had nothing else to do (Luke 6:12).

Prayer is the primary means through which our Heavenly Father has ordained to perform his will in our lives. Jesus said, "The Son can do nothing by himself" (John 5:19). The same is true with us, and how much more so! Our Heavenly Father wants us completely dependent on him, and when we learn to pray we are saying, "I understand your way and I humbly accept it."

Learn to pray and you will be unstoppable. You will see the humanly impossible come to pass before your very eyes—the unchangeable irreversibly altered, and the unmovable suddenly in motion. You will learn the secret that led Moses back to Egypt with only a rod in his hand, the power that sustained Daniel in the lion's den, and the strength that routed whole armies before David's men, though outnumbered three to one. You will come to know a God who is ready and waiting to do anything through anyone who will just believe, "Lord, your kingdom come, your will be done; your throne be established, your glory be exalted; have your way in everything, have your way in me."

LEARNING TO ASK

Ronald Reagan was a movie actor who would later be used of God to bring about an end to communism in Eastern Europe and the Soviet Union. Millions came to Christ as a result of these lands

Just Ask

opening up to the gospel. How he became president, and one of the most loved in history, has left many a little bemused. But his staff could tell you why. They knew his secret. They would often see him in the middle of a meeting bowing his head, closing his eyes, and quietly praying. Whenever there was a problem, an impasse, or a difficult issue needing heavenly wisdom, Reagan would take it to the Lord. No matter where he was or who was around, he would pause and say, "Lord, we need your help."

Many people don't ask because they genuinely think God has more important things to look after. They say, "I can't bother God with the small things of my life." But the truth is, such people have a small God! God is so great and awesome, your small things are the very things he wants to hear about. A small God can only handle so much. The God of the Bible is much different. Before him there is no difference—small things and great things are all the same! That's how big our God is.

My grandfather was one who learned to ask God for everything, small and great. Interestingly, it was the small things that meant the most to my dad. He and his friends would always play baseball in a nearby empty lot. The back of the lot was overgrown with ivy and weeds. Many times the ball would get lost back there, and my dad and his friends would search and search until in despair they would come running to my grandpa. He never failed to find that ball. He would say, "Children, let's ask the Lord to help us find it." Then he would pray and the Lord would show him exactly where the ball was. Later, when my dad was in a desperate time in his life, and not yet fully surrendered to Christ, he cried out, "O Lord of the lost ball, I need you now!"

Learning to pray is all about bringing "lost balls" to the Lord and growing in faith as you see his awesome power at work. Oftentimes the testimony of the small things has the greatest impact on those needing the Lord. For if God is concerned about such a thing as a lost ball, then certainly he is concerned about all the other "important" things in your life. It is by learning to pray such a simple prayer as "Give us this day our daily bread," that you begin to understand what it means to pray "Your kingdom come, your will be done *on earth as it is in heaven.*" In bringing to God even the smallest things of your life, you give him the opportunity to show how much he loves you, and as a result, you will learn to trust him more and more for greater and greater things.

The Lord delights in building the faith of his children, especially those who are the youngest and the smallest. One night, my brother Paul was in bed moaning and groaning because of the pain in his ear. The pain was so great he could not get any sleep. My little sister Mary was up getting some water when she heard him. So she went in and prayed and asked the Lord to heal him. Then she left and went to the kitchen. On her way back she peeked inside his room. He was sound asleep and completely healed.

That night my sister learned the most important lesson of her life: God is listening! Very closely. Everything we say, and every thought we make, is heard by God and taken into account. The Bible says, "Men will have to give an account on the day of judgment for *every* careless word they have spoken" (Matt. 12:36). It sounds a little scary at first. Why do we have to be so careful about what we say? But the answer is profoundly life-changing. Scripture says, "If anyone is never at fault in what he says, he is a perfect man, able to keep his whole body in check" (Jas. 3:2). Our words affect everything about us. Words are powerful—God has made them to be so. Words can change the course of eternity. What we say, or don't say, what we pray, or don't pray, will determine who we are and who we will become. Not only that, our words can determine who others may become as well. Jesus said, "By your words you will be acquitted, and by your words you will be condemned" (Matt. 12:37). For better or for worse, the tape is rolling, the mics are up, and the record light is flashing. How many of our words will be counted for us? How many conversations mattered for eternity? How many breaths were used for prayer and intercession and communing with the Lord?

Like every heavenly gift, prayer comes with a great responsibility. Scripture says, "You do not have, because you do not ask God" (Jas. 4:2). Now ponder on this for a moment. It will forever change the way you think about prayer. There are things which God wants to do in your life, but you will never see them until you ask him. Some people wonder, "What's the point of praying if God already knows what needs to be done?" But the *purpose* of prayer is not to "get God's attention" or "educate" him or "empower" him. Bringing our problems before God is an expression of our faith in his promise. He says, "If you pray, *then* I will answer."

In this sense, prayer is like a thermometer of our spiritual condition. The temperature of our faith can be measured by the heat of our prayer life. Since God commands us to ask, seek and knock—to persevere and cry out, the matter is very simple. If we believe God, we will pray, and if we don't believe him, then we won't.

By our prayers we will be acquitted or condemned. Prideful people don't understand prayer; it remains a mystery to them. Spiritually lazy people will never intercede; its purpose escapes them. Faithless people consider prayer a mere ritual; they bless the dinner table and not much else.

The number one thing Satan wants to do in your life is to keep your prayer life as powerless as possible. There is no greater means to hindering your spiritual growth than to keep you off your knees in prayer. What a tragedy to give him the victory! And yet for many believers, the purposes of God in their lives are being kept at bay through an unwillingness on their part to invest the time and effort before the Lord in his presence, humbly accepting his method for working in their midst.

OVERCOMING IN PRAYER

Many people have the experience of being distracted when they try to pray. They set aside time to be alone with God, but it seems they hardly get any praying done because their mind constantly wanders. There is a good reason for this and it should give us pause and make us think. The moment you set yourself to pray, there is someone who will try to stop you—every time, without exception. He won't stop until your eyes are heavy, your lips are silent, and your thoughts are far, far away in never-never land.

Prayer is dangerous to Satan, and the enemy will do everything possible in his means to keep you out of the presence of God. The lessons you learn in this struggle will become the most valuable part of your growth in Christ. The investment here is an eternal one. Learning to pray is the most important thing you will ever learn to do in this lifetime. As far as we know, this is the only time in eternal history where intercessory prayer has significance. That makes it all the more important for us to prioritize this discipline in our lives.

A million years from now you will not be able to pray for your lost relatives to be saved. Ten thousand years from now it won't matter if you want to pray for the fulfillment of the Great Commission. And if history continues in its present course, one hundred years from now you will be with the Lord. And then it will not matter how much money you had in your bank account, or what degree you majored in, or what people thought about your hairstyle. If eternity was not your priority during your stay here on earth, there will only be one thing on your mind as you stand before the Lord, "If only I had known what I know now, I would have lived a radically different life." And if given a chance to live it again, I know beyond a shadow of a doubt, the number one thing you would do is learn to ask in faith and prayerfully seek after his Kingdom.

I know of people who spend hours in prayer every day. I used to think praying 20 minutes was next to impossible. How I struggled when I first began! Now, years later, prayer is not a burden. It is a joy. For I know that as I pray, God is silently at work within me, developing and fashioning my spirit for an eternity of glory with him.

I have learned to pray with a much different perspective. I will often pray at least three hours a day, and it has nothing to do with having enough time. This spiritual secret came to me through the life of Martin Luther. He also learned to pray at least three hours a day, not because he had the time, but because he *needed* the time. He said on one particular day, "I am so busy today, I don't have time to pray. Therefore, I am too busy *not* to pray!"

Here is one of the most profound truths about God I have ever learned. It took me a long time to get it, and now I will never let it go. My strength, and also my weakness, is that I am naturally a very driven person. I like to get things done as quickly and efficiently as possible. If it were up to me, I would say a few short prayers at the beginning of the day and get to work. But I have learned a valuable lesson. If I will spend more time with the Lord, my day will be even more productive. In this way, God has turned my weakness into a strength. My drive to excel has brought me to my knees—to the place where all lasting purpose finds its true beginning.

As a result, prayer is a joy to me because I see God answering throughout my entire day. I can be thankful in every circumstance because I see his hand in everything. Prayer is a way of experiencing the presence of God throughout every moment of your life. I have learned to make a record of specific prayers and the answers God brings. I believe the Lord delights in this. He loves to build our faith, but our memories are so short! As we remember what God has done, he can use these examples to help us overcome the uncertainties we are sure to face. That's the whole purpose of the Bible. The more you understand what God is willing to do, and the more you apply this understanding in your life, the more you will grow in faith and the more your prayers will have an impact.

One of the most courageous things you can do by faith is to take a portion of your busy schedule and give it to God. Rest assured, he will honor you. The Lord delights in making our lives a demonstration of his power. Looking back, you will find this devotion has become the most rewarding and fulfilling aspect of your life. It will be the one thing you will look back on from eternity with a smile. All other things will fade from memory, but the dividends of prayer will live on with you forever.

Of course, prayer is hard work. It takes effort. But in the midst of all that work and expended energy, there is a joy beyond description. It's like playing basketball. For some people, playing the game is pure drudgery. But for others, they are out there playing basketball like it's the most exciting thing on the planet. They give it all they've got. All their energy, skill and talent are going into the game. All their competitive will power is going into getting that basketball down the court and into the basket.

In the same way, your attitude in prayer will go a long way toward overcoming Satan's resistance, which is sure to come. Prayer requires your highest dedication and greatest resolve. But at the end of the day, it's always worth it. You come to enjoy the discipline, appreciate the practice, and long for the next encounter with the Lord. When done properly, and with the right perspective, prayer is the most exciting endeavor imaginable. It's connecting with God and being changed for eternity. It's the best deal and the greatest opportunity we've been offered this side of heaven.

THE LAW OF INTERCESSION

Wesley Duewel was a pioneer missionary to India and a great man of faith and prayer. One Sunday afternoon, God began to burden Wesley to pray fervently for the salvation of his son, who was now studying in America. Time and space seemed to disappear as he entered the presence of God. At that moment he knew God was going to do a great work in his son's life. He felt as if the Spirit of God was allowing him to kneel beside his son with his hand on his shoulder. Then the assurance came, God had fully answered his prayer! He got up from his knees with joy and thanksgiving, knowing his son was in the Kingdom of God. The next day, Wesley received a telegram from his son. It read, "God is my Captain. Quiet but sure decision. Thanks for the heritage, love and prayer. John." In tears he dropped to his knees to thank the Lord. Later, Wesley received a letter from his son with more details. He had given his life to the Lord at the exact moment his father was interceding, so many thousands of miles away.[2]

This same testimony of prevailing prayer could be told a thousand times over, perhaps a million times. The Lord wants you as his partner and he is serious about enlisting as many intercessors and prayer warriors as are willing to sign up. There is no greater honor than to join this courageous band. The Lord has given us the weapon of prayer and faith to demolish all that stands in his way.

Prayer connected to the will of God is the most powerful force in the world. Prayer activates the will of God in a particular situation or person's life. But prayer by itself accomplishes absolutely nothing. It's only words, air vibrating, futile human energy. Prayer only has power when connected with God's purposes and the promises of his Word. That's why the Bible says we are to "Take the sword of the Spirit, which is the word of God. And pray in the Spirit on all occasions" (Eph. 6:17).

There is no more powerful weapon given to man. God has set up the universe to operate according to his laws, and of all these laws the spiritual ones are the most important. Spiritual laws are those which affect both this life and the life to come. They impact the temporal and the eternal at the same time. The Law of Intercession is by far the greatest and most powerful spiritual reality in heaven and on earth. Through this law we are saved, and through its power we are transformed.

This Law was at work on Calvary when Jesus prayed, "Father, forgive them, for they know not what they do" (Luke 23:34). This Law stayed the hand of God when he was about to destroy an entire nation. Moses interceded and the Lord replied, "I have forgiven them, *as you asked*" (Num. 14:20). This Law saved Job's friends who had spoken against a righteous man. The Lord said, "My servant Job will pray for you, and I will accept his prayer and not deal with you according to your folly" (Job 42:8). This Law saved King Abimelech when he took Sarah into his household, not knowing she was Abraham's wife. God spared him saying, "Now return the man's wife for he is a prophet and he will pray for you and you will live" (Gen. 20:7).

When you consider all the evidence, it is not hard to imagine why the Law of Intercession brings with it the most grave responsibility given to man. Samuel said, "As for me, far be it from me that I should *sin* against the Lord by *failing to pray* for you" (1 Sam. 12:23). Oh, that more people today would take prayer as seriously as Samuel did! When prayer is a priority it affects your entire life. The Bible tells us Jesus "offered up prayers and petitions with loud cries and tears" (Heb. 5:7). We learn of Epaphras who was constantly "wrestling in prayer" for the Colossian believers (Col 4:12). Prayer is not a past-time or a "hobby-when-I-get-around-to-it" sort of thing. If you're a follower of Jesus, prayer is your lifestyle and primary assignment. It is your highest calling.

The greatest arrogance in the world is to pray half-heartedly or not pray at all. The greatest tyranny against the cross and the Kingdom is to squander its power. Imagine having the capacity to do good and refusing to do so! Such is the prayerless life. Believers who refuse to pray do more harm, more damage, more destructive work to the cause of Christ than they will ever know until eternity. Prayer is an awesome trust and costly stewardship, demanding your full attention. It calls for the highest level of consecration. It requires patience, endurance, determination, and persistence. It will bring you to your knees, shed tears from your heart and soul, and stir your entire being. It demands your time and will task your emotion. Prayer is a sacrifice of the highest order.

Without exception, we have *all* been given the capacity to intercede as followers of Jesus; it is our greatest inheritance and strongest obligation as his disciples. Your capacity to pray will grow as you exercise it, but therein lies your responsibility. It is the calling and the responsibility of everyone in Christ. It is the *primary* responsibility! Everything else is secondary, for whatever else you may believe God wants you to do on this earth, none of it can be accomplished but through faithfully seeking his will in the stillness of his presence.

God has so ordained it that we must remain completely reliant on him throughout our entire stay here on this planet. No endeavor will succeed without him.

One of the greatest men of faith in Scripture was the apostle Paul. But we have more prayer requests from this man of faith than from any other person. To every major church in his day, Paul requested that they pray for him.[3] Men of faith are not superheroes with extraordinary powers. They are ordinary people with an extraordinary God who listens to the prayers of his people. Paul urged the Church in Corinth, "On him we have set our hope that he will continue to deliver us, as you help us by your prayers" (2 Cor. 1:10-11). To the Church in Rome he wrote, "I urge you brothers, by the Lord Jesus Christ and by the love of the Spirit, to join me in my struggle by praying to God for me" (Rom. 15:30).

The war we are engaged in can only be won through the deliberate and faithful intercession of God's people. How many souls are being lost, how many missionaries ministering ineffectively, how many believers experiencing spiritual drought because they have not learned the lessons of prayer? The Lord says, "*If* my people will humble themselves and pray, *then* I will turn and heal their land" (2 Chr. 7:14). Notice the condition. Mark the order. God's conditional will is one of the most misunderstood aspects of his character and much disobedience results from this confusion. But one of the primary reasons God has given us his Word is to demonstrate this very aspect of his will *so that* we will endeavor to do our part.

There are some things about God which are *unconditional*. God will never stop loving us. He will always be faithful. He will never lie. God will always do his part.

But he will never force you to love him. And as a result, there is much that God will not do until we ask him. God's desire is that all men should be saved, but we have to receive heaven's offer for his will to be activated in our lives. In the same way, God has ordained that we should pray—and pray daily, for his will to be done (Matt. 6:10). He does this for an important reason. Having stated his terms, the condition of our heart becomes manifest to all based on our response. For to not ask God, in light of all he has told us, then becomes the highest form of arrogance known to man. In the most declarative way, prayerlessness is telling God, "I don't need you, I don't believe you. I'll get along without you."

FAITHFUL IN PRAYER

Sometime ago, a Christian businessman and trader from Armenia was traveling through a place called Kurdistan, the traditional homeland of the Kurdish people. This group is entirely Muslim and somewhat infamous for their hostility toward Christians. So when a group of Kurdish bandits found out about this Armenian trader, they began to follow him. At night they descended on his camp intending to kill him and take his possessions. But when they arrived, to their amazement, they found 20-foot walls surrounding his entire camp. Puzzled, they went back into the hills and decided to keep following him.

The next night they returned to rob him, but once again the same 20-foot walls were in place! By now they were beginning to get a little curious about this phenomenon. So they all decided to try once more the next night. This time their persistence paid off. Once again the walls were there, but there was a breach on one of the sides where they could enter. The bandits took the trader by surprise and demanded to know his secret. Of course, he had to admit that he knew nothing about the walls. But he explained, "Every night before I go to bed, I ask the Lord Jesus to protect me. But tonight I really prayed a half-hearted prayer and that must be why there was a breach in those walls!"

That very night, each of those Kurdish bandits prayed to receive Christ as their Savior. It's an incident with a grace-filled ending, but with a gentle reminder as well: Our daily and fervent prayer *does* matter. When the great missionary Paul heard about the believers in Colosse, he immediately added them to his prayer list. He said, "Since the day we heard about you, we have not stopped praying for you" (Col. 1:9). Even though he had never met them, he joined with them in their witness for Christ every day. Scripture says, "Encourage one another *daily*" (Heb. 3:13). I can think of no greater way to encourage people than through prayer. How many times have I been lifted up and surrounded by God's presence because of the faithful prayers of his people? More than I can count, to be sure. I am forever grateful to those who have committed to pray for me daily and as the Holy Spirit leads them.

On the day before my twentieth birthday, my mom felt an intense burden to begin praying for me and my brother. At that very moment my brother and I had a blowout on the freeway. We spun around in circles across five lanes, hit the center divider, and ended up in the emergency lane. I don't know how it happened, but our car was perfectly parked in that lane—headed the other way! All I can do is say thank you to the Lord for my awesome praying mom!

We may never fully understand it, but there is something about daily interceding for others which is more important than anything else we can do for them. Prayer engages the "spiritual forces of evil" in a way that is impossible for us to comprehend. But we know this much: there is no more deadly and dangerous force in the entire universe as far as the enemy is concerned. Every lasting Kingdom victory has been won at the price of great intercession. The power of Christ-centered, Holy Spirit enabled prayer is immeasurable. Through it we have access to the great work of his Kingdom in every village, street corner and home. We're unstoppable. We can't be shut out!

In Revelation we see a picture of angels before the throne carrying golden bowls of incense, "which are the prayers of the saints" (Rev. 5:8). How precious are those offerings! And what an honor to be a part. There is still time and there are still bowls to be filled. Much intercession remains before the end. Even now, great strongholds remain to be conquered. Great challenges await us. Tall giants still defy the armies of the Living God. But the Lord has given us the answer. He has given *you* the answer, and how you use it will make all the difference in the world. It's an incredible responsibility and an unequaled opportunity of eternal value. Each of us will be called into account for how we employed it.

Two thousand unevangelized ethnic groups still await faithful intercessors to take up their plight. Billions remain without a hope, without a prayer, without a faithful intercessor to stand in the gap on their behalf. They are hopelessly bound, but you and I hold the key! Will we learn to use it? Will we play a part in the greatest moment of eternal history—preparing the way for His coming? Or will we let the drowsiness and busyness of this world render us powerless and spiritually paralyzed? The time you spend alone with God, interceding before his throne with all your heart, soul and mind, will tell you the answer.

Billy Graham once said, "If you don't feel like praying, it's probably a good indication you should start praying immediately." It sounds obvious, but there is great truth behind it. Scripture says, "Always pray, and never give up" (Luke 18:1). There are incredible forces at work to keep you from being faithful in prayer. It is their primary mission. Satan and all his demons are dedicated to making the Church as impotent and weak as possible by destroying any dedication to prayer. To the extent they succeed, our life will diminish, our hope will fade, and our joy will disappear. To the extent we are faithful, the harvest will increase, Satan's forces will be routed, and our Lord's Second Coming will be hastened. The choice is ours, and what a choice! We can pray or watch TV, intercede or go back to sleep, rise up and conquer or shrink back and surrender to defeat.

The blessings of being an intercessor reach far into eternity. When Jesus talked about the final days before his coming, he asked his disciples, "Will not God bring about justice for his chosen ones, who *cry out to him day and night?*" (Luke 18:7). But then he warned them in the next breath, "However, when the Son of Man comes, will he find faith on the earth?" According to Jesus, the difference between these two—between those who fall away and those who stand firm in the end—will be found in the substance of their prayers and in the dedication of their hearts.

Someone once said, "The measure of a person is not in what he has accomplished, but in who he has loved and who has loved him in return." Scripture says the same: "We love because he first loved us" (1 John 4:19). I can think of no greater expression of love than to intercede for another as Christ did for me—*he gave it all that I might be redeemed!* Can I possibly do any less for those who don't yet know him as Lord and Savior? Can I possibly be indifferent when such love has saved me?

Amazingly I can! But may I never, for an instant, be guilty of such a crime. Rather, may *his kind* of love for me, and my love for him, be of one heart, mind and spirit. May I be "joyful in hope, patient in affliction, *faithful in prayer*" until he comes (Rom. 12:12).

CHAPTER THIRTEEN

∼

SPIRITUAL REALITIES

"Put on the full armor of God so that you can take your stand against the devil's schemes." (Eph. 6:11)

*E*lisha's servant was in a panic. The city was surrounded by a strong army whose commander had been sent with only one mission by the King of Aram: capture the so-called prophet of Israel and bring him to me. Perhaps they didn't know any better, or perhaps they simply couldn't believe the rumors they had heard. But whatever they were thinking, there they were in full array—"a strong army of chariots and horses," who had come by night to surround the city and force a surrender (2 Kings 6:14).

The terms were simple: "Give us the prophet and we'll go home." So it was only natural that Elisha's servant would be slightly alarmed. But Elisha wasn't moved in any way. He said to his servant, "Don't be afraid. Those who are with us are more than those who are with them" (2 Kings 6:16). Imagine the faith of this man! Here was a guy who looked at kings and generals in their armor and saw old men in red long underwear. He knew who was standing with him and he wasn't going to back down before anyone.

Elisha had come to see into the spiritual dimensions. He knew he was immortal until the moment God decided to bring him home. So he prayed for his servant, "O Lord, open his eyes so that he may see" (v. 17). I suppose at that moment Elisha's servant, next to his master, was one of the most blessed people on this planet. For the Lord answered Elisha's prayer and his servant "looked and saw the hills full of horses and chariots of fire all around Elisha" (v. 17). That day he witnessed an entire army defeated and captured with one prayer from the prophet. "Strike these people with blindness" was all he heard the prophet say (v. 18). Just a simple request from one friend to another and it was done.

I don't know about you, but I would love to have been there that day! And I would love to know the Lord the way Elisha did. The promise is there. Jesus said to his disciples, "I have given you authority to trample on snakes and scorpions and to overcome all the power of the enemy; nothing will harm you" (Luke 10:19). What an incredible promise! But do we believe it? Are we living it?

Now this promise does not mean we are exempt from suffering. Jesus went to the cross, Paul had his head removed, and Peter was crucified upside down. Just the same, what it does mean *absolutely* is that Jesus has all authority over *all* the power of Satan. And as we are abiding with the Lord, we are guaranteed to have complete spiritual protection. In the midst of every trial we *will* have joy. In the midst of confusion and deception we *will* have heavenly wisdom. In the midst of compromise we *will* have moral resolve. We will overcome every plot of the evil one designed to stop us. We may die, we may have pain, we may encounter uphill battles. But we will never lose. We will always prevail.

This is what Jesus wants us to see. Once we get it, we'll be unstoppable. But how do we get there? Each of us needs to have our eyes opened to see what Elisha's servant saw that day. The good news is, we're only a prayer away. Opening eyes is the Lord's work. It's supernatural. You might not see chariots of fire. But then again you may. It's up to the Lord. If you need it, you'll see it.

The gift of spiritual vision is the most important one there is. Ask for it continuously. Then keep your eyes open to what you *can* see. Study what you learn and meditate on it. Ask questions. Seek answers. Find out what God is doing and never stop wondering and believing, "Lord, will you do it for me!"

There is no greater question you can ask than this one. The Lord has given us the witness of Scripture and history for this very reason. They are a guide to our faith—to let us know what God is willing to do, so we can pray with confidence. Sometimes we forget that the God of the Bible is the same God of today. We believe in the God of the past, but not the One of the future! There is a great divide in our faith, and we need to overcome it in the Lord's power.

Our responsibility is to study what God has done and keep it with us. We should especially study what he is doing all over the world today in answer to the prayers of his people. One of the ways you can do this is to keep a record of the miracles which you hear about and which God has done in your own life. Then meditate on them regularly. I have assembled what I call a "miracle notebook" with hundreds of miracle stories I have collected over the years. I can't tell you how many times I have been blessed by reading through these stories and how much my faith has grown from this practice.

There is much we can learn from what God is willing to do through those who have put their trust in him. In this chapter I have selected twelve miracle stories (or what I call "field observations") that illustrate important principles about spiritual realities. As you read them, you should find the big picture coming into view, or at least a bigger picture than perhaps you had previously observed. All accounts here are true and have been completely researched and documented by our organization. Following each is a brief analysis from the Scripture.

Field Observations 1-2   Locations: India and USA

Case One: Recently, four Christian evangelists were mobbed and beaten in a Hindu town in North India. In many parts of India today, it is not uncommon for Christians to face severe persecution while the government looks the other way. In many states and districts, Christians are without legal rights. So when Hindu militants announced they would return in a few weeks to "finish off the Christians," the believers in this town took it seriously. They gathered together for a period of prayer and fasting, asking God for his deliverance.

True to their word, on the appointed day, hundreds of militant Hindus gathered at the temple of Kali to ask for her blessing. (Kali is a black, naked Hindu goddess who drinks the blood of men and young virgins. The Christians in this town would be her victims.) As the ceremony proceeded, a goat was sacrificed and the blood given to a woman to drink. Soon she went into a trance and became demon possessed. Then the priest spoke to her, asking, "Mother! Shall we attack the Christians? Will you lead us?"

She shouted, "Oh, no! There is a huge white angel standing at the town square, and he has a huge sword in his hand. We cannot defeat him!"

Enraged, the crowd went to another temple of Kali in the same town. The ceremony was repeated with another woman and the question asked again. The woman who drank the blood said, "I see every square in town manned by white angels carrying swords. They are too powerful for us." One by one, the crowd turned away and went back home, perplexed and shaken.

Case Two: A friend of our family related the following story to us. Her nephew was visiting her from another state. He was not a believer, but as he was walking down the street, he felt a strange presence come on him. He knew it was an evil spirit, but he was powerless to do anything. As he was walking by our home, he felt the peace of God around our place. So he stepped onto our driveway. Immediately the evil presence left him. It only returned the moment he stepped foot off our property. This experience became a powerful testimony to him, and he gave his life to the Lord soon after.

Analysis: Demons fear the presence of God's holy angels. The Bible says the angels of God encamp about his people (Psa. 34:7, 91:11). We don't know how angels and demons engage in battle. But we do have pictures of blazing swords and chariots of fire. In Revelation we see a picture of God's angels engaging Satan's forces. We read, "And there was war in heaven. Michael and his angels fought against the dragon, and the dragon and his angels fought back. But he was not strong enough, and they lost their place in heaven" (Rev. 12:7-8).

The demonic realm is referred to as "dominions and principalities," suggesting a hierarchy of authority and geographic influence (Eph. 6:12). Satan and his forces are dug-in, so to speak, all over this planet. This is all they have and they are defending it with their very lives. They are divided up over every village, town, city and nation. Nothing is given up without a fight—not even the smallest community or neighborhood.

The armies of God are the invading forces coming into their territory. We are *not* on the defensive! All authority in heaven and on earth has been given to Jesus. Satan and his demons are usurpers of this authority. They stand on shaky ground. They have been defeated at the cross, and as believers we shall overcome them by the "blood of the lamb" (Rev. 12:11).

Field Observations 3-5 Locations: Peru, China, Zululand

Case One: Jesuel was a church planter sent by his church in Brazil to Peru. As he was praying one evening, he had a vision. In his vision an evil spirit appeared before him claiming to be the prince of Peru. "Return to your own country or you will die here," the spirit said. Within one week he became so ill the doctors said he would not recover. He could not understand why God would send him to Peru only to be defeated so quickly. As he cried out to God for help, another pastor across town was in prayer. He knew nothing of Jesuel, but as he was praying that night the Lord gave him a vision of this young man and told him to find him and pray for him. He obeyed and Jesuel was completely healed that night.

Case Two: J.O. Fraser was a pioneer missionary to the Lisu tribe of China. For many years he labored without much fruit. His first disciples had fallen back into sin and demonization. He came under great oppression himself and was on the point of suicidal despair. He realized he needed great help, so he wrote to his mother asking her to gather together some Christian friends who might intercede for the Lisu people. Over the next few years a great spiritual breakthrough began among the Lisu and in Fraser's life as these faithful believers kept praying. Tens of thousands came to know Christ, and the Lisu became a great missionary sending nation to other tribes in

China. Fraser's biographer writes, "He came to the place where he asked God to take away his life rather than allow him to labor on without results. Then he told me of the prayer forces that took up the burden at home and the tremendous lifting of the cloud over his soul, of the gift of faith that was given him and how God seems suddenly to step in, drive back the forces of darkness and take the field."[1]

Case Three: Erlo Stegen worked for many years among the Zulu in South Africa without any results. He felt as if the spiritual oppression in that land was too great and he was defeated. He says, "I cried out to God to come down or I'll die." Soon after this moment of brokenness before the Lord, the Holy Spirit came upon him and his team in a mighty way one evening as they had gathered for prayer. The presence of God was so powerful in their midst, people from nearby homes were also affected and came out to see what was happening.

One of those affected was a witch. She belonged to a Satanic group which controlled the spirituality of the entire area. She showed up at their door and said, "I want Jesus to set me free." As the team began praying for her, the demons within her were forced to manifest themselves. "We are 300 strong warriors," they declared defiantly. "No one will force us out." In the name of Jesus they were commanded to leave, which they did in the most dramatic way, screaming with loud cries and shrieks. Immediately the woman's face changed. What had been an ugly, terrifying face turned into a peaceful and happy expression, as if she had been a believer for many years.

After this spiritual showdown with the forces of darkness, a great revival began throughout Zululand. Tens of thousand came to know

Christ. A hall was built which seats 15,000 and is packed out every weekend to this day.

Analysis: There are great spiritual forces assigned to keep whole groups of people in bondage. Just as individuals can be influenced by evil spirits, whole societies, towns and ethnic groups can be kept under the influence of a unified force of demonic presence.

Jesus said, "*No one* can go into a strong man's house and plunder his goods unless he first binds the strong man" (Mark 3:27). This binding of the strong man is what happened in the case of the Lisu and J.O. Fraser. In the case of Daniel, he was led to pray and fast for three weeks while Gabriel and Michael battled against the prince of Persia. Gabriel notes, "The prince of the Persian kingdom resisted me twenty-one days. No one supports me against them except Michael, your prince" (Daniel 10:13,21). From this we can learn two important things. First, the war angels are engaged in is *real* warfare! There is real resistance and real struggle. And second, we can see that prayer and fasting can bring about spiritual breakthroughs in the heavenly realms.

A strong man is the principality with authority over all demonic activity in a particular area. When a strong man is "bound," people become more receptive to the gospel. Jesus said, "Whatever you bind on earth, will be bound in heaven." (Matt. 16:19) Scripture says we have been given "divine power to demolish strongholds" (2 Cor. 10:4). These strongholds of the enemy have been established through deception and cruel slavery to sin.

It is only on our knees that we receive the required power to communicate clearly and effectively into people's lives, going past the darkness and deception and into the life-changing mechanisms of their hearts and minds. This is God's prescribed method for rescuing people. It requires hard work and serious dedication. It will measure our resolve and test our commitment. It forces the question: How much do I really love the lost? How much effort will I invest to see them reached?

Field Observations 6-7   Locations: Philippines, Malaysia, Zululand

Case One: Paul was sharing the gospel on the island of Jolo, located in the Southern Philippines, when he was asked to pray for the largest mosque on that island. There were several evil spirits manifesting themselves in the mosque, and the local people could not get rid of them. So they asked Paul if he could do something about it. Paul went into the mosque and prayed in Jesus name that the evil spirits would be bound and cast out. The next month, the local governor decided to construct the biggest mosque in Asia on the site of that mosque. He had the entire mosque leveled to the ground. Soon after he did this, he ran into financial and political trouble and had to abandon the project. To this day that mosque is a heap of rubble. The local people attribute this to the prayer of Paul!

Not long after this, a member of a neighboring island asked Paul to pray for the trees on his island. They had stopped bearing fruit for many years and there was nothing anyone could do about it. So Paul prayed for the trees, asking the Lord to heal them in the name of Jesus. One month later all the trees on the island started bearing fruit! Believing Paul must be a prophet, the Muslim leaders on this island invited him to come share with them about his faith and who Jesus really is.

Case Two: In 1986, a Chinese Buddhist temple in Malaysia erected a 100-foot statue of one of the goddesses they worship. Amazingly, this statue began drawing turtles to it and as a result became a huge tourist attraction. The local believers, recognizing this was a spiritual battle, decided to take the issue to the Lord in prayer. They gathered together and prayed the prophecy of Isaiah 47, which declares against the "eternal queen" of Babylon, "Your nakedness will be exposed and your shame uncovered" (v. 3). Within a week, the newspapers began to report of a mysterious crack that had appeared in the cement skirt of the statue. Despite efforts to fix it, the entire skirt and outer form of the woman fell to the ground, leaving only a grotesque head at the top and an ugly column of concrete going down to the base.

Analysis: Spiritual realities often have physical manifestations. When there is a spiritual breakthrough, you can expect to see physical changes as well. Equally, when spiritual resistance is mounting, you can expect to see some manifestation of it, such as with the case of the 100-foot statue being erected in Malaysia. These manifestations are important to the enemy. They become symbols of faith in a false belief system. In the same way, when they are destroyed you can be sure the enemy is being routed and the armies of God have the upper hand. The Word of God is very powerful in guiding your faith toward such victories. The only part of the armor of God that is offensive is the "sword of the Spirit, which is the word of God" (Eph. 6:17). When the believers in Malaysia prayed the prophecy of Isaiah over this spiritual battle, they were employing a weapon far more powerful than the enemy could withstand.

Field Observations 8-9   Locations: South Africa, USA

Case One: Paul Dell was a missionary to the Kanwani and Gazankulu tribes of South Africa. As he entered a particular village, he was immediately confronted by a witch doctor who told him he must leave because this was his territory. He declared to Paul, "I will curse you! In two weeks time you will be dead!" Under the anointing of the Holy Spirit, Paul looked at him in the eye and said, "The curse you pronounce on me I turn back on you in the name of Jesus!" Two weeks later, the witch doctor became deathly ill. As a result, over 60 witch doctors renounced their practice and a great revival began.

Case Two: For years, a good friend of mine, Larry Boggan, struggled with a disabling back problem that would sometimes leave him paralyzed (once while driving!). One day the Lord spoke to him and promised he would heal him. That same evening he attended a Christian concert. In the middle of the concert, one of the band members asked if anyone needed prayer for anything, and if so, to stand up. In faith, my friend rose to his feet. As he did so, he felt excruciating pain in the back of his neck. He said it was as if the Devil was telling him to forget about it and sit back down. But because of God's promise he remained standing. As he stood there praying, he suddenly felt a "hand" enter his lower back and begin moving his discs back in place. From the bottom of his back, all the way to the top of his neck, he could feel the hand of God restoring his spine completely as he stood there.

Analysis: Many intercessors have observed that when God's people first begin to pray for something, the problem may sometimes become much worse before it gets better! But in every case, victory is sure to come when we persevere. Satan knows he is defeated, but he wants to keep us from believing it. We have to call his bluff. Jesus has called us to be involved in a heavenly conflict just as real and dangerous as any physical conflict. As it is in earthly combat, so it is in our heavenly one: when you attack the enemy he must respond in kind or lose the battle. In the same way, when we begin to pray, when we take up our positions and invade his territory, our enemy will do whatever is possible to discourage us by increasing the opposition. But the truth is, the enemy *must* give way before the name of Jesus! He cannot stand against the One who has all authority in heaven and on earth. Therefore, the only difference between victory and defeat in spiritual warfare, lies in the substance of our convictions on this simple truth: Jesus *is* the Mighty Warrior, the Lord of Hosts, and the King of Kings. *No one* can stand against him!

Field Observations 9-12   Locations: China, Kenya, Borneo

Case One: Isobel Kuhn and her husband worked among a large tribe in southern China. They experienced great opposition and saw little fruit from their hard labor. Then one day, the situation suddenly changed. Warring clans made peace with one another and hundreds began turning to Christ. A little later they found out why. They received a letter from one of their friends who explained how she became gripped with a tremendous prayer burden for them and their ministry. It was such a strong conviction she called one of her friends. Remarkably, her friend confessed that she had felt the same burden. Recognizing the Lord was speaking to them, they called one more friend and together these three began to intercede. It was at that exact same time the breakthrough began among the Kuhn's ministry in southern China.

Case Two: In the 1960s, missionaries Matt and Lora Higgens were traveling from Nairobi, Kenya during the Mau Mau uprising. About seventeen miles outside of the city their Land Rover stopped and they were unable to repair it. As darkness descended, Matt and Lora prayed the prayer of Psalm 4:8: "I will lie down and sleep in peace, for you alone, O Lord, make me dwell in safety."

The next day they were able to repair the car and continue their journey. They thanked the Lord for his protection, but had no idea what had really happened that night. A few weeks later, as they were preparing to leave for furlough in the United States, a local pastor came to visit them. A member of the Mau Mau had confessed to him that he and several others saw the Higgens' car that night and had planned to kill them. But when they crept up to the car they saw sixteen armed men surrounding it. In fear they ran for their lives.

A little later, Matt and Lora found out even more of what had happened that night. After they returned to the United States, one of their friends and supporters, Clay Brent, came up to them and asked if they had been in any danger on March 23rd—the exact day when their vehicle broke down. He then explained that on this day he felt a great burden from the Lord to pray for them. He called the men of the church together and sixteen gathered to pray until the burden had lifted.

Case Three: In the town where he was staying, George Birch was invited to the home of a Chinese family whose daughter had not eaten for three days. An evil spirit had possessed her and was demanding that she become a spirit-medium, or she would die. When George arrived at the home of the family, the initiation ceremony had already begun with a master medium. George asked the father of the girl if he might intervene and the father consented. Meanwhile, the sorcerer was chanting loudly and swaying back and forth over the girl. George approached him and asked him politely to leave the house. But the sorcerer paid no attention to him and just continued right on. Then in the power of the Holy Spirit, George said, "You unclean spirit, in the name of the Lord Jesus

Christ, I command you to keep your mouth shut." At that exact moment he stopped chanting, went to the back of the room and just sat on the floor. Then the evil spirit was cast out of the young girl and she was well again. Her appetite immediately returned!

Analysis: The Great Commission is an urgent rescue operation. It wasn't without purpose that the Lord burdened Clay Brent and fifteen others to pray for the Higgens family on March 23. Isobel Kuhn's three friends could tell you the same. And what if George Birch had not been there that day to intervene and confront that master medium? A young girl would have remained in bondage to evil spirits, perhaps for the rest of her life.

God is calling people all over the world to join him in an urgent mission to rescue people from every nation, tribe, language and people. Whether we stay or go, there is a mission to accomplish. As you learn to intercede in the Spirit's power, you will come to understand more and more of what every great man and woman of faith has come to believe. Jonathan Edwards, the great revival preacher of the 18th century, put it this way: "There is no way that Christians, in a private capacity, can do so much to promote the work of God and advance of Christ as by prayer." If the history of mission advance has taught us anything, it is the enduring truth of this reality. Wherever we happen to be, or whatever our circumstances, we can see great works accomplished for the Lord simply by letting his Holy Spirit intercede powerfully through us.

FINAL ANALYSIS

There is one thing to remember about spiritual realities, and I think it should be obvious: You must be careful! The demonic realm is real and dangerous. When the sons of Sceva, a Jewish chief priest, attempted to cast out a demon, they were physically harmed because they did not have the backing of the Holy Spirit. One demon possessed man overpowered seven people and "gave them such a beating that they ran out of the house naked and bleeding" (Acts 19:16). I know of a believer who went into a Hindu meditation ceremony and began speaking against them. He was cursed and immediately lost his senses. For many years he was kept in a mental institution. Without holiness, faith, and the power of the Holy Spirit, you will be completely destroyed if you attempt to engage the enemy in your own way.

Just the same, have no fear of the enemy. Trust in the Lord, and let him show you how to demolish strongholds in his power. Seek out guidance and pray with experienced intercessors whom you know are living godly lives. Be absolutely sure! Confess your sins before the Lord, and ask him to build your faith and increase your spiritual vision. Then pray very humbly! Ask the Lord Jesus to do the work of binding Satan and his evil forces. The Bible warns us of bold and arrogant people who are not afraid to slander celestial beings, yet "even angels, although they are stronger and more powerful, do not bring slanderous accusations against such beings in the presence of the Lord" (2 Pet. 2:10-11). We also read, "But even the archangel Michael, when he was disputing with the devil about the body of Moses, did not dare to bring a slanderous accusation against him, but said, The Lord rebuke you!" (Jude 1:9). So we, too, must be careful as we engage the enemy, pleading the blood of Jesus and praying with the Scriptures, which were given to us for this very reason. Satan *can* be destroyed and his forces *will be* routed as we connect with the Lord's power made available to us through the cross.

Scripture says we need to be aware of the enemy's schemes "in order that Satan might not outwit us" (2 Cor. 2:11). You need to know what the enemy is capable of and what you can do about it. The short testimonies told in this chapter are but a few of the many thousands which you can learn from. Begin to take note and search the Scriptures to find out how to be more effective as a soldier of Jesus Christ. The Lord wants to do great and awesome things through you. He has big plans to fulfill in your life. But you must be aware of what you are up against. Take the time to find out and you will save yourself a lot of problems.

I know of many missionaries who learned about spiritual realities the hard way. Many have the same story to tell: "I wish we had known about spiritual warfare *before* we left for the field!" However, the truth is, it doesn't matter where you are. Satan is operating everywhere. But the difference in experience lies in what is being attempted for the Kingdom. The fact is, *anyone* who attempts to do *anything* for the Lord *anywhere* on this planet will encounter spiritual resistance from the enemy. Count on it, expect it, but most importantly get ready for it. Learn how to pray, develop your spiritual eyesight, and continually ask the Lord for an enduring faith to fight on until the battle is won.

You have his promise, "Nothing will harm you." "You will tread upon the lion and the cobra; you will trample the great lion and the serpent." "You will overcome all the power of the evil one." (Luke 10:19; Psa. 91:13).

He wouldn't have said it if he didn't mean it!

CHAPTER FOURTEEN

GROWING IN FAITH

"We ought always to thank God for you, brothers, and rightly so, because your faith is growing more and more." (2 Thess. 1:3)

*T*he following conversation actually took place between George Müller and a ship captain:

"Captain, I have come to tell you that I *must* be in Quebec on Saturday afternoon."

"Impossible," the captain replied. "The fog is too dense. We cannot go any faster."

George smiled and then told the captain what he believed.

"If your ship can't take me, God will find some other means to take me. You see, I have never broken an engagement in fifty-seven years."

Amazed at such faith, the captain shrugged and said, "I would help if I could—but I am helpless."

"Let us go down to the chart room and pray," George suggested. The captain couldn't believe what he was hearing. But before he had time to think about it or object, he found himself following George to the chart room below. Together they got down on their knees to pray. George began in a quiet and confident voice: "O Lord, if it is consistent with your will, please remove this fog in five minutes. You know the engagement you made for me in Quebec on Saturday. I believe it is your will."

After praying this short prayer, George stood up. "Open the door, Captain, and you will find the fog is already gone," he said. The captain did as he was told, and opening the door, received the surprise of his life. The fog had completely disappeared. He ordered the sails to be hoisted and the ship arrived on time.

* * *

Would you like to have faith like that of George Müller? Well, you can! Scripture tells us the secret. In story after story, the Bible gives us examples to remind us of one basic truth: *What God has done through one of his servants, he is willing to do again!* The Bible says, "Elijah was *a man just like us.* He prayed earnestly that it would not rain, and it did not rain on the land for three and a half years" (Jas. 5:17). Elijah came to understand something about God that distinguished him from all those in his generation. The same thing happened to George Müller. And the same thing can happen to you.

As a man of faith, Elijah couldn't stand by and do nothing while a pagan rain god, Baal, took glory away from the Lord. So Elijah claimed the promises of God in prayer. The Lord had warned his people that idolatry would shut the heavens tight (Deut. 11:16-17). Elijah took hold of this promise by faith and *fervently* declared, "Lord, may it be so in this generation!"

The prophet Daniel did a similar thing. The Lord had promised his people that the Babylonian captivity would last for just seventy years (Jer. 25:11-12). Daniel believed God, and like Elijah, he too began to cry out to the Lord to fulfill his purposes. Daniel writes,

Growing In Faith

"So I turned to the Lord God and pleaded with him in prayer and petition, in fasting, and in sackcloth and ashes" (Daniel 9:3).

The Lord had declared it, but one person believed it. And the sign of this belief was that he *asked* for it. God has given us his promises for this very reason. They are meant to inspire the intercession of his people and ignite fires from generation to generation. God had spoken his promise to Jeremiah, and 70 years later a man named Daniel *petitioned for it.* God had spoken to Moses, and 600 years later a man named Elijah *fought for it.*

Faith is contagious and electrifying. Through the faith of one, God can change an entire nation. After three and half years of drought, God said to Elijah, "Go present yourself to Ahab and I will send rain on the land" (1 Kings 18:1). The leaders of Israel assembled on Mount Carmel, and without any wavering in his faith, Elijah told his servants to soak the sacrifice in water. He drenched it with water—in the middle of a drought! Then the fire of God fell, consuming the sacrifice and all the water that had been poured upon it. The priests of Baal were rounded up and their temples destroyed, bringing revival throughout the land.

But still, something was missing. For God had given his servant a promise. So once again, Elijah got down on his knees, and this time he began to pray *for* rain. He sent his servant back and forth to a high mountain to see what was happening as he interceded. (Now remember, God had already said it was going to rain! But Elijah's response to this heavenly decree was to get down on his knees and *pray* for God's will to be done—*until* it was done.) Then after the seventh time, his servant returned and reported only a small cloud the size of man's hand. But at last the breakthrough had come! It grew and continued growing as Elijah fervently prayed. He just kept asking until he was answered and the rain came pouring down.

That's what faith and prayer are all about. They are the means by which we participate in the will of God. When George prayed with the captain that day, he received the assurance in his spirit that the prayer was answered. In the same way, Elijah knew absolutely that his earnest prayer would shut the heavens tight for over three years. He said confidently to King Ahab, "There will be neither dew nor rain in the next few years except at my word" (1 Kings 17:1). Elijah's earnest intercession gave him an unshakeable confidence from the Lord. Prayer of this sort comes from a deep fellowship and communion with the Spirit of God. Faith springs from such communion. The closer you get to God, the more you become aware of his presence in every aspect of your life. The more aware you are of his presence, the more in tune you are with his will. For his Spirit begins to guide your spirit. You just know that you know. George Müller knew without a doubt the fog was gone.

Faith is knowing, *really* knowing. For all knowing comes from faith. Everything you "know" to be true comes from faith in someone you have learned to trust. When I was young, my mother told me not to touch the pot on the stove. She told me it was hot and if I touched it I would burn myself. I had never been "burned" before, but I trusted her just the same. I had no reason to doubt her love and concern for me. In the same way, believing God comes from knowing him and experiencing his trustworthiness. The more you experience God, the more you will trust him.

George Müller didn't wake up one day with a faith that could "move mountains." He learned to trust God as he gathered orphans off the street. And as he saw God answer prayer, he learned to trust him for even greater things. The same story could be told with everyone who has grown in faith, and your story will be no different. You must begin where you are, and let God take you from there.

Growing In Faith

Faith produces results and all people of faith are people of action, without exception. The two go hand in hand, they both produce and reinforce one another. Faith comes in direct proportion to our involvement in something God wants done. His vision for you is so big you can't do it without him. God wants to do extraordinary, humanly impossible, incredibly amazing things through *you* to fulfill his mission here on earth. But you have to believe it and seek the vision he has for you. Without a vision to stretch you, your faith will *never* grow and will ultimately die. But as you step out in pursuit of a God-sized vision, he will *give you* a faith so big, demons will tremble at the very thought of your prayers.

Such a person in our generation is Brother Andrew. While a young man he began to grow in faith as he smuggled Bibles into Soviet Russia. He would pack his car full of illegal merchandise and prayerfully drive right over the border and through the checkpoints. Slowly but surely he began to realize that the same God who got him through those checkpoints could also remove them altogether. As his faith began to build, he decided to ask God for this very thing. In 1983 he called on Christians everywhere to begin a seven-year prayer campaign to tear down the Iron Curtain. Seven years later it was a done deal!

The following year in 1991 he issued a call to his prayer partners to join him in a ten-year prayer campaign for the opening up of the Islamic world to the gospel. Ten years later, Muslim terrorists boarded jumbo jets and crashed them into the Pentagon and World Trade Towers. As a result, the nations of Afghanistan and Iraq, two of the most closed countries in the Muslim world, became opened up for the gospel through the U.S. led response. Within a year, thousands had come to know the Lord in the city of Kabul, once the center of Islamic fundamentalism.

Eternal Vision

WHERE FAITH BEGINS

George Müller, Elijah and Brother Andrew all have something in common. Each has seen God do the impossible. There is no doubt in their minds that God exists. There is no doubt he answers prayer. And there is no doubt he will do whatever they ask as they pray according to his will.

The number one thing God wants to do in your life is give you the same resolve. Jesus said, "If you believe, you will receive whatever you ask for in prayer" (Matt. 21:22). Now that's an incredible promise! God wants this promise to be a reality every moment of every day in your life.

So how can it happen? Where does faith begin? When the apostle Peter wrote a letter to encourage the faith of the suffering Church in Asia, he began with something you won't find in most counseling textbooks. He began with theology. It might sound like a strange way to comfort someone, but nothing could be more powerful. He writes, "To God's elect, strangers in the world . . . who have been chosen according to the foreknowledge of God the Father" (1 Pet. 1:1).

Peter was writing to believers whom he describes as having "had to suffer grief in all kinds of trials" (v. 6). And yet his perspective on their suffering was absolutely incredible. He goes on to explain, "These have come so that your faith . . . may be proved genuine and may result in praise, glory and honor when Jesus Christ is revealed" (v. 7).

Peter was looking at the big picture. He was seeing life from heaven's perspective. People of faith are focused not on themselves and their needs, but they are focused on God and his glory. That's why they receive whatever they ask for, because they are seeking only what will result in the praise, glory and honor of Jesus Christ.

Growing In Faith

They are God-centered, not self-centered. They are interested only in what will reveal more of God and his goodness.

Faith flounders when we turn our eyes away from God and begin to doubt the genuineness of who he is—the essence and nature of his character. In the midst of tragedy, how do we respond? When faced with uncertainties or unanswered questions, where do we turn? What do we think about God when the unthinkable happens?

A friend of mine was raped while in high school. Armed men broke into her house and repeatedly raped her and her friends. Her father was a pastor and out conducting a Bible study when it happened. I can think of nothing worse for a father. I can imagine nothing worse for my friend. And yet she and her family have done the unthinkable through the grace of God. They have forgiven their enemies. When the men were found and arrested, they prayed for them. They led them to Christ. Today this family is serving the Lord in the most incredible way—literally thousands have come to Christ because of their faithful ministry.

Perhaps you also have experienced something in your life that has caused you tremendous pain. You may be crying out inside and asking God to reveal his purpose. Like Job, who did absolutely nothing wrong, you may be completely innocent. What has happened to you may be entirely for a purpose beyond your own life. And without minimizing what you have experienced, there is something very important you need to understand. This event in your life can either hinder you or help you. It can either be a gateway to faith, or become a "root of bitterness" (Heb. 12:15). Left unsettled, and questions about God's trustworthiness can become cataracts in your spiritual vision. But once you settle the issue with God and humbly acknowledge his sovereignty over everything, your relationship will grow in quantum leaps. Remember, Jesus also was innocent, and yet he went to the cross for us all. In the same way, the Lord will take your suffering and use it for his glory if you will offer it to him and surrender everything to his eternal plan.

Every person of great faith has come to this same crossroad. But when all is said and done, people of faith remain optimistic about their heavenly Father. They can't explain everything, but they refuse to doubt his goodness, compassion, love and mercy. They refuse to limit his capacity and awesome power. They refuse to blame him for the evil in this world and they refuse to be paralyzed by it. They will not accept evil in any form and they will not be overcome by it. They will challenge it in faith and they will see God's awesome redemption.

People of faith have a positive outlook on the future. They're believers like Paul who said, "Be joyful always; pray continually; give thanks in every circumstance, for this is God's will for you in Christ Jesus!" (1 Thess. 5:16-18). Paul was one of the greatest missionaries in history, but he claimed no rights for himself. He was also one of the most mistreated missionaries. Nonetheless, he refused to let his joy in the Lord be compromised. As a result, what the enemy intended for evil, God used for good. What was intended to break his spirit served only to increase his faith and trust in the Lord.

There is an important connection here between Paul's character and his faith. The apostle says, *"Be* joyful always." Note the grammar. It's a command! Being joyful is a decision you make. It begins with the seeds you plant in your heart. And what you've planted comes from the attitudes you have chosen to harbor and nurture.

For example, if I have a bad attitude about something—let's say I'm not content with how much money I have—it is because I doubt a part of God's character—in this case his willingness and ability to provide for all I need. In fact, most character flaws and wrong attitudes come from a disbelief in some aspect of God's character. Disbelief in God's true character can produce a very dangerous kind of "faith" that is the exact opposite of Christ-centered faith.

There is a "faith" which will connect you to Satan's power and it will destroy both you and those around you. The Bible speaks of a faith that "can move mountains" but has not love (1 Cor. 13:2). This kind of empty, *self-centered* faith may produce "signs and wonders," but it will lead you away from the Lord and bring glory to yourself and to man instead of to God (2 Thess. 2:9). *Christ-centered* faith connects you to the love of God and leads you into complete trust and dependence on him.

Moses was called the most humble man in the world. He was also a great man of faith, and there is an important connection here. He came to understand how much he needed God in his life. There was absolutely no way he could accomplish the mission he had been given. Only with God's power could he possibly lead two million people in the desert (who were only days away from famine) for over forty years!

Walking with God produces a great humility within us. You come to realize the truth of what Jesus declared, "Apart from me you can do nothing" (John 15:5). Once you realize this, you are well on your way to taking giant leaps of faith. For Moses it took forty years of herding sheep in the desert before he was ready! Then at eighty years of age, God called him to do the humanly impossible. But he was completely broken, no longer trusting in himself or his own strength. All that remained was the Lord.

That's where God wants you to be as well. He wants you to let go of yourself and let him have his way with you. He's thinking about *you*. He's interested in the eternal part of who you are. He knows the real you better than anyone else. Not only that, he really likes you. He knows everything there is to know about you, and whatever's not worth remembering, he's already forgotten. The very thought of you brings a smile to his face. He's on your side and he'll always be.

I have a friend who thinks of God this way all the time. The joy in her life is indescribable. Though many terrible things have happened to her and her family, she is truly someone who has learned to "give thanks in every circumstance." As a result, she is one of the most positive people I know.

Not too long ago, her car was broken into while she was studying at her college campus. Many important things were taken, including her wallet. Upon discovering this, her first response was not anger or even questioning God. She actually believed, "God is going to teach me something through this." She went to her dad that afternoon and they agreed together in faith that God could do anything. If it was his will, she prayed that she might get back at least her license and a special picture album which meant a lot to her. That same day, a courier from the school where she attends was delivering a package on the other side of town. As he was walking, he looked down and saw a college ID which caught his attention. Sure enough, it was my friend's ID and scattered nearby were the very things she prayed about!

Now I believe God let all this happen to bring him glory. It is of course easy to see that after the fact. But remarkably, my friend saw it all from the beginning. And that's what faith is all about. It's letting God open your eyes to see what he's up to and trusting him to use every situation to bring him the greatest honor and praise. People who are concerned about the glory of God will naturally have great faith. When other people look at a problem and ask, "Where is

God?" people of faith look at a problem and see "divine opportunity" written all over it. It is when evil is most insurmountable and seemingly unstoppable, that attitude, character and faith all work together to produce and reinforce one another and bring God the greatest glory possible.

THE PLACE OF FAITH

The Bible tells us three important facts about faith that are important to keep in mind. First and most important, faith is a gift from God. We are responsible to act according to the "measure of faith" given to us (Rom. 12:3). Second, you can grow in faith. The more you grow in faith, the more God can do through you. (2 Cor. 10:15; 2 Thess. 1:3). Third, the faith you possess you can lose. Scripture speaks of those who have "shipwrecked their faith" (1 Tim. 1:18-19).

There is no standing still in the Christian walk. You are either moving forward, or being swept away in the tide. Faith begins with participation in the will of God and it ends when we step outside of it. We participate in God's will when we ask, "Lord, how can I be a part of your purposes for this generation? How can I bring you the greatest glory with my life?" When I'm thinking this way, I am operating in the Place of Faith. When I remove myself from that place, God waits patiently for me to return.

Jesus used this kind of language when his disciples awakened him during a storm. He asked, "Where is your faith?" (Luke 8:25). As if to say, "What have you done with it?" Faith is something God has given us, but we have to possess it and use it. I may have a dozen gifts under the Christmas tree, but if I never pause to unwrap them, I will never benefit from them. The gift of faith becomes activated when we participate in something God is accomplishing.

Eternal Vision

Many people say, "Increase my faith, Lord, and I will do great things for you." But God says, "Attempt great things for me and I will increase your faith accordingly."

In one particular tribe in Papua New Guinea there was no word for the concept of "believe." The missionary searched and searched for this all important word so he could translate, "I believe in Jesus." But he could find none. Finally, he decided on a description as the best way to translate the word. So he put it this way: "I am hearing, thinking about, grasping hold of and following the talk of Jesus continually all the time."

Sometimes I think Bible translators end up with a better understanding of what words really mean than anyone else! They are forced to rethink everything so they might communicate meaning cross-culturally, and as result, they come to understand Scripture in a very deep way. In this particular case, a Bible translator who was working to serve a very small group of people has come across something very useful to the rest of the Body of Christ.

"Believing" in Jesus means far more than we think it does. The same is true with love. How do you define it? Like many meaningful words in our language, it's impossible to sound its depth with a simple definition. When God defined love, he told us what love does, what it produces. Love produces acts of kindness, patience and humility. The same is true with *believing*. When Jesus sent out his disciples, he was careful *not* to say, "Go into all the world and get people to believe in me." Certainly that is what happens, but the evidence of faith's existence cannot be found in the recitation of creeds or the chanting of sacred mantras. Rather, it is in the eternal substance of our *deeds* that faith finds its truest form. That's why "faith without works is dead" (Jas. 2:26). Faith produces obedience, and as we obey, our faith continues to grow. It's "walking the talk" as the Bible translator came to understand. For this reason, Jesus said, "Teach them to *obey* everything I have commanded" (Matt. 28:20).

Faith flounders when we stop obeying. Faith requires us to take the initiative. It makes us listen and softens our hearts. Then once we know what we ought to do, and where we should be going, we need to *act* on it. For if we ignore the Lord's leading, and stay at home with our fears, worries and excuses, we will quickly wander from the Place of Faith simply by staying right where we are!

This happened to David when he fell into temptation with Bathsheba. The Bible says it was the time "when kings go off to war . . . but David remained in Jerusalem" (1 Chr. 20:1). The Ark of the Covenant was out on the field, but David stayed at home. This great warrior, who had seen God do so much, decided to take it easy and hang up his armor. After all, wasn't he far too important now to be risking his neck on the battlefield? So he stayed behind. One of his Gentile officers, Uriah the Hittite (who had come to know the Lord and was one of David's 37 "mighty men"), had more spiritual depth and insight than David did at this time. He said, "The Ark and Israel and Judah are staying in tents . . . and camped in the open fields. How could I go to my house to eat and drink and lie with my wife? As surely as you live, I will not do such a thing" (2 Sam. 11:11).

You know the rest of the story. It is the most scandalous and shocking story in the Bible. Part of me wishes it wasn't there and it never happened. But the truth of the matter is, *no one* is exempt from what happened to David. If any of us turn aside from our God-given calling, if we refuse to fight in the battles he has called us to, we will find ourselves in greater danger and risk than we could ever have imagined possible. Not only that, we may also put others at risk as well. The whole nation of Israel felt the effects of David's sin before the Lord.

Faith matters because there is much that depends on it. There is a world that needs it. There are people to be won for Christ, strongholds to be challenged, battles to be fought. Jesus said, "*Whoever* has faith in me will do what I have been doing. He will do even greater things than these . . ." (John 14:12). Ponder on the depth of what that means! Jesus didn't make any qualifications here. He said *whoever has faith*. That means you and I can literally do even greater things than Jesus did. But are we willing? Are we attempting greater things? Are we claiming the promise? It's an open invitation to all who would come!

God is calling you to *live* a life of faith because you *must* live such a life. He is calling you to *do* the things he did and to *walk* as he walked because he needs you to join him in his mission. Jesus didn't call us to vegetate. He called us to enlist in his unit and fight right alongside him. And when you are doing that you will find something remarkable taking place. Because faith grows in direct proportion to our awareness of God's presence in our life. Peter didn't wake up one morning and decide to jump out of the boat and walk on water. He saw Jesus and seeing him inspired his faith. Then he jumped. Faith comes alive when we become aware of who is with us and who has *always* been with us and who will *never* leave us.

Living in God's presence results from participating in his will, his mission, and his plan for this earth and its lost inhabitants. You see God when you need him, and you need him when you are about his business. As you seek the Lord he will give you opportunities to bring him glory, and in these moments your faith will grow as never before.

When I was in high school the Lord taught me this principle, and I will never forget it. I used to be terrified of speaking in front of a group of people. But once I had given my life to the Lord I realized

I had no choice but to proclaim his Word. In the beginning of my ninth grade year, I was confronted with an atheist teacher who was determined to influence us against Christianity and faith in Jesus. Suddenly the Lord gave me boldness to answer all his questions and accusations.

When the time came for us to give research reports to our class, I did mine on "creationism vs. evolution." For the first time in my life as I stood before a group of people, I was not nervous or shaky, but instead I had a calmness and peace of mind from the Lord. I spoke with conviction and authority. From that day on I have never been intimidated to speak in public. After this the Lord led me to begin a Christian fellowship on campus and from there he led me into full-time ministry. I remember my father saying to that teacher, "Sir, I want to thank you. You've made my son a better Christian!"

ASKING FOR MORE

Jabez asked for more. He prayed, "Oh, that the Lord would bless me indeed and enlarge my territory!" (1 Chr. 4:10). Now at first that might seem a little selfish. But it wasn't in any way. According to Jewish tradition, Jabez was the younger brother of Caleb, also known as Othniel the Judge. His generation was given an assignment by God to take possession of the promised land. Othniel became Israel's first judge and he left behind a legacy for generations to come. He made a difference because he knew what God wanted done and he was determined to be a part.

Biblical faith combines two realities in perfect harmony: contentment with the ways of God and discontentment with evil and inactivity in God's mission. Many times we sit content in a position of theological rhetoric which amounts to little more than "Christian fatalism." We say through our actions and sometimes we actually say it—"What will be, will be." This attitude has nothing to do with biblical faith. In fact, it is a heresy. Faith does not say, "Well, I hope God will use me to do something, but if not, then whatever." Faith is being "sure and certain" the Bible says (Heb. 11:1). Faith is conviction. Faith says the gospel is the only hope of the world, there is no other way, and I'm going to *live* my life accordingly. Regardless of what others may say, I'm going forward. As Martin Luther put it, "Here I stand, I can do no other." People of faith are compelled to stand. They will not be moved. Only a bullet can stop them, but even so they stand, with even more power than before.

One person with real convictions *can* change the world—for good or for evil—and history has proved it time and again. Consider Michael Borodin. He was just a school teacher in Indiana, but he changed the course of human history when he applied the teachings of Christ and the apostle Paul to Marxist Communism. He moved to Russia and became friends with Lenin. In the 1920s, Lenin sent him to China to help organize the Communist Party. At that time there wasn't much happening and skeptics were easy to find. An American reporter once came to interview him and asked mockingly, "Don't tell me you seriously mean to take over a fifth of the human race? You're only a handful with no knowledge of the land or the language. You'll never do it in a thousand years."

Borodin replied, "I used to read the New Testament. Again and again I read it. It is the most wonderful story ever told. That man, Paul, he was a real revolutionary. I take my hat off to him. But where do you find him today? . . . I am not interested in a career or a fortune like the Americans. I serve an ideology. And with an ideology it is not numbers that count. It is dedication."[1]

Mr. Borodin looked at Christian history and saw what a few dedicated people could do to change the world. He studied our faith. He read the words of Christ and admired the life of Paul. This school teacher from Indiana changed the world because he would not be quiet, he refused to be shaken, and he grabbed hold of the tide of history. But he applied what he learned to the wrong vision!

Faith is seeing beyond yesterday, today and tomorrow and looking at decades past and decades to come. Not only did Mr. Borodin succeed in "conquering" China, but Viet Nam as well. One of his disciples was Ho Chi Minh. His small group of revolutionaries were all ordinary people who got connected to something that was ready and waiting to sweep the world. They knew history was on their side. And as far as Communism was concerned, Mr. Borodin, Lenin and Ho Chi Minh were absolutely correct. But they were also absolutely wrong. For their faith lacked depth and their vision lacked perspective. For if they could have seen a little further, they would have witnessed the year 1989. They would have watched the Iron Curtain crumble and the Soviet Union collapse in a single year. They would have heard the cries of millions starving in North Korea. They would have watched in horror as capitalist markets invaded Shanghai and Beijing.

And if they would have kept watching, they would have seen something else—something destined to sweep into eternity. For Jesus said to his disciples, *"The meek* will inherit the earth" (Matt. 5:5). Not revolutionary Communism, not militant Islam, not venture capitalism—you! The meek, the humble, the gentle in Christ. He said of his Kingdom there shall be no end. If we really understood what Jesus was talking about, we would have millions of Mr. Borodins out there riding the greatest tide of history there has ever been or ever will be. They would be asking for more and expecting more; they would reach for the impossible and see it fully realized in their generation.

The Second Coming of Christ is the only hope of the world. It is the only vision that fills biblical faith. All Christ-centered faith is focused on this purpose. For only complete victory over the forces of darkness is a lasting victory. In World War II, victory did not end on the shores of Normandy. Victory was taking Nazi central command in Berlin and annihilating it. Hitler lost Germany because he could not take the world. Communism lost in Russia because it did not prevail in America and Western Europe. The same principle holds true today in the mission we are engaged in.

A heart like God's is a heart that has the world, the *whole* world, in focus. It's a heart that continually asks for more until the job is done. That means all of us are called to enlist in God's *global* mission. We can't be content with what has been accomplished. We can't sit back and relax while vast fields remain unharvested.

To become a Global Christian is to expand your vision far greater than you ever thought possible. It's joining a whole host of angels and millions of believers now in heaven with only one thing on their minds: the final completion of the Great Commission in this generation. It's a big goal and a giant task. Skeptics are easy to find. But keep in mind that skeptics and doubters are the losers of history. History has always been written by those who would not be moved from their convictions. In the same way, becoming a Global Christian is to take up that same legacy and rewrite the future by faith. It's saying, "The tide is with us, we *will not* fail."

DENYING THE SKEPTICS

There is a war going on for your faith. The enemy wants to quench your passion and shake your vision. That's why you need to be careful who you listen to. Just as people of faith inspire faith in others, people of doubt become spokespersons for the evil one. The great-

Growing In Faith

est enemies to your faith may be your closest friends. It's happened before. Our Lord's own mother and brothers thought he had lost his mind. Faith, by definition, is seeing the unseen. It's *wanting* to see. The world is not blind because they have to be, but because they choose to be—because they prefer to be. And that's why faith will get you into trouble. In a land full of blind skeptics, the person with one eye will find himself terribly annoying.

Consider Robert Morrison. He was the first Protestant missionary to China, and he went there in spite of all the would-be theologians who told him to stop messing with God's plan for their damnation. Like William Carey, who was also told to "sit down and be quiet," Morrison was a simple shoemaker. (Interestingly, he and Carey died in the same year.) Why God decided to use two shoemakers to pioneer the gospel in the two greatest lands the world has ever known, India and China, is something to ponder for all those who think they aren't qualified!

But in spite of all those who opposed him, Morrison believed God wanted the gospel to enter China. So he began to pray about it, and sure enough, God made a way for him to get there. It wasn't easy. Like Carey, he also was refused passage by the East India Company. Undaunted, he went to America to find a ship that would take him. One ship owner sneered at him, "So then, Mr. Morrison, you really expect to make an impression on the idolatry of the great Chinese Empire?" Robert replied, "No sir, but I expect God will!"

The Lord honored his faith and perseverance. Mr. Morrison did find his ship and eventually made it to the mainland. The Lord so gifted him linguistically that within two years he had become an indispensable translator for the very company that refused him passage! He now had both a legitimate right to be in China and a good salary on top of it all.

Carey and Morrison helped lay a foundation that has brought millions into the Kingdom. It's an undeniable fact. Through the determined faithfulness of a few men, literally millions have been impacted for eternity. Even Mr. Borodin might have scoffed at the tiny Chinese Church of his day. But he didn't have the faith of Robert Morrison or Hudson Taylor. Indeed, there are more Christians in China today than there are members of all Communist parties in the whole world combined!

So how about us? What kind of vision do we have? What do we believe in? If faith is being "sure of what we hope for" (Heb. 11:1), where do we see the future headed? How many today can see the 2.7 billion unevangelized of the 10/40 Window as harvest fields where tens of millions can come to know Jesus in our generation? And here's the bigger question: How many really care enough to do something about it? How many are willing to sacrifice their lives as Carey and Morrison did to bring it in? As in the days of Elijah, God has reserved a remnant who have not bowed the knee to Baal. But from what I can see, they are far and few between. For if we really believed God wanted millions more to be saved in this generation, would not every one of us be fully consumed with this priority? And yet how many are even thinking about it, much less doing something about it?

If only Carey and Morrison could be here to speak with us today. How easy we have it compared to them! Morrison not only set out to learn one of the most difficult languages in the world, he translated the whole Bible into Chinese in less than a decade! Carey translated the Bible in over thirty languages by the time he put down his pen and breathed his last. Morrison prayed, "Lord, I want to be stationed in that part of the field where the difficulties are the greatest and to all human appearance the most insurmountable." Imagine if all of us today would pray such a prayer! The whole world would soon be evangelized. The truth is, we have so much more than Morrison and Carey did, and yet somehow we excuse ourselves with doing so much less.

Sometimes I wish Paul, Peter and John were here to preach a message to us today. The tears would flow from even the strongest critic. There would not be a dry eye in the house. How is it that they labored so hard and long, only to find us relaxing comfortably while billions in the 10/40 Window remain in darkness? What excuses and compromises are we standing on?

Could it be that our inactivity is an expression of where our faith is? For Christ-centered faith sees the future as God sees it. Faith is having hindsight in the present. I hope with all my heart that this generation learns to pray with faith and ask for more. If God does not want anyone to perish, can we really excuse ourselves and remain content while 50,000 souls are perishing every day without Christ in the 10/40 Window?

We need to ask, "Lord, what do you expect from us?" And I know there is only one answer. He expects initiative. He will give the faith. The generation that fulfills the Great Commission will be a generation of prayer and concern for the glory of God. They will refuse to back down, refuse to compromise, and refuse to let any obstacle stand in the way of full obedience to the cause of Christ. May it be so with us! May we be those who "long for the day of his appearing" (2 Tim. 4:8). May we work hard to "speed its coming" (2 Pet. 3:12). May we never compromise with the skeptics of our generation. Let us silence them by faith, and with the sound of that great Trumpet, which will soon be heard when the last man of the last village of the last tribe is reached with the gospel in this final generation before our Lord's coming.

WHY FAITH MATTERS

Satan loves to manipulate people. He has been doing it for thousands of years, so I guess that makes him an expert. Now you and I happen to be alive on this earth toward the finale of his career. I suppose that's the bad news. But the good news is we know exactly what he's up to and we have plenty of history we can learn from.

If there is one thing we have observed, it is this: Satan loves to confuse people about spiritual matters—it's his number one priority. That's because spiritual deception is the most subtle; it's like sugar-coated poison. All over the world, people are being manipulated by evil spirits into seeking false solutions to their problems. Through "signs and wonders" and temporary fixes, the evil one seeks to keep people perpetually bound to his power.

The Great Commission is a battle between light and darkness, truth and deception, hope and despair. It's an engagement of faith and spiritual authority. Believers who think they can just walk in and set the captives free without the power of the Holy Spirit are in for a big shock. Paul said to the believers of Corinth, "My message and my preaching were not with wise and persuasive words, but with a demonstration of the *Spirit's power*" (1 Cor. 2:4). Only true faith in Jesus Christ can set anyone free from "darkness to light and from the power of Satan to God" (Acts 26:18). Faith inspires faith. That's why God needs us to be his witnesses. He wants our lives to be living demonstrations of his power to save, heal and transform.

The situation of the lost is more tragic than any other human plight. Demons delight in tormenting human beings, and every single person outside of a personal relationship with Jesus is subject to their harassment and manipulation. Believers who take trips to the 10/40 Window are forever changed. One trip to India for even a few hours is enough to change anyone for life. If you ever had the notion that people without Christ are okay, just visit a Hindu village on one of their holy days.

Last week, a friend of mine wrote me about a Hindu festival in the town where he ministers. His description broke my heart:

> "It is now a time where I am gripped with sadness as countless friends and even some of the kids we are working with ask me to join in the fun. Ganesh (a Hindu god who received the head of an elephant for sleeping with his mother) is even packaged like Santa Claus here with ads saying, "He's done so much for us this season, let's do something for him," or, "He listens. He hears. He understands . . ."
>
> You see, the Indian government has decided to implement an aggressive campaign in the schools here to teach Hindu thought, mythology and all the aspects of worship as the school curriculum starting at Kindergarten level. Third graders have graphic pictures in their Hindu heritage books of the gods ripping each other open and slaying demons. Every Hindu festival is heavily geared towards the kids with games and contests around the idol or related to this holiday celebration."

Why does faith matter? Because people matter. Without exception, there is *no other way* for them to be rescued unless you and I proclaim the gospel with power. God is ready to give it to all who would ask for it. People are often amazed at the miracle stories they hear about on the mission field, as if they were limited to such places. Jesus said, "According to your faith will it be done to you" (Matt 9:29). It doesn't matter *where* you are, it matters *Who* you're with. We could see the same miracles here at home (and some do), but most aren't asking, seeking and knocking. For wherever there is faith, miracles will follow, and wherever there is action in the pursuit of God's glory, there will be faith.

There are many people who have attempted great things and have received great faith as a result. But there are many still who once grew in faith and who are now content to stay where they are. God has so much more to do through them. Continually seek his face to know his will for you. As long as you are here, you're not done! There is no such thing as retirement in God's Kingdom. Continually ask him to do even greater things through you. The Bible says we do not have because we do not ask (Jas. 4:2). And we do not ask because we do not believe there is anything more. But there is—there is *so much* more for *every one* of us.

Our faith can only rise as high as our doubts linger against what God wants to accomplish in and through us. But keep in mind what faith is all about. Remember why God wants you to have faith. As long as you are breathing on this planet, as long as there is a Great Commission to be completed, as long as there are souls perishing without the gospel, there is a reason to seek the Lord's face and find out what he wants done in this final harvest before he returns. It is imperative that you grow in faith! It is not an option really for followers of Jesus. It is your primary responsibility. Ask for more, seek to do more, work hard until the end. You will never regret it. You are the sum of what you believe for an eternity to come.

CHAPTER FIFTEEN

SATAN'S TOP FIVE LIES

"Satan himself masquerades as an angel of light. It is not surprising then, if his servants masquerade as servants of righteousness." (2 Cor. 11:14)

The Bible tells us in the last days people will abandon truth to follow things taught by demons (1 Tim. 4:1). We are told that many people, perhaps even the majority, will gather around themselves a great number of teachers to hear what their "itching ears want to hear" (2 Tim. 4:3). What is frightening about all of this is that these people claim to be followers of Jesus, but in fact they are not. Without becoming too paranoid, we need to be seriously thinking about the direction popular Christianity is headed today. Could it be that we are fast approaching the days we were warned about? Might we actually be living in them! We need to keep from being lulled asleep into thinking everything is the way it ought to be, when in reality it is not, and perhaps even far from it.

So how do you tell a fake from the genuine thing? You have to know, *really* know, what the real thing is. Jesus has one objective and that is the fulfillment of the Great Commission. The enemy has one objective as well, and that is to stop it. All lies of the enemy, all false teaching, all developments in our world center around this conflict. This is the *real thing*, the genuine article that Satan wants to confuse you about. If you don't know what Satan is trying to accomplish, if you don't know the objectives of the war, you will make a lousy soldier indeed. But if you know the goal of your enemy, you can follow his plan, take your stand, and fight accordingly.

Now of all the ideas Satan has propagated to stop the Great Commission, there are a few which have proved their worth time and again. Chances are you have been familiarized with these in one form or another, so they should come as no surprise. You may even have been taught to believe them. But just the same, I think it is important to ask ourselves what the Bible says about what we sometimes declare emphatically to be true. Then in the end, it is not I you must deal with (and you are sure to find fault with me), but Scripture itself and its Author.

Lie Number One: It's okay to be a lukewarm Christian.

I hear this all the time after a person has died: "Well, he might have been a Christian. We're just not sure." The biblical truth is, if there is any doubt on the matter, you can be sure that person *wasn't* a follower of Jesus. Call them whatever you like, invent categories for them, but don't water down what it means to be a disciple of Jesus. Jesus said, "You are either with me or against me" (Matt. 12:30). You are either cold or hot. Lukewarm people don't make the cut. Amazingly, we have not taken Jesus very seriously on this. Today in Christianity there are tens of millions who think it is perfectly all right to live without the lordship of Christ in their lives. Very few have the boldness to tell them otherwise. Instead, we call people who live like Jesus did the "saints" of the Church. But the Bible calls them *Christians*, followers of Jesus, disciples. There is no other category, no other gospel than the one of sacrifice, and no other assignment than the one Christ gave us.

It is *not* okay to be a lukewarm Christian. It is *not* okay to lower the standard. It is a mockery of the life of Christ to suggest that a disciple is anything less than what Jesus said it was. The enemy wants us confused about this for one simple reason: real disciples of Jesus are the only thing he fears down here. The Lord wants to fill you with his power and ignite a revolution through your life. Lukewarm Christians settle for less. The promises of God were for another day, another time, certainly not for me. Satan delights in such people. There is nothing that warms his heart more than a Christian who has said, "Hope it all works out in the end, I'm going fishing."

Lukewarm Christians play when they should pray. They laugh when they should weep. They give up when they should press on. They turn away when they should pay attention. They close their eyes and shut their ears to anything that might unsettle their comfortable world. Jesus said of such people, "Why do you call me Lord, Lord and do not do what I say?" (Luke 6:46). Isaiah prophesied, "When you spread out your hands in prayer, I will hide my eyes from you; even if you offer many prayers, I will not listen. Your hands are full of blood" (Isa. 1:15).

Imagine it! Is it really possible for our worship to be unacceptable to the Lord? Is the blood of the unreached nations and the lost on our hands? To suggest such a thing makes some people angry. Jesus doesn't really mind. He didn't come here to reinforce people's fantasies about themselves. He came to set the record straight. He spoke to the heart of the matter and they crucified him. But he accomplished his objective just the same. He came to divide the house of God between those who were on the Lord's side and those who were not.

I think we need to be careful about being harmfully polite to our fellow believers who have cast their faith into the pool of shallow Christianity. Sure, we have a natural compulsion to water down what it means to follow Jesus when it comes to funerals. I'll just leave that one alone. But what about the rest of the year? Must we leave our Sunday services sanitized of anything unsettling? Honestly, my Bible doesn't read like a 2nd grade Sunday school lesson. I would rather worship with a group of five people who are seriously grappling with Great Commission realities than a group of 100,000 who can only think, pray and sing, "Oh, bless me, bless me, Lord—how I need you, how I want you, how I love you—just don't ask me to do anything or go anywhere or talk to anyone that might burst my bubble."

Lie Number Two: God doesn't need you.

On a street in New York City, Kitty Genovese was raped and murdered in broad daylight with the full knowledge of dozens of people. For 30 minutes her cries and screams went unanswered and unacknowledged. She cried, "I'm dying, I'm dying." No one called the police. Some even closed their windows. No one got people organized. No one said a word. Perhaps everyone thought their neighbor would do the calling. Or perhaps they simply didn't care.

I would like you to consider for a moment what might be the most important lie the Devil could convince you to believe. Of course there are many lies he will try to sell you throughout your life and some will be more effective than others. He will try to discourage you, make you think there's no point going on, try to convince you that somewhere down the road you missed it, when in fact you are right where you should be. There is no end to the things he will try to sell you in his desperate attempt to keep you from moving forward and fulfilling God's mission. But there is one thing that you may believe at the very outset of your journey, and you may in fact be very sincere and genuine in believing this. It may actually be a very important part of your theology. Well, far be it from me to tamper with anything sacred! But just this once please permit me to ask some questions. I believe God needs you and wants you in his mission. But time and again I have heard statements to the contrary coming from the lips of very sincere people. More often than I care to recount I have heard the lofty statement: "God doesn't need us to complete the Great Commission." It's a very comforting sentiment, but it doesn't ring true in my heart *or* the Scriptures.

So I have some questions about all this. I would like to know why it is so important for us to believe such a thing. Why do we feel the need to convince ourselves that God doesn't need us? Has God asked us to do such a thing? Could it be that we have sanctioned the very philosophy of indifference that led those New York citizens to do absolutely nothing when Kitty Genovese was raped? Are we giving our disobedience a covering under the sovereignty of God?

While it is true that God works all things together for good, he is *not* the author of evil. "In him is no darkness at all" the Scriptures declare (1 John 1:5). Imagine the Devil getting us to blame God for the evil we have committed! Can you think of anything more sinister? I honestly cannot. But that is exactly what can happen when we have a corrupted or incomplete view of God's sovereignty.

Brother Andrew writes, "This is why I am concerned about Christian fatalism. . . . Fatalism is a paralyzing disease that has invaded the Body of Christ with disastrous consequences. It infects its victims with complacency and apathy that immobilize their will to resist evil while eroding their determination to accomplish the great work of Christ."[1]

Eternal Vision

I believe Brother Andrew is absolutely correct about this. There is a kind of Christian fatalism which infects much of our thinking. But the Bible speaks directly against it. The Bible tells us specifically and emphatically that God does need us. In fact, you will find that every lie of Satan is specifically targeted against an important truth in God's Word.

The Bible tells us that Christ is "the head of the body, the Church" (Col. 1:18). And, "You are the body of Christ" (1 Cor. 12:27). And also, "[God] appointed him to be head over everything for the church, which is his body, the fullness of him . . ." (Eph. 1:22). The concept of being interconnected in a Church body is one of the most important principles we can come to understand. We *are* needed and our participation *is* required for the success of the mission. So Scripture makes this conclusion for us, "The eye cannot say to the hand, 'I don't need you.' And the head cannot say to the feet, 'I don't need you'" (1 Cor. 12:21). Now if Jesus, who is the head of the body, cannot say to us, "I have no need of you!" who are we to say such things on his behalf?

Equally, if God has chosen us to be his hands and feet, we cannot say back to him, "You have no need of us." (Yet we say this very thing more often than we realize.) To do so is a violation of God's revealed purpose. While it is absolutely true that God is all powerful, it is also true that God *chooses* to limit himself in certain areas. One of these is the Great Commission. God has chosen to limit himself to our obedience in making disciples of all nations.

Scripture warns us about those who have "lost connection with the Head, from whom the whole body, supported and held together by its ligaments and sinews, grows as God causes it to grow" (Col. 2:19). Imagine having a body that doesn't do what you want! Feet that go left instead of right, hands that hang limp, and arms that won't budge. Such is the person who has lost connection with the Head and abandoned God's purposes for this generation. Thus we cannot excuse ourselves and say, "Well, if things go undone in God's harvest field, it must be his will." To the contrary, God is "not willing that any should perish" (2 Pet. 3:9). The problem is with us, not the Lord.

Scripture says, "There is only *one* body" (Eph. 4:4). There is only one way, only one life, only one method for saving people. "We are therefore Christ's ambassadors as though God were making his appeal through *us*" (2 Cor. 5:20). Therefore, we can only conclude with the Scriptures that unless we go, unless we are faithful, unless we preach the word to the lost, the Great Commission cannot and will not be completed. For how can they believe, and how can they hear, and how can they call—if no one is sent?

Now this is a very important concept to the enemy. There is nothing more important to him than to keep you out of the action. If somehow he can convince you to believe a false understanding of God's prescribed methods, then he has you right where he wants you: compromised and ineffective. Lies are like viruses. They stay dormant, then spring to life and multiply when we are weakest. They work together with fear and doubt to form a lethal potion of indifference. Our responsibility is to come to terms with what God has required of us. Not to question why, not to assume everything will work out anyway in spite of our disobedience, but to take seriously the reality that unless we are faithful, terrible consequences may, and probably will, take their inevitable course.

Saying God doesn't need us is no different than saying God doesn't love us. God has chosen to need us, just as he has chosen to love us, and he has chosen to need us *because* he loves us. There is no greater honor than to be called according to his purpose. He has chosen to make us his partners in the fulfillment of the Great Commission. All the more should we be concerned! If we properly understood it, we would all say with the apostle Paul, "Woe unto us if we don't preach the gospel!"

I have no quarrel with those who want to defend the self-sufficiency of God. It is absolutely true that God needs nothing to be God. He exists in perfection, with or without us. But it is *not* true that God will complete the Great Commission without our involvement. He absolutely will not. It's like saying that God could save us without cross. It's none of your business to question him on the matter. He has chosen to involve us and he will not and *cannot* go against what he has declared to be his eternal purpose in Christ and his Church, "which is his *body*, the fullness of him" (Eph. 1:23).

Lie Number Three: If you don't go, somebody else will.

Next in line to "God doesn't need us" is another related lie, "Don't worry about going as a missionary someplace because God will send someone else." Like every good lie, this one has a little bit of truth in it, but of course that only makes it all the more sinister. The more truth you can put in a lie, the better.

The Great Commission *will be* completed, no doubt about it. Jesus prophesied, "This gospel of the Kingdom *will* be preached in all the world" (Matt. 24:14). It is entirely his initiative, his business, his show. But he will *not* do it without us. And that means he will wait. So while it is true that God will send someone if you don't go, it may not be in this generation.

Millions have perished in lands of darkness, having never heard the gospel, even though the Christian church had the personnel, the funds, and the capacity to reach them. But we didn't take them the gospel. Now whose fault is it? Can we blame God? Can we say God didn't want them to hear the gospel? Or is it more likely that God called people to go who never went?

When God called Ezekiel, he warned him about the consequences of not fulfilling His mission. He said, "I will hold you accountable for that man's blood" (Ezekiel 3:18). He didn't say, "If you don't go, I'll send someone else." He said, "That man will die for his sin" (v. 18). In the same way, we have been entrusted with a message from the Lord that is literally a matter of life and death—heaven and hell—for those who are perishing. There is no Plan B for delivering that message. You and I are the only plan!

One missionary to Africa was mightily used of the Lord to bring thousands to Christ among a particular tribe. It was a great honor to be used of the Lord in this way, but for some reason he had this feeling that this honor had been previously reserved for someone else. For some reason he always felt that God had called someone before him who didn't go. This conviction was so deep he would speak of it wherever he went. One Sunday, an elderly man came up to him with tears in his eyes and said, "I am the one. God called me to that tribe when I was a young man, but I didn't go."[2]

Jesus said, "As the father has sent me, I am sending you. If you forgive anyone their sins, they are forgiven. *If you do not forgive them*, they are *not* forgiven" (John 20:23). Jesus said virtually the same thing to Paul. He said "I am sending you . . . *so that* they may be forgiven" (Acts 26:17-18). Now what is the implication of this? It is no more or less than what the Bible says: "Faith comes from hearing the message, and the message is heard through the word of Christ. But how can they believe if they have not heard? And how can they hear without someone preaching to them?" (Rom. 10:14-17).

Has God called you someplace? Have you felt his tug on your heart? Don't shake it off. Don't put it aside. Take it seriously. God *is* calling people—each day his voice goes out to any who will pay attention. He is calling the believers of this generation to take the gospel to the least reached areas of the world. But how many are listening? How many are going in the opposite direction like Jonah? How many are in the storm and still not repenting? How many are in the belly of the whale? How many are still thinking it over and wondering if it's all worth it?

Like Nineveh, a death sentence hangs over dark regions like the 10/40 Window. Who will take the light? How many have been called and yet delayed? How many wonder if it really matters? We have the capacity to reach them, but will we? Will the next generation look back on this one and ask, "Where was the Church, where were the people of God, what were they thinking?" Will the 2.7 billion unevangelized of the 10/40 Window rise up on Judgment Day to accuse us? What will we say to them? What will *you* say to them?

Lie Number Four: Believers will not be judged.

This is a lovely lie. It too has great truth in it, but it will prove to be the most shocking letdown of them all. Who is the wicked and lazy servant that Jesus talks about (Matt. 25:26)? Was he not entrusted with his master's business? Was he not given an assignment? Paul makes an important observation here, "What business is it of mine to judge those outside the church? Are you not to judge those inside?" (1 Cor. 5:12). Jesus will come as judge and judgment begins with the House of God, with those who call themselves by the Name, and who claim Jesus as their Lord (1 Pet. 4:17). But will all measure up the same? Will everyone hear "Well done, good and faithful servant"? Or will there be some surprises?

Why did Jesus say to the Church, "But if you do not wake up, I will come like a thief"? And, "Blessed is he who stays awake"? And most significant, "My reward is with me" (Rev. 3:3; 16:15; 22:12)? Is it possible that there is more to his coming than we realize? We are told to prepare ourselves for this day. Believers are warned to "make every effort to be found spotless, blameless and at peace with him" (2 Pet. 3:14). Why should we have anything to worry about? After all, we are saved by grace and justified through his blood. We've prayed the prayer, we've been *immersed* in the baptismal, we've even "re-committed" several times just to be sure.

But there is such a thing as "trampling on the grace of God" and "using the grace of God as a license to sin" (Heb. 10:29; Jude 1:4). How many people are convinced that because they have said the "sinner's prayer" they can live however they like and everything will work out in the end? Jesus spoke directly against this. He warned of those who will be called "least in the kingdom of heaven" because they disregarded his commands (Matt. 5:19). The Bible warns us about such people with the most graphic of language: "He himself will be saved, but only as one escaping through the flames" (1 Cor. 3:15). Now these "believers" will be with us in eternity, but they are in for a shock when they get there. Consider this well: If it is justifiable that people should perish forever in hell, is it not equally justifiable that those who did nothing to save them, and who lived according to a false gospel, should be made to think about the consequences of their indifference during that same eternity?

Having said that, let us also keep in mind that there are going to be some "believers" who will not make it all. The "wicked lazy servant" was cast out into outer darkness. Jesus warned his followers for a good reason, and he wanted them to be concerned about the consequences of disobedience. He said, "But the one who hears my words and does not put them into practice is like the man who built a house on the ground without a foundation. The moment the torrent struck that house, it collapsed and *its destruction was complete*" (Luke 6:49). This person was building but it was swept away. Others built with hay and stubble but the fire came and burned it up (1 Cor. 3:14-16).

So who are we to think we can play games with eternity? Is there no fear of God left in our hearts? No respect for his Word and his warnings given time after time? Will we be among the wise servants who labored hard with their talents; will we be counted among those who carried an extra supply oil; will we be awake with those who would not rest until He came? There is great danger in assuming too much about what God will *not* do, when he has told us plainly what he *will* do. There are many people today who are building all kinds of "houses," constructing all manner of pleasant theologies to protect their comfortable lifestyles. But what Jesus wants is obedience. He said, "Why do you call me Lord, Lord and do not do what I say? Then I will tell them plainly, 'I never knew you. Away from me, you evildoers!'" (Luke 6:46; Matt. 7:23).

Lie Number Five: The lost will be given a second chance.

This generation is the most theologically curious of them all. We have theories for everything. Anything God has omitted to tell us we have eagerly devised theories for. We fill in the blanks and in a matter of time ordain it as gospel truth. One of those theories is about what happens to those who have never heard the gospel. We would rather not believe they will go to hell. Now to be perfectly honest I would love for this lie to be true. I would love to be able to say that God will save everyone in the end. But I cannot in good conscience say it. For whatever reason, God has chosen to tell us the opposite. Now you may say, "Well, he doesn't really mean it. Us enlightened people know better."

But suppose you are wrong. Suppose people really do go to hell. Suppose there is no second chance. Does it really make a difference? If so, what might that difference be? The difference lies in what may be our response to their plight. Now one may say, "Should it not be motivation enough that people are under the power of Satan and living in darkness? Should that not be enough to thrust us out in earnest?" Indeed, it should be. But those who don't go, and stay uninvolved, are as unconvinced about the condition of the lost as they are about hell. Yet suppose you *are* convinced that the lost are hopeless without Christ and that Satan has them under his power. If that is so, I would like to propose that you think about this a little while longer before you conclude that people who die under this condition are going to be okay. Because it just might be significant. God doesn't waste ink. The Bible says they are "Without God and without hope," and "It is appointed unto man to die once and after that to face judgment" (Eph. 2:12; Heb. 9:27).

If there is even the slightest possibility that these people could go to an eternity in hell, if there is even a lingering of doubt on the matter, then that is precisely the reason why you ought to work and live as though eternity is on the line for those without Christ. We are not to second-guess God and assume that everything will work out okay in the end for those who have never heard. Our responsibility is to assess the potential risk of our disobedience and let the full measure of that reality sink deep within our hearts.

When the rich man died and was sent to Hades, he looked up into heaven and asked that Lazarus might come to his aid. Gabriel's response is incredible. He says, "Between us and you a great chasm has been fixed, so that those who want to go from here to you cannot, nor can *anyone* cross over from there to us" (Luke 16:26). Now who fixed this great chasm? Who made the rules? Was it not the all-loving, all-merciful God? The Bible says the rich man was "in torment." His suffering was real and continuous, and there was nothing anyone could do to stop it. Even all the angels in heaven could not have saved that man. God made a decision and it was final. There was no crossing over, no turning back, no possibility of escape. No repentance possible.

Now consider well what this rich man wanted to do. He wanted to become an evangelist. He wanted to warn his unbelieving family members about that terrible place. But it was too late. There was no way possible for him to leave and tell them. For us, however, it is not too late. And if we could visit hell, we would be unstoppable in our witness for Jesus Christ—the only way, the only truth, the only life, the only name under heaven by which we can be saved.

Today in our seeker-sensitive churches we speak much of God's love. That's important. But there is another aspect of God's character which we tend to overlook, that of his wrath and justice. Scripture speaks of those for whom "blackest darkness has been reserved forever" (Jude 1:13). We are warned that those not in Christ will be "shut out from the presence of the Lord" (2 Thess. 1:9). We are told of others for whom "no sacrifice for sins is left, but only a fearful expectation of judgment and of raging fire that will consume the enemies of God" (Heb. 10:26-27). Why would Scripture tell us again and again of God's wrath if it were not so? Are we not to take this seriously?

The possibility that eternity is settled in this lifetime is a real one. The Bible has given us every good reason to believe it. The fact that we don't live like it testifies clearly against us. But be forewarned, all of us—without exception—will be called into account for every Truth we choose to disregard, disobey, and theologically explain away.

KNOW THE TRUTH

The Bible calls Satan the father of all lies (John 8:44). The first recorded words from his mouth were a lie. His purpose was to distort the Word of God and he did it masterfully. I would like to propose that he has not changed. His number one target is to specifically challenge the Truth revealed to us in Scripture. I have gone out on a limb here to challenge what I believe are inroads of the enemy in our thinking. I have done so with one enduring perspective: Satan doesn't want the Great Commission completed. Any theology, or teaching, or popular belief that works against that mission is a candidate for suspicion.

There are many more lies of the enemy I can think of which work against the Great Commission. I won't list them all (because I have to choose my battles carefully!), but I'm quite sure you can think of them. We need to understand just how seriously and persistently Satan works to keep us from obeying. The first step to failure in any war is to underestimate your opponent. In one of the creeds of the U.S. Special Forces, the following resolution is made which I think is very relevant to us:

> "In battle, I eagerly meet the enemy, for I volunteered to be up front where the fighting is hard. I fear no foe's ability, *nor underestimate his will to fight.* I will never surrender."[3]

Satan is absolutely terrified that your heart may turn toward the Great Commission. He fears the passion and fire that the Holy Spirit is kindling within you. He wants nothing else than to stop you this very moment. Don't underestimate his will to fight you to the very end. His lies are all about surrender. They are a battle for the mind and the will. They are the subtleties that keep us out of the ac-

Eternal Vision

tion and turn us away when the going gets tough. They are the justifications for a life without real purpose. They are the compromises with unsurrendered desires. They are the cataracts that narrow our vision to just getting by and settling for less.

The antidote for any lie is the pure and simple, unadulterated truth. The reason so many people remain out of the action, and out of the inner circle of true friendship with Christ, is they remain unconvinced about the truth of what Jesus really said. Whenever we remain unconvinced about the truth, we become a candidate for being deceived. Whenever we read something Jesus said and believe, "Well, he couldn't have actually meant that," we doom ourselves to a life of mediocrity. Rather, we should take in the full force of his words and say, "Lord, I'm not sure what all this means but I want to. And if it means what it says it means, help me to understand what that means for me and how I ought to be living." Re-read the words of Christ as a personal letter to you. Re-read his instructions to his disciples and say in your heart, "Lord, open my eyes. I want to see the truth. I am willing to turn aside from anything that keeps me from fully knowing you and serving you the best I can. I want my life to matter for you and your Kingdom!"

CHAPTER SIXTEEN

GETTING DIRECTION

"Stand at the crossroads and look; ask for the ancient paths, ask where the good way is, and walk in it." (Jer. 6:16)

*H*ave you ever wished God would send you a letter telling you exactly what you're supposed to do with your life? I know I would. It makes perfect sense to me. But God in his wisdom has chosen something better. He has chosen the path of ups and downs, mountains and valleys, raging rivers and wooded forests. He has chosen the Journey and the Relationship. Of course, it may seem a whole lot safer the other way—to have everything laid out, nice and neat. But God is an adventurer at heart, and he has designed for you an awesome journey—full of faith, hope, love and trust in him.

Every good relationship depends on some kind of interdependence. And so God has made us dependent on him while he has allowed his mission to be dependent on our obedience. He wants us to take the initiative—to ask, to seek, and to knock. He wants us to find out what he's up to, where he's going, and follow his lead. Most importantly, he wants to bless us for all eternity. He wants our lives to matter, because that's why he made us. He wants us to be the very best we can be, and he knows how to get us there.

Recently, a friend wrote me an e-mail along these lines. He said, "I want to live a life that will have "HUGE R.O.I." (Return On Investment). Here is a portion of his letter and my response:

> David, like I mentioned last Saturday there was this one thing you talked about in one of your talks about how God sometimes molds us to be ready for a work of service that can be just for ONE moment. Did I understand that right?
>
> In any case, I know my life is not about me, it's about Him. Then if so, that should change my entire perspective on what must be done next and next and next. I just don't want to waste my life you know. I want to live a life that will have HUGE R.O.I. and I mean heavenly ROI, I just don't know what that will mean for me. I really long to live the extraordinary life—the one that God will delight in—I am soooo not there yet, but if you can give me some clues, please tell me. —Mark

After I prayed, the Lord gave me the following answer:

> Mark, one of my favorite verses is a kind of obscure one buried like the Prayer of Jabez in one of those long lists of names: "The sons of Issachar understood the times and knew what Israel should do" (1 Chr. 12:32). I can think of no more important thing for today than to understand the time in which we live. Once we understand this, everything else begins to fall into place. For example, if you knew that Jesus was coming back in your lifetime, how might that affect your plans? Would you take that reality into every decision you made? How could you not! But the trouble with us is that we

Getting Direction

remain unconvinced about the significance of how close we are—the "what we should do" factor. So despite all the attention given to the second coming of Christ, so few people are actually adjusting their lifestyles and priorities accordingly. It reminds me exactly of the parable of the ten virgins. All were eagerly expecting Jesus to return. All understood how close they were to his coming—the signs were obvious, but unlike the sons of Issachar, not all understood what they were supposed "to do." Not all took enough oil and their supply ran out. Not all made the right preparations.

So here in a nutshell is my advice on seeking God's will that we might better understand the times and prepare ourselves for action:

First: Learn to pray at least two hours every day. Now I say "learn" to pray! I believe with all my heart that the best way to understand God's will for you and to think clearly (there is no greater gift than rational thought!) is to spend much time in quiet "closet room" prayer with the Lord. I would begin by asking the Lord to teach me how to pray and especially how to intercede for the lost and for his purposes in the world. Most people do not learn how to pray with faith and power because they are not asking for and seeking this all important gift. It really is a great tragedy, because there is no more important thing we can learn to do as believers down here at the present time.

Second: I would ask the Lord to show me how I can best participate in bringing the gospel to the least reached peoples of the world. Most of these are in the 10/40 Window: think of Hindus in India, Buddhists in Tibet, Muslims in Saudi Arabia.

In all, there are 2.7 billion least evangelized people in the 10/40 Window. These people groups must become our top priority. While there are many good things we can do, we must never lose sight of this immediate and urgent rescue operation. I would begin by praying for the unreached nations of this region and asking the Lord to fill me with a burden for those furthest from the gospel (be assured he will answer!).

Third: I would get rid of all distractions to the greatest extent possible. The greatest enemy of priorities are all the petty, seemingly "urgent" things which pop up here and there. We must remember that Satan also has a plan for our life! His plan consists basically of diversions, anything to keep us off course from the mission God has planned for us. I would also include here some advice for people like us, whom you might call "high-energy" people. We have a tendency to try to accomplish too many things at once. This is a mistake. We need to focus on the top priority and make sure it is being done (e.g., learning to pray 2 hours every day!).

Fourth: I would get myself ready for ministry. There are so many rusty Christians out there, it makes me very annoyed. We need to be equipping ourselves for our three most important tasks as followers of Jesus: Prayer, Evangelism and Discipleship. Most Christians go through life without winning anyone to Christ! There is no greater tragedy than Christians who drift through life clueless about their top priorities. Learn how to disciple believers from the infant stage to maturity. Find out how to raise up more leaders for the Kingdom, and become one yourself!

Getting Direction

Fifth: I would ask the Lord to send me into the frontiers of his harvest field, into those places where the gospel has not yet gone, where people are living in greatest darkness. Then I would prepare myself with "reckless abandon" to get there as soon as possible. If it were up to me, I would send four of every six "recruits" (real followers of Jesus!) into the 10/40 Window. Here is a region filled with thousands of unreached peoples and billions who have yet to hear the gospel.

As one missionary put it, "So many risk takers for gold, so few risk takers for God!" What the Lord needs right now are people with the courage to say, "Lord, send me! I'll go anywhere and do anything for you (no strings attached)."

— David

Mark is now preparing for ministry somewhere in South Asia. I hope and pray he makes it. The difference between those who make it and those who don't is one simple thing: bold initiative with the Holy Spirit's power. Most people are not hearing because they are not asking—*really* asking. Nor are they seeking. They are not taking the time to develop the ministry skills required to be useful in the Lord's service. Seeking is a big part of asking. We must be faithful with what we know we should be doing. Seeking is more than just uttering a few words in prayer. Seeking new answers from the Lord is about being faithful with the ones we have already been given. Most people mistakenly take a passive approach to knowing the will of God for their lives: no need to ask, no need to seek, no need to keep knocking. Such people will wander in circles for most of a lifetime and will look back on the years wasted wondering where they all went.

Eternal Vision

Whatever may be the specific role God has given you, there are some basic things that every follower of Jesus *must* be doing, without exception. If you're neglecting the basics, then I can tell you right now, without a doubt, you are not being led where God wants you to be. Take, for example, the three priority skills every believer should develop: Prayer, Evangelism and Discipleship. Now examine your life very carefully. To what extent are you being equipped to win people for Jesus? Are you being trained to make disciples who will win others and make more disciples? Are you striving to grow in faith and holiness so your prayers might become deeper and stronger and more effective?

Whatever might be your situation, if you're not being *fully* equipped, it's up to you to find a place where you *will be* equipped. I think it's unfortunate that most people have to join para-church organizations before they will be equipped to be followers of Jesus. If you are a pastor, I hope you will remedy this deplorable situation. Not that there is anything wrong with para-church ministries; I belong to one myself and I believe we need them. But what if every church rose to the level of a mission society? And why not? Is that not what the first church looked like? Isn't that the kind of fellowship Jesus formed with his disciples?

People say, "The local church is a hospital for the hurting, a mending place for the broken, a shelter for the weak. You can't turn it into a basic training camp." But they are only partly right. The local church is indeed a basic training camp, and it happens to have a hospital on it. But the hospital is not the main focus, it's not the main program. Training people for action in the Great Commission is what the local church is all about. With all due respect to the hurting, the broken, and the weak, I would like to suggest that these are precisely the people God wants to use and super-charge to reach a hurting, broken, and dying world. Furthermore, there is no greater healing that takes place when we begin to help others. There is no greater strength we will find than in seeking to extend the grace of God into the lives of others who are hurting just as much as we are, or once were. Recovery begins with purpose. If you have a reason to get well, you are well on your way.

WHAT YOU ALREADY KNOW

While I can't tell you specifically where God will send you, or give you a guarantee that you won't make any mistakes, I can remind you of what you already know (or at least should know from God's Word!). Our responsibility is to be faithful with the opportunities God has given us and to do what we know we should be doing. Being faithful *here* is the first step to getting over *there*—to that place or ministry where God wants you to invest your life.

Step One: Sharpen Your Focus Jesus has given his Church one assignment to complete: the fulfillment of the Great Commission. This is your top priority. All of your plans must fit within it. Whatever may be your current plans, however good your intentions may be, you must ask yourself and measure your plans by this standard: "How will this thing I want to do contribute to bringing the gospel to those who have never heard?" Many people go through life seeking to do only what is best for themselves. They can only think of what will make them happy and comfortable. Sacrifice is out of the question. Hardships and problems are to be avoided. But as followers of Jesus, our calling is much different.

Jesus said to his disciples, "*Seek* first the Kingdom" (Matt. 6:33). Here is the most important principle every disciple of Jesus must learn to master. The Kingdom comes first in everything. Post this on the wall and think about it. Ask yourself, "Am I really doing this? Am I truly seeking? Am I taking the initiative?" Seeking first the Kingdom is asking "What does Jesus want done?" and then finding out how you can fit into His program. Secondly, it's also asking "What *remains* to be done?"

Followers of Jesus are concerned about the *completion* of the Great Commission. They are not content with disobedience or half-hearted measures. They want Jesus back again! He will return the moment his Great Assignment is completed, and not a moment sooner. Imagine a group of people working on a 70-story skyscraper and 65 floors have been constructed. They're so close to finishing, but there is a rumor afloat that it won't be done. The creditors won't foot the bill. So a few have decided to call it a day. "We're all finished," they exclaim. "Now where's the Champagne?"

In a similar way, some of us have forgotten about our contracts with the Kingdom of God. We've signed up to *finish* a job. The sooner we remember where we are, and why we're here, and get to it, the better. Jesus said to his disciples, "My food is to do the will of him who sent me and to *finish* his work" (John 4:34). There are all kinds of things we can do with our lives—all kinds of *good* things, but how many of them actually contribute to "finishing" the work? Make this your focus, your passion, and you'll be right in step with the Master.

Jesus talked about finishing his Father's work in the context of reaching an unreached people group, the Samaritans. His disciples were surprised to find him making the effort (a people for whom they had no great love). In fact, they had only one thing on their minds: Come on, Lord, let's have some lunch! But Jesus brought their attention from the temporal to the eternal and said, "Look you guys, here's what's important: let your hunger, your desire, your appetite be for the work of the Father and *finishing* it." Then he added this amazing statement as a warning and a challenge, "Do you not say, 'Four months more and then the harvest'? I tell you open your eyes and look at the fields! They are ripe for harvest" (John 4:35).

Imagine going to sleep during the greatest harvest of eternity? That's precisely what Jesus is talking about. This is your top priority; it's the *only* priority. It won't be harvest time for long—each harvest has a season and each can be lost. How much more should we be alert and focused as we see the end drawing near? The situation is urgent and the need is imperative. All hands are needed, and you and I are no exception!

Second: Re-evaluate Your Priorities Peter wrote, "The end of all things is near, *therefore* be clear minded and self-controlled *so that you can pray*" (1 Pet. 4:7). From the time Jesus entered into this world, a new age in human history began. A final countdown was launched that could not be stopped. The "day" would give way to the "night" and the harvest would be over. The Son of God came to warn us and to show us how to live and work "as long as it is day" (John 9:4). And believe me, if it was a priority to be "devoted to prayer" in the first century, how much more so today! Those who overcome in this final generation will be a people of prayer. Those who fall away will be characterized in the same light: those who would not, cared not, and did not.

The Second Coming of Christ is the one event we have been commanded to "hasten" (2 Pet. 3:12). We should be thinking about it all the time. The Bible says we should be *longing* for it (2 Tim. 4:8). Seeking his soon coming means we don't mind our lives being interrupted. It's saying, "Lord, this is your show, your life, your time. It's all about you. I want you back again—you're all that matters!"

So we need to examine our priorities in light of his soon coming. We also need to keep from deceiving ourselves about what is really our top priority. There is one simple way to find out. Prayerfully make a list of what *should be* your top priority in seeking first the Kingdom. Then make another list of what are currently your top priorities. What takes up most of your time? What things are you doing to help fulfill the Great Commission? How much time is spent on "temporal" concerns over eternal priorities?

Much time is wasted on things that don't really matter for eternity. Many people spend more time working on their bodies than they do on the eternal part of who they are. Others spend more time getting input from the world's discipleship program than from the One who died to set them free from its power.

So ask the Lord to help you examine your life. If you will honor him, he will honor you. Bank on it. He says, "Take care of my business and I'll take care of yours." Of course, this does not mean we neglect our responsibilities to others. It simply means that we strive to eliminate all hindrances in our lives and all unnecessary entanglements that might keep us from the eternal priorities God has for us.

Third: Develop Spiritual Disciplines Jesus said of his disciples, "They *will* fast" (Matt. 9:15). It is a characteristic of true disciples of Jesus that they are willing to sacrifice for the cause of Christ. I can think of no greater discipline than the combination of prayer and fasting for producing spiritual breakthroughs. Jesus fasted forty days before he began his ministry. John Wesley made it a discipline of fasting two days a week. He said, "The man who never fasts is no more in the way to heaven as the man who never prays!" John Calvin fasted for the conversion of Geneva and the Lord granted it. There was not a home without a praying believer by the end of his life. Charles Finney, who was used by the Lord to bring revival throughout America, would regularly fast and pray three days before he would preach.

Like these men of faith, you can dedicate your fasting to something God wants done. In the time you might spend eating, you can pray about God's purposes. You will be surprised at the results! I know I have been. You really must experience this to believe it. I have never failed to find an answer from the Lord this way. Keep in mind that fasting is not a substitute for prayer, nor is it a way of earning God's grace. Fasting is simply a reminder to us of our weakness and complete dependence on God for everything (Psa. 35:13).

Spiritual disciplines are something which will prepare you for greater works of service. Wherever you happen to be and whatever you are doing, learning to prioritize your relationship with the Lord is the most important lesson you can learn. On his final day with the disciples before he endured the cross, Jesus made this very clear. He said to them: "If a man remains in me and I in him, he will bear much fruit. . . . If you remain in me and my words remain in you, *ask whatever you wish*, and it will be given to you" (John 15:5-7). The key to a fruitful life is abiding with Christ. The key to answered prayer and direction for the future is your personal relationship with Jesus. There is no substitute, no shortcut, no other way for being effective in His service than seeking the Lord right where you are and asking him to bless the work of your hands.

You can have as much of Jesus as you want, and the more you have of him, the more he will do in you and through you. This great promise comes with a great responsibility. For you can surely limit what God wants to do through you by not abiding. Jesus said, "If anyone does not remain in me, he is like a branch that is thrown away and withers" (John 15:6). Abiding in Christ is not a suggestion.

It is a requirement and a mandate—a solemn warning from the One who bought us at the highest price.

Fourth: Learn to Love Have you ever had the experience of losing sight of a small child? Immediately, a sense of urgency comes over you as a dozen frightful possibilities flash through your mind. Did someone grab her? Is she hurt? Did someone find her? Nothing else matters. Nothing else could.

One time my family and I were attending a hometown event called the "Rose Parade." Around one million people gather on the streets to watch dozens of "floats" covered in flowers make their way down Colorado Blvd. Marching bands from across the country fill in between the floats to launch the new year with a bang. After the parade, two of the best college football teams battle it out in the Rose Bowl to the applause of over a hundred thousand spectators.

Well, this one year we all happened to be there in Pasadena and most of the family was able to go. Midway through the parade, we were all so excited and distracted by everything, we allowed our little sister Lydia (about three years old at the time) to wander off without anyone seeing it. When my dad finally noticed she was missing, she was nowhere to be found. Suddenly everything changed. Where a moment before we had been laughing and joking, we were now concerned and worried. None of us cared about the floats or the marching bands anymore; they were now a terrible nuisance. My dad said, "I'm going out there and stopping this parade." He was serious, too, and he would have done it! Fortunately, just as he was about to make good on his intentions, one of us spotted Lydia. A kind stranger had taken her by the hand and was leading her to us.

That day we all discovered something very interesting. We loved Lydia a whole lot more than that parade. We would have searched for her and done just about anything to get her back. Her condition became our *only* priority. It demanded our full and complete attention.

That's exactly the way God wants us to be with the Lost. They *are* lost. They *must* be found. When we are focused where God's heart is focused, a lot of the confusion about what we should do with our lives begins to clear up. There is only one priority: those without Christ. There is only one mission: bringing them the gospel. Everything else is a nuisance and a distraction. We have all eternity to amuse ourselves. We have a few years to rescue people who are drowning, who are lost, who are being held hostage by a malicious liar and psychopath.

The Good Shepherd leaves everything behind *to seek* that which is lost. He says goodbye to the ninety-and-nine, and sets off on an undeterrable mission. It matters not how difficult the terrain may be. The dangers are irrelevant, the lost one is what matters. He's not coming back without it. He will fend off wolves and challenge any attack that might come between him and the one he seeks to rescue.

That's the kind of Shepherd we have and as his disciples we will follow his lead. So let's ask ourselves, "Are we making progress?" Do we share his passion, love and concern? Are we out there on the search with him? Are we seeking the lost as though nothing else matters? Have we taken up the lifeline that was thrown out to us? Are we *learning* how to use it? How odd it would be to take up tennis instead! And yet how many rescued people, figuratively speaking, have done this very thing?

Fifth: Get Ready for Sacrifice Paul said, "I resolved to know nothing while I was with you except Jesus Christ and him crucified" (1 Cor. 2:2). Here is the most profound and utterly amazing statement any disciple of Jesus can come to understand. Many people do not see from the Lord where they should be and what they should be doing because they are not focused in their vision. We want to know and do so many things, but only one thing really matters at the present time: Christ and him crucified. Until we are willing to die to all else, save this vision, we will limit what God wants to do in and through us.

Dying isn't easy. Everything in you says no way. Many people go through heart-wrenching experiences before they finally surrender everything to the Lord. But it is nonetheless the most important thing that can happen to you here on this earth. Ask for it! Seek it with all your might. Don't delay it. Desire it. Pursue it with reckless abandon until every day your prayer and your life becomes, "More of Christ, less of me."

When we learn to focus our attention on what really matters in the light of eternity, many things begin to clear up. We begin to see the slimy tentacles that have grabbed hold of us. We begin to see the cataracts that blinded us. We start to recognize and feel the heat and the imminent danger of the sinful, fallen world we live in. We become thankful, for we were like blind and numb creatures destroying ourselves at every turn, with little understanding of what was happening. We only had this sinking feeling deep within that we were dying. But now with our eyes wide open we have a new perspective: Christ and him crucified is life more abundant! It is the only life worth living.

The sooner we take hold of it, and the sooner we die to blindness and numbness, the sooner we can see and know "his incomparably great power for us who believe" (Eph. 1:19). That power will come as you are led into greater sacrifice for his Kingdom. Those who suffer for the Lord are granted tremendous grace. So don't shy away from hardship and trial. Discipline yourself and be disciplined by the Father in the midst of difficulty. God's training program for you will involve the unexpected and the unexplainable. It will involve soul searching and tears. He delights in a broken and contrite heart. For these are the people he can use most to do the most for his glory. And there is nothing more important, and more urgent, than seeking his power for greater service in this final harvest before his coming.

Jesus said, "Every branch in me that *does* bear fruit he prunes so that it will be even *more* fruitful" (John 15:2). There are no exceptions here. Every believer will go through pruning by the Lord so that he might use them more effectively. Pruning is painful for the branch! But it is the best thing for it, and God will take the suffering you have endured and cause his life-giving power to flow through you into more and more fruitfulness.

EVERYBODY'S NEEDED

Billy Graham once said, "God's not going to take me home until he's done with me." I really admire Billy Graham. Here is someone who never stopped working hard even though he had every right to retire. He understood why he was here and what mattered most. Hudson Taylor is another good example. He tirelessly labored for China until the day he died, and never shied away from danger for the gospel's sake. He said, "I am immortal until God decides to take me home." God is going to keep you alive for as long as he needs you here. If you're here on this planet, you're needed. *No exceptions!*

Many people limit themselves unnecessarily because they think they aren't qualified. This is a great mistake. They say, "God couldn't possibly use me; I'm all *messed* up." Or, "God couldn't possible want me; I'm all *used* up." What these people don't know is they are exactly the people God wants to use. They make the cut, they pass the bar, they have the qualifications! People who don't see themselves as they are have much to learn. People who recognize their limitations, their complete inadequacy and inability, are the very people God can and will use.

There is no such thing as retirement in God's economy—no matter what your age! Especially the kind of retirement where people just go on vacation after 65 and play with their grandkids. Of course there's nothing wrong with vacations and grandkids, but I'm talking about your focus—your vision and purpose, and the investment of your time in the most crucial moment of eternal history. Besides all this, it is a simple fact that people who stop working fall apart like abandoned ships, eventually lose their minds to sit-coms and their wallets to slick-selling infomercials, and finally end up in nursing homes where they are slowly medicated to death. But even if that were not so, the simple reality is, if you're still alive on this planet, if you still have breath in your lungs and blood rushing through your veins, you have an important part to play in fulfilling the Great Commission.

Not too long ago, I was in Malaysia where I met an Irishman in his seventies who had just baptized three Iranians. "What are you doing here?" I asked in amazement. "The Lord is moving powerfully among Iranians all over the world," he explained. "I want to be a part of it!" Than he told me of his recent trip to Iran. He was flying from Dublin to Tehran when a lady across the aisle interrupted his Bible reading. She inquired, "Excuse me, sir, is that a Bible you are reading?" At first my Irish friend was a little amazed that a Muslim woman would be speaking to him, let alone asking about a Bible. He acknowledged that it was indeed a Bible and she began to get very excited. "Would you read to me from your Bible?" she asked. He agreed, and for an entire hour he read to her from the life of Christ. At the end of the trip, as the plane was about to land, he asked, "Would you like this Bible?" Tears started streaming down her face as she was given the first Bible she had ever held in her hands. Two weeks later she became a born-again Christian.

Now what is amazing to me about this exchange is that I would never have been able to do this. This young, married woman would not have been able to speak to me. In her culture it's practically impossible. But because of my friend's age it was not a problem. He was not a threat, and what's more, because of his elderly appearance he was accorded great respect. What is even more amazing is how God used the mere presence of a believer in Iran to change an entire family. He didn't know Persian, but this lady and her family knew English. God put them together. He was just a tourist, not a professional missionary. But by making himself available to God, he accomplished a great work for the Kingdom.

The world is changing rapidly and we need to catch up. Traveling and living overseas are not the chores they used to be. Thanks to globalization, fluent speakers of English are increasing in every major city. God is preparing the way for the greatest harvest the world has ever seen. He is calling us to be salt and light, and as we obey him, he will set up the opportunities. You just have to be there. Just show up! Meet the people, pray for their needs, and share your story.

I believe God is awakening all parts of his Body for this final in-gathering of souls. Whether you're old or young, it doesn't matter. God has a place for you. If you're a young person, you have an unprecedented opportunity to do something which no other generation has ever witnessed. A global youth culture is emerging that is perhaps the most significant development for world evangelization there has ever been or will be. A wide cultural gap is emerging between the two generations that will rapidly break down traditions and social restrictions. Nations that previously seemed unreachable like Japan and Thailand are going to see explosive church growth among this new generation. Sixty percent of those living in the frontier areas of the world are under the age of 25!

There is a vast harvest ready and waiting to be brought into the Kingdom. The only question is, "Will you and I be a part?" Are we willing to let the Lord increase and expand our vision far beyond what we ever thought possible? Are *you* willing to ask the Lord to use *you* to reach hundreds and even thousands with the gospel?

Every great work in the Kingdom has been birthed by those who learned to try and refused to give up. The same will be true in your life. There are no substitutes for personal initiative in response to the Holy Spirit. If God is leading you to do something, don't expect him to *make* you do it. Expect help and guidance, even gentle prodding (or if you need it, not so gentle prodding). But eventually you must make the decision to obey. So *begin* where you are, with what you have, and watch his hand guide you to complete victory. The secret to finding God's will for your life is not knowing the future, it's understanding the present and your place in it. It's making a difference where you are, and asking God for more.

CHAPTER SEVENTEEN

I AM RESOLVED

*"Be patient and stand firm,
because the Lord's coming is near." (James 5:8)*

One thing I have committed to do before the Lord, and something which has affected my life more than any other discipline, is to get up no later than 6 a.m., no matter what time I go to bed. Even when I am traveling, even on holidays, whatever the situation, I'll be up by 6 a.m. to spend time with the Lord. Recently, I was surprised to find one of the leading salesmen in the United States advocating this same discipline for another reason. He recommends to everyone who struggles with prioritizing their time (and I think that's almost all of us), "You need to join the 6 o'clock club!"[1]

It really is incredible what begins to happen around two weeks into this. Your body gets used to it, and even likes it. Now you might think it's a little legalistic to never break this habit, and I would partly agree, so I am giving myself one or two grace days per decade. But other than that, don't mess with the 6 o'clock club! The reason is, this commitment will help you say "no" to those who would ask you to stay up later than you ought to.

John Wesley tells a funny story along these lines. He was once meeting with the king of England. It was getting late and so he begged to excuse himself. The king was really enjoying Wesley's visit, so he asked him to stay a little longer. John Wesley replied, "Your Majesty, you really must excuse me. You see, I have an appointment with another King tomorrow morning!"

Whatever you decide is best for you, one thing is for sure, the disciplines you practice each day will shape who you are and who you will become. For this reason, I am very careful to develop disciplines which will influence my character and lead me into Christ-likeness. One practice, which has helped me immensely to stay focused, is to prayerfully read the following statement of faith each morning after worshiping the Lord and reading his Word. I highly recommend this practice and encourage everyone to write their own statement of faith as soon as they can (even sooner!). It's a great way to remind yourself daily of your eternal priorities as you read it over before the Lord. Mine goes like this:

I believe:

Jesus is coming back soon and time is short.
He gave us one assignment to complete.
The only reason he has not returned is because that assignment has yet to be finished.
But we're closer than ever. We *are* winning!

Therefore:

I must abandon all distractions, desires and fantasies that might keep me out of the most exciting endeavor in eternal history: the final fulfillment of the Great Commission, culminating in the Second Coming of Christ.

I Am Resolved

I want my life to make a difference—as big a difference as possible for those who are perishing. I want to be resolved to entertain no fanciful notions, however prettily stated, that might derail my focus and passion.

By the grace of God, I will keep the following eternal realities and principles deep in my heart and endeavor to live like they matter more than anything else in this world:

I am resolved . . .

- To never forget why I am here. Fifty-thousand people perish without Christ every day among unreached peoples. I must never forget that I have been called to a rescue operation. This single fact must guide every decision I make about how I will use my life and my time.

- I am resolved to make prayer the priority of the day. Anything that prevents me from praying in a particular day is an obstacle to be challenged and overcome. I must *learn* how to pray in faith and perseverance. Learning how to pray and trust in the Lord is the most important objective of my life.

- I am resolved to be discipled and actively *learn* how to *make* disciples. I must not limit what God wants to do through me by avoiding his training program. I must commit myself to learning everything I can about how to rescue as many lost people as possible before Jesus returns. Being discipled and *making* disciples is not an option for followers of Jesus, it is a mandate!

ETERNAL VISION

- I am resolved to adjust my lifestyle in such a way that I can give the most money possible to advancing God's mission. I will not forget why God has blessed me: so that all nations on earth might be blessed with the saving knowledge of Jesus Christ.

- I am resolved to be ever alert to the temperature of my passion for Christ and his mission. My enemy is the Devil and he seeks only the destruction of my soul and the prevention of my participation in his ruin, which is the fulfillment of the Great Commission. Therefore I will not shrink back from this engagement, and I will not hide when courage is needed for the gospel's sake.

- I am resolved to allow nothing to disqualify me from running the race to the end. If I allow my fears to dictate my priorities, I have lost the race and run in vain. Therefore I must identify and prayerfully eradicate each and every fear that prevents me from fully serving the Lord Jesus with all of my heart, soul, mind and strength.

- I am resolved to make the Final Frontiers my priority. Jesus will come back the moment the Great Commission is fulfilled. Therefore I have no other objective but to bring the gospel to the remaining unreached peoples of the world and to every unevangelized person I can find.

- I am resolved to *seek* the lost and utterly refuse to be silenced about their plight. Bold initiative is how the Kingdom of God moves forward. People with unshakeable convictions, who will not be denied a hearing and will not be silenced, and who will not bend their knees before the gods of comfort, security and compromise, are the only kind of people who will stand firm in the end.

- I am resolved to be worthy of calling Jesus my Lord. If Jesus is Lord of my life, I cannot hold anything back from him, including my life itself. I must be prepared to give my body for the sake of the gospel.

- I am resolved to live like eternity really matters in my life. If I am going to live forever, what must I do *now* that I can never do again after I die or after Jesus returns? Every decision I make about how to use my life must remain accountable to this question.

- I am resolved to hasten his coming! The Second Coming of Christ must be the preoccupation of my life and my constant desire, prayer and vision.

- I am resolved to have zero tolerance for sin. This world is so corrupt and contagiously evil, I must be ever vigilant and awake to its potential influence in my life.

- I am resolved to always keep in mind that I live in a unique time in eternal history. I have been called to participate in the final battle of the last war that eternal history will ever know. Nothing must ever distract me from this primary focus.

- I am resolved to hear from the Master, "Well done, good and faithful servant. You have been faithful in a few things; I will put you in charge of many things. Come share my joy!"

ETERNAL VISION

FINISHING THE RACE

We are in the final 100 meters of a 4,000-year-old marathon race. We have been passed the baton by generations before us who have sacrificed and given their lives to bring us where we are today. We are well within sight of victory.

There is no greater honor than to be alive in this generation. But remarkably Jesus warns us that not everyone will recognize the time in which they live. Not every believer will adjust their priorities. Some will keep right on sleeping. Many will find good excuses, which are nothing more than clever ways of hiding the truth: I'm not really interested, I don't really care, I have more important things to do.

The Lord's main objective for you right now is to maximize your potential in this final campaign. This is not the time for business as usual. This is a time for bold initiative to reach as many lost people as possible before our Lord returns. All the prayers stored up for centuries, all the grace, mercy and power to be released before the end are available to you. They are yours for the asking. Everything that must be done and will be done is going to be done now, in your lifetime—you will live to see it. How can I be so confident? Because the world is headed for meltdown. We are being warned with multiple signs in every arena—from the environment, to the buildup of military armaments, to the breakout of new and deadly diseases, to the development of bio-technologies that will influence human behavior and control it.

Indeed, the Lord *must* come back. Or nothing will remain. But though the great *Titanic* is headed for the bottom of the ocean, it is being restrained for a time—just enough time to knock on every cabin, wake up every sleeping passenger, and present a plan for their salvation. Such is the time in which we live. Business as usual on the

I Am Resolved

Titanic is ballroom dancing, five star accommodations, and full dress dinners. But the ship is sinking! It's time to throw off the tux and put on some overalls.

There are many reports that some passengers on the *Titanic* were so drunk they went right on dancing as the ship sunk. Our world is no different. So don't be deceived about where you stand. Our Lord clearly warns us many times about the final generation before his coming. He says, "Watch out that you do not lose what you have worked for, but that you may be rewarded fully" (2 John 1:8). And, "Each of us *will* give an account of himself to God" (Rom. 14:12). Now you may say, "Then we're all doomed!" But what God is interested in—the means by which he balances his scales—is not with failure on one side and success on the other, but with blatant disregard and disobedience of his commands, over and against heartfelt repentance and resolve to live 100% for the purposes of his Kingdom.

The Lord will weigh our hearts on that day, not by our standards or perceived motives, but by his knowledge of what we could have done and should have done, yet neglected to do because of fear and doubt. The Bible says, "Such a man should not think he will receive anything from the Lord. He is a double-minded man, unstable in all he does" (Jas. 1:7-8). He is a man of many excuses:

"My wife won't let me sell this house. I know I ought not to live in it, but what can I do?"

"I know I should pray more, but I've got so many problems. I just can't find the time."

"If only I had more money, I would be able to give to the Lord."

He is already defeated. Scripture calls them double-minded, unstable, and as far as the Kingdom is concerned—"by their actions they deny him, they are unfit for doing anything good" (Tit. 1:16). Now you may say, "Wait a minute there, buddy, that's a bit harsh. The God I know would never say such a thing." But I beg to differ and so does God's Word. Many will come and claim all kinds of things about being "believers." They will say, "Lord, Lord, didn't I do this for you and go there for you and 'prophesy in your name, and in your name drive out demons and perform many miracles?'" (Matt. 7:22). And these very people who claim these very things will be told, "I never knew you. Away from me you evildoers!" (v. 23). These people were deceived. Someone told them they were going to be all right. Someone convinced them they were on the right track. But they neglected obedience to what Jesus commanded. He said of these people, "But everyone who hears these words of mine and does not put them into practice is like a foolish man who built his house on sand" (v. 26).

So what does all this mean? Keep in mind, this person was *building*. He was a church member. He was in the community; he was busy in ministry; he was prophesying and performing miracles in the name of Jesus. But he lost his reward. Now actually most Christians aren't like this guy. That is, they are not prophesying and performing miracles. But Jesus chose this particular person for a reason. He was a big shot. Perhaps he was a great pastor, a well-known evangelist, a world-class faith healer. But Jesus isn't impressed with how big your ministry is, or how giant your "faith" is, or how famous you become. He is interested in whether or not you put into practice what he commanded. He gave us one assignment to complete: Go make disciples of *all* nations. And he promised us, when you have finished doing this, I will return. Jesus is not interested in your legacy or the 40 million dollar church you may be building. It's all going to burn up! Every cathedral will be smoked! There is one thing and one thing alone that stands in the way: the fulfillment of the Great Commission. So if you must build something, keep it plain and simple. Invest your time, personnel and resources carefully, especially so as we see the end approaching.

Every one of us will be called into account on this one simple reality. The great deception in our age, the great falling away that has begun, is a pre-occupation with what will bless us and a disregard for our responsibility to bless the nations who have yet to be reached. We have become consumed with revivals for us, buildings for us, celebrations and feasts *for us*. But what Jesus is consumed with is a passion for the 2.7 billion lost souls who have never heard the message of salvation. And so he warns us:

> Woe to you who are rich,
> for you have already received your comfort.
> Woe to you who are well fed now,
> for you will go hungry.
> Woe to you who laugh now,
> for you will mourn and weep.
> (Luke 6:24-25)

We need to re-think the way we are living. We need to re-think a lot of things before it's too late. We who are rich, well fed, and carefree need to seriously re-examine the direction our lives are headed. Is Jesus pleased with our lifestyle? Is he concerned with our spending? Our gluttony? Our amusements? We need to find out.

I would encourage you to make a covenant before the Lord to serve him faithfully in this final generation. Write it out. Make it personal, let it cut deep into your heart, let it bring you to full surrender before the Lord. I'll give you an example of what I mean. Here is my personal covenant before the Lord:

Covenant of Consecration

Heavenly Father, I covenant before you today to live a life of full obedience to you and to your mission here on this earth. Every individual deserves to have someone praying fervently for their salvation as someone did for me. Every person on this planet, no matter who he is, what language he speaks, or where he may live, deserves to have someone working hard and strategizing to reach him as was done for me. As long as there is even one person alive today who doesn't know the gospel, I have a mission to accomplish. I cannot excuse myself. I cannot say, "Let someone else take care of it." It is *my* responsibility. I will not assume that everything will work out okay. I will find out. I will assess what's being done, and what's not being done. I will refuse to live in ignorance. I can't do everything, but I will maximize what I *can* do. I will define my priorities and work hard within them. I will refuse to compromise them or step outside of them.

I want my life to make a difference—as big a difference as possible. I covenant today before you Lord to work hard in your harvest field. I will use my time wisely, my money carefully, my opportunities effectively.

I want to pray with fire in my spirit! I want to pray like Elijah did. I want to live like Paul did. I want to die with honor in your service. I will not tiptoe through life. I will be obnoxious for you!

May it be said of me wherever I go, "Jesus was here." Lord, I covenant today to be your hands and your feet. May it be said of me as it was the disciples, "And they took note that these men had been with Jesus" (Acts 4:13). Let them be astonished, Lord! I want to walk like Jesus walked, live like he lived, say what he said. May his words fill my entire being and saturate my soul. May I become a living testimony of what he said and did.

MY PRAYER FOR MY LIFE

I would also encourage you to change the way you pray for yourself and for others. Pray with boldness and conviction. Below are examples of how I pray for myself and how I intercede for God's people and for the nations:

"Heavenly Father, I want to know you! Fill me with passion for your glory. I want unshakeable conviction. I want to know in my heart of hearts what I'm supposed to do with my life. I want to know beyond a shadow of a doubt that you have called me, and every true follower of Jesus, to a life of *full* consecration to your mission. I want your purposes to be the only thing on my mind. I want to see you come back! I want to work hard toward that end. I want to hear, "Well done, David! I'm so proud of you!"

May I never compromise with anything that subtracts from my being used of you to bring the gospel to every remaining unreached "tribe, language, people and nation," wherever they may be or however difficult it may be to reach them (Rev. 5:9). May I take no rest from this mandate and give no rest to any until this thing is done.

Change my attitude, change my heart, change my thoughts! Keep them in line with your desires. Fill me with holiness, clothe me in your righteousness, renew my mind, refresh my spirit, restore my soul, strengthen me in every way. Equip me for your service and anoint me for your will. Fill my life with so much joy that all who encounter it will see only you and your glory. Show me how to live day by day in your power, grace and mercy.

Eternal Vision

My Prayer for Your People

"Lord, let your revival fire fall! Consume us with your power. Remove from us any wicked and rebellious spirit. Change our hearts. Make us tender. Let our eyes be filled with tears, and our spirits, O Lord, let them cry out! Forgive us, O merciful Father, for we have wandered far from your ways. You called us to bring your light to the nations. We have kept it. Forgive us, O Great King, forgive us. Have mercy on us this day and turn our hearts from the things of this world. We have taken a spirit of mockery, jest, scoffing and revelry. We have compromised with the idols of comfort, materialism and greed. We have worshipped the gods of entertainment and have lusted for the things your soul hates. Lord, how far we have wandered! Forgive us, O Lord, forgive us. Place a right spirit within us."

My Prayer for the Nations

"Lord Jesus, I want the nations to know you! The Kurds, the Arabs, the Fulani. Lord God, they will praise you. In their languages they will acknowledge that Jesus Christ is Lord! Heavenly Father, you sent your Son to die for these nations. They need to hear about you. O Lord, thrust out laborers! Raise up an army of prayer warriors. Pour out your spirit on all flesh, and may the ends of the earth resound with your praise! Lord, shake the nations. Tear down the strongholds. Demolish the deception. Illuminate the darkness with your wonderful light. Fill the 10/40 Window with your love and mercy. Send us, O Lord! Fill us with your power. Let there be miracles, visions and dreams. Let there be courage, faith and conviction. Build your Church, O Lord! Bind the evil one, Lord Jesus. Loose the bonds that hold the captives. Open our eyes and lift them up to the fields, white and ready for harvest!"

I Am Resolved

MY ACTION PLAN

There is so much to do, so many to reach, but so few who are willing to go. So where does one begin? As always, the journey starts right where you are. If the Lord has awakened your spirit, you can be sure he will use you as a flash point of revival in your church and community. Get ready and stay consecrated. God is calling you to change your life. He is asking you to sacrifice something. I don't know exactly what it is, but you probably have an idea. All of us have been given something to give back to the Lord. It may be a gift, an inheritance, or a physical ability. He says, "Test me in this and see if I will not open the floodgates of heaven and pour out so much blessing that you will not have room enough for it" (Mal. 3:10).

God wants to bless your life and raise you up to be a blessing. He wants your whole being to overflow with joy and satisfaction in him. But there's something you need to do, and it won't be easy. You have to set aside the first fruits he has given you. Then his power and blessing will flow through you, unrestricted and without limit.

God says, "Test me in this." What might be the first fruits in your life? They are the things you want to do. They are the talents God has given you, the obvious opportunities, the desires within. They aren't bad things. But they are first fruits. They belong to the Lord. And you must give them back to him.

When there is a rescue operation going on, many things must change. Each day, fifty-thousand people perish without the gospel among the least-reached peoples of the world. This is *your* problem. It is *my* problem. It's not going to get any better the longer we wait. So what can we do? What *ought* we to do? There are three steps I think we should all take to find out:

Eternal Vision

Step One: Ask! Cry out to the Lord, "Heavenly Father, what can I do *now* to further the completion of the Great Commission? Teach me how to pray. Teach me how to ask, to intercede, and to listen. Teach me to follow your lead. May I hear your voice alone. Guide me in your way each moment of every day."

Step Two: Seek! Take a look around you. What remains to be done in your immediate area? Jesus told his disciples to begin in Jerusalem and then move out into Judea, Samaria and the ends of the earth. (Luke 24:47; Acts 1:8). Jerusalem is your city, your neighborhood. The Book of Acts tells us the disciples visited *every home* in Jerusalem sharing the gospel (Acts 5:42). Has this been done in your city?

Next, you have Judea. Here is a place filled with neighboring towns and teeming with people. Do they have a church? Is the gospel going from home to home in those cities? The Bible says Jesus and his disciples went teaching from "village to village" (Mark 6:6; Luke 9:6). They were systematic. No one was left out.

And then there's Samaria. It's not going to be easy! Here is the place not many want to go. They are the despised and neglected, the outcastes, the feared and hated. Are they being reached? Are they being loved as Jesus loves them?

And finally, *the ends of the earth*. "Lord, may the earth be filled with the knowledge of your glory as the waters cover the sea!" (Isa. 11:9). Every tribe, people and language must be reached. What can you do to reach one?

Two thousand ethnic groups still await "faithful" messengers to lead them into the light. What can your church do about it? What *ought* they to do without delay!

Step Three: Knock! What will you do with closed doors? There will be many of them. They will either turn you away or inspire you to knock. The Lord wants to open them. He wants his glory to be made known through you. Be resolved to persevere. Be determined from the outset not to turn back. Refuse to surrender. Move continually forward. Don't abandon hope. "Be joyful always; pray continually; give thanks in all circumstances!" (1 Thess. 5:16-18). We were destined for glory! The glory of the impossible through Christ.

Finally, *be resolved* to love the Lord with all that you are. Find out what that means. Don't settle for less. Leave no ambiguity in your consecration. Give it all! This *is* that time. This *is* that moment. Lives depend on it. A mission awaits you! Eternity lies before us and is ready to greet us. But for a brief few moments of that indescribable eternity, we have been given a glorious opportunity to say, "I love you, Jesus!" with all our hearts. As he did for us, let's say it with our very lives.

CHAPTER EIGHTEEN

FINAL COUNTDOWN

*"I am coming soon. Hold on to what you have,
so that no one will take your crown." (Rev. 3:11)*

*T*here is an urgent and massive rescue operation needed to save the 2.7 billion least-evangelized living in the 10/40 Window. They are a special priority for the Church because they have the least missionaries going to reach them, the least believers sharing the gospel, and the least resources committed to them. It is the single greatest tragedy in the world today and the most unnecessary. There are over 550 million evangelical Christians who can reach them!

Might God be calling you to do something about it? Imagine having an eternal impact on an entire nation now living in total darkness. The Bible tells us we *will* win in the end! The gospel *will* be preached. There *will be* representatives of every people, tribe and language standing before the throne, worshiping the Lamb and declaring his praises (Rev 7:9). The vision of Revelation 7:9 will be the greatest sight you will ever see. Picture hundreds, and even thousands of people, coming up to you and embracing you as a brother or sister in Christ. People from Tibet, Saudi Arabia and India saying,

"I am here today because you prayed. Thank you for listening to the Lord and obeying his voice. Thank you for caring about me and working hard to reach me. You are truly a faithful disciple of the Lamb!"

Thousands of unreached groups still await someone like you to take up their plight. While you can't reach them all, you can play a big part—the most important part of all. Here in this final chapter is a list of 365 groups, which are the largest, least-reached ethnic groups in the world. We have assigned one group to each day of the year in what is called the *10/40 Window Prayer Calendar*. By using this calendar you will be joining with millions of believers around the world who are committed to praying for spiritual breakthroughs in this region.

We have also grouped these 365 least-reached "mega-peoples" into 12 affinity blocs and assigned one affinity bloc to each month. For example, this January the focus will be on the Muslim peoples of Central Asia. We are encouraging believers to meet monthly in prayer groups to pray for the assigned affinity bloc of that month. In this way you can stay accountable to one another and spread the vision by recruiting new intercessors.

Then, connected to these 365 large ethnic groups are thousands of smaller groups, nearby or related to the larger groups assigned to each day. We will be praying for them as well. For example, on January 2nd we will be praying for the 25,000,000 Muslim Pashtun of Afghanistan, as well as the nearby Jakati (a Muslim group of 210,000) and the Waneci (a Muslim group of 100,000). In effect, throughout the year you will be asking the Lord for the fulfillment of Revelation 7:9!

Would you be willing to commit your life to praying for spiritual breakthroughs in these least-reached ethnic groups? You can do this by becoming a member of the 10/40 Window Prayer Alliance. This special prayer alliance involves three important components:

1. Adopting one of the least-reached groups for prayer
2. Praying through the *10/40 Window Prayer Calendar*
3. Becoming an advocate by recruiting others

This Alliance will bring you into prayer partnership with believers from all over the world. Twenty-four hours a day, in every time zone and continent, believers will be praying for the same group you are praying for. Thousands of others will be joining you in adopting the group you have adopted.

As you become an advocate for the unreached peoples, the Lord may even use you to bring renewal to your church! One lay leader, Dr. Mike Buehler of Westminster Presbyterian Church, recently commented, "Adopting an unreached people has affected our church more than anything in the last twenty years I have been a member here. Our mission budget has grown over sixty percent!"

The Lord might also give you a burden like he gave to Greg, Sally and Mark. They meet every lunchtime to pray for their adopted group. Though they are professionals and very busy people, they take the time to intercede for a people group they may never meet until heaven.

Or perhaps you will go even further like Dan did. He learned about an unreached Muslim tribe in the Philippines with no believers. Though he had a busy practice as a dentist, he reduced his work load so he might devote time to this Muslim group. He began organizing visits. He put together a slide show and started recruiting others to adopt them. They formed a partnership of believers, churches and mission organizations. Soon they found a believing nurse who was willing to go live among them and set up a health clinic. Two years later, there are now over 150 believers in 20 house-fellowships!

As you learn to pray for the nations, you will be surprised at what the Lord will do with your commitment. Just like Brother Andrew, who recruited others to pray in a seven-year campaign for the tearing down of the Iron Curtain, the Lord will use you to ask him for the impossible. In hindsight we can all say of the Iron Curtain, "Well, of course God can do that!" But how many have the faith to believe, "And God can do it again!"

There are still walls that need tearing down. These are the times for mountain-moving faith in the Kingdom of God. It's time to say, "Lord, the 10/40 Window and the unreached peoples within will no longer be frontiers! They *will* be reached! They will *no longer* be neglected by your Church!"

As you begin to pray, the Lord will begin to prepare you for even greater things in his kingdom. Some will be called (perhaps even you!) to go and give up everything. But what a great feeling it will be to know that thousands are already praying for you as you minister among one of the last remaining unreached peoples. Over 50,000 churches have already adopted their own unreached people group. Churches in Singapore, Brazil, Korea, the Philippines, and dozens of other countries have signed up for the cause.

When our organization first began this initiative, we had no idea the Lord would spread it around the world so quickly. The concept of unreached peoples is now known in almost every country, denomination and mission organization. All of this can only mean one thing: the Lord is getting ready to take us home! Even in the secular world and media there is an increased emphasis on the peoples and ethnic groups of the world. The Lord is the one doing the work. He is using CNN, the White House, and even terrorists to bring into our living rooms the unreached nations of the 10/40 Window. The

Lord of the Harvest is the one fulfilling His Great Commission and he is the one asking us today: "Won't you join me? You don't want to miss out on this one!"

GETTING STARTED

As you begin to pray through the *10/40 Window Prayer Calendar* each day, ask the Lord to burden your heart for one or more unreached people groups to pray for regularly. I pray for the Muslim Bengali of Bangladesh and India. I ask the Lord to raise up more workers, to build his Church, and to raise up more intercessors to adopt them in prayer. As I learn to pray for this group, I learn how better to pray for the other groups on the list. Praying for the Muslim Bengali has been the most exciting endeavor of my life. When I met my first Muslim Bengali believer in Jesus, my heart leapt for joy! After many years of praying, it was confirmed recently that a great spiritual breakthrough is underway in this unreached group of 120 million. Thousands have come to know Christ and several mosques have been converted into churches!

When you adopt your people group, you will want to find out as much as you can about them. You will want to connect with missionary teams working among them and sign up to get regular prayer updates. One place to begin is by registering your adoption commitment at www.prayeralliance.org. This will bring you up to date with the history of evangelization progress among your adopted group and help you stay accountable. Here at this site you can register the time you have prayed for your group each week. This will help you stay accountable and will help the Body of Christ stay informed with the progress being made.

I would encourage you to order a copy of the *10/40 Window Prayer Calendar* as soon as possible so you can begin praying strategically for the unreached peoples of the world and find out which specific group the Lord wants you to adopt. These calendars are available free of charge, but you must make a commitment to use them! (You can request these online at the same website.) Praying through this calendar is very strategic. Here you will stay in touch with the big picture. You will ask the Lord of the Harvest to thrust out laborers and raise up more intercessors for un-adopted groups. You will graphically and visibly see the progress of both mobilization and evangelization efforts to bring the gospel to all peoples.

Next you may want to become an advocate for these unreached groups. You can show the monthly video highlighting the affinity bloc being prayed for. You can organize a special prayer fellowship in your home. You can become an adoption recruiter and mobilize others to take up the challenge of an unreached group. You can contribute to the Frontier Mission Fund. This fund is designed to "fill in the gaps." Where there are unfunded projects or special opportunities, this fund is used to make up the difference and quicken response time to pressing needs in frontier areas. (See p. 338, Appendix B, for more details.)

IT CAN BE DONE

The most exciting reality of our day is the feasibility of bringing the gospel to every people group and every village and every person in our generation. This has never happened before in history, but it could happen in your lifetime! Most people are unaware of the significant advances of the gospel all over the world. In Africa, Asia and Latin America there are now over 400 million evangelical Christians and 2 million congregations.

This is the fruit of great sacrifice. In China, over 10,000 missionaries labored for over 150 years. When missionaries were expelled after the Communist takeover in 1949, many were unsure as to what might happen to Christianity in that country. Churches were closed down and most pastors were either imprisoned or killed. For decades there was silence and few knew what was going on inside closed China. But as the country began to open to the outside, the news began to trickle out. The Church in China was exploding! It was growing in leaps and bounds. The Chinese government estimates there are over 2 million baptisms a year—and they are being conservative!

The largest evangelical congregation in the world is now in Seoul, Korea, with over 1 million members. Korea is now the second largest foreign missionary sending nation in the world, right behind America and closing in fast! Every day hundreds of thousands of believers in Seoul rise up at dawn to meet at their churches to pray for world evangelization. The second largest local church in the world is in Argentina, with over 200,000 members. Latin American evangelicals now send out 2,500 missionaries all over the world!

The success of missions is one of the greatest arguments in its favor. If you could read the stories of those who pioneered these lands for Christ, if you could see how they willingly endured great trials and sacrifices, it would inspire you to give everything to the Lord. For their sacrifice has brought millions into the Kingdom. Though many did not live to see it while here on earth, they are seeing it now! They are rejoicing with countless angels and praising the Lamb who was and *is* worthy of it all.

The sacrifices of these pioneer missionaries have brought us to the place where finishing the Great Commission is well within sight. We are joined by churches all over the world that are filled with the power of the Holy Spirit and the knowledge of the gospel. The final push is becoming a global effort made up of pioneer missionaries from every corner of the earth—Brazil, Korea, India—you name it. And don't count out the Americans or the Europeans! Even missionaries from formerly closed countries like China are now being sent out by the hundreds. There will soon be thousands! The Lord is building an end-times army of believers from every continent and country. He is opening closed doors and pouring out his Holy Spirit upon the nations. The greatest soul-harvest in history is ripening all over the world. These are the most exciting times to be alive!

IT OUGHT TO BE DONE

1.3 billion Muslims, 800 million Hindus, 500 million Buddhists, and 150 million Animists need your immediate help. They speak over 4,000 languages and 12,000 dialects. They are scattered across islands in Indonesia and river banks on the Ganges. They are tucked away in the world's deepest valleys of Nepal and Tibet. They are troubled by civil wars and government coups. Their poverty is unimaginable. Their diseases are rampant. Their water can be deadly, and their food—well, what can I say, it can be hard to swallow (and keep swallowed!). Some of their languages are pretty peculiar.

You might say, "That's why they're unreached!" But the Bible tells us something else. The physical realities are a mere shadow of the spiritual realities. They live in lands that have been cursed by sin and demonic presence. Their cultures and traditions are prisons of shame and guilt. In one particular Muslim tribe, in the country where I am staying, evil spirits are invited to come enter the child at birth. They are hopeless and helpless from the moment they enter this world.

But you have the key to reaching them! You have the capacity in Christ to set them free. You have the light, the cross, the blood of the Lamb, and the power of prayer. You have the helmet of salvation, the breastplate of righteousness, and the sword of the Spirit. You have the Word of God and the hope of Christ. They have only superstitions and worthless prayer beads. You have the name of Jesus and the love of the Father. They have only mute idols and filthy demons to call upon. You have the authority to bind and loose. You hold the keys. You are on the winning side, and you are living in the most exciting moment in eternal history. You have the victory in Christ—the only hope the world. You can never be defeated!

IT MUST BE DONE

If the Apostles were here with us today, what might they say? If Isaiah could stand before us, what might he prophesy? There is no doubt in my mind their message would be the same: You guys are *so close! Don't give up!* Work hard, for the night is coming when *no one* can work. Stay in the race and finish it!

The apostle Paul referred to running seven times in his writing.[1] He wrote, "Run in such a way as to get the prize" (1 Cor. 9:24). We are in the final few moments of an incredible race. Finishing this race will require all the intensity, focus and discipline of a marathon runner. So keep your eyes on Jesus, the author and perfecter of our faith. Abide in his strength, spend time with him daily, and soak up his Word. Learn to pray with fire and passion in your soul. Seek out the lost and win them over in love. Disciple them into maturity and get them ready to meet Jesus.

Honestly, I can't wait to go to heaven and see my Savior face to face. I want to be gathered around the throne and to worship the Lord with all those Bengali believers I've been praying for. I want to see the victory parade from every nation, tribe, people and language. I want to worship Jesus with the all the angels and all the redeemed from the ends of the earth.

Eternal Vision

It will be the most exciting moment of our lives. But getting there is going to require hard work and discipline. It will require dedication and faithful commitment—but the Lamb is worthy of it! He is worthy to receive all honor and glory, riches and power, praise and adoration.

So ask yourself today: What can I give to the Lamb? What honor or power or riches do I possess? What capacity have I been given to bring His salvation to the ends of the earth? What can I do? What difference can I make? These are the most important questions you can ask. They will demand your utmost for His highest. They will call for sacrifice and consecration. They will bring you to your knees before the Lord and make you cry out: What am I doing *today* to hasten your coming? How am I living *today* to win the nations for your glory? What am I doing *today* that I can never do again throughout eternity?

Because . . .

> "It *can* be done.
> It *ought* to be done.
> And therefore, it *must* be done!"
> D.L. Moody

So let's go do it!

10/40 Window
Prayer Calendar

A Daily Guide to Praying
for the Least Reached Peoples
of the World

10/40 Window Prayer Calendar

Represented here in this prayer calendar are 3,700 least-evangelized ethnic groups, encompassing 2.7 billion people. Among them are 2,100 Muslim groups, 1,400 Hindu groups, 150 Buddhist groups and 450 tribal groups.[1]

Each of these groups has been clustered around one of the 365 largest groups in their area. Listed here are the names of those largest groups and the corresponding day we are praying for them. For a complete list and for specific prayer details for each day you can go to www.prayeralliance.org and view the specifics there or sign up for a weekly prayer e-mail.

12 Affinity Blocs and Their Assigned Month

Month	Affinity Bloc	Population	% Chr
January	Central Asian Muslim Peoples	220,000,000	0.03%
February	Hindu Middle Caste Peoples	300,000,000	0.07%
March	Least Reached Peoples of East Asia	200,000,000	0.35%
April	Buddhist Peoples	500,000,000	0.65%
May	West African Muslim Peoples	120,000,000	0.05%
June	Hindu Lower Caste Peoples	200,000,000	0.85%
July	South Asian Muslim Peoples	400,000,000	0.01%
August	East African Muslim Peoples	100,000,000	0.02%
September	N. African and Mid East Peoples	320,000,000	0.01%
October	Tribal Peoples of South Asia	100,000,000	1.05%
November	SE Asian Muslim Peoples	200,000,000	0.02%
December	Upper Caste Peoples of South Asia	200,000,000	0.01%

www.prayeralliance.org
info@finishthetask.org

[1] Because research is ongoing, the total number of peoples listed in this calendar is rounded.

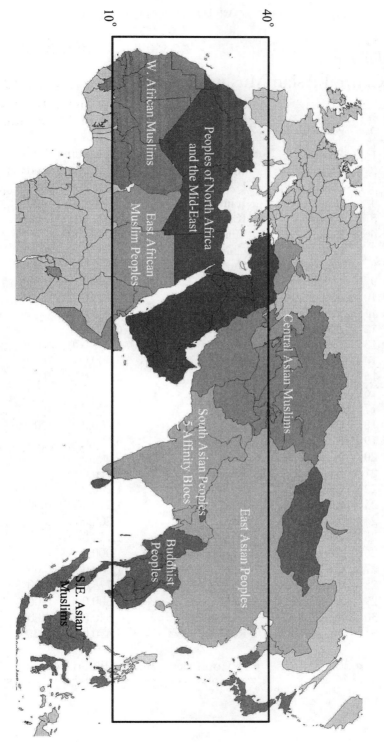

10/40 Window Prayer Calendar

January
Central Asian Muslim Peoples

Day	People Focus	Hub Country	Population	% Chr
1	Persian	Iran	30,000,000	0.07%
2	Pashtun	Afghanistan	25,000,000	0.00%
3	Uzbek	Uzbekistan	20,000,000	0.01%
4	Iranian Azeri	Iran	15,000,000	0.00%
5	Kazakh	Kazakhstan	13,000,000	0.04%
6	Tajiki	Tajikistan	11,000,000	0.00%
7	Hui	China	11,000,000	0.00%
8	Turkish Kurds	Turkey	10,000,000	0.00%
9	Uyghur	China	9,600,000	0.00%
10	Baloch	Pakistan	7,300,000	0.00%
11	Turkmen	Turkmenistan	7,000,000	0.00%
12	Azerbaijani	Azerbaijan	6,850,000	0.00%
13	Tatar	Russia	6,200,000	0.00%
14	Iranian Kurd	Iran	6,000,000	0.00%
15	Luri	Iran	5,000,000	0.00%
16	Iraqi Kurd	Iraq	5,000,000	0.00%
17	Hazaragi	Iran	4,000,000	0.00%
18	Gilaki	Iran	3,800,000	0.00%
19	Kyrgyz	Kyrgyzstan	3,600,000	0.06%
20	Mazanderani	Iran	3,000,000	0.00%
21	Bashkir	Russia	1,700,000	0.00%
22	Chechen	Russia	1,200,000	0.00%
23	Circassion	Russia	1,200,000	0.00%
24	Nawar	Iran	1,200,000	0.00%
25	Bakhtiari	Iran	1,150,000	0.00%
26	Aimaq	Afghanistan	1,000,000	0.01%
27	Qashqai	Iran	1,000,000	0.00%
28	Quchani	Iran	775,000	0.00%
29	Avar	Russia	600,000	0.00%
30	Karakalpak	Uzbekistan	540,000	0.00%
31	Lezgi	Russia	450,000	0.01%

- 300 Groups • 13 Countries • 220 Million People

10/40 Window Prayer Calendar

February
Hindu Middle Caste Peoples

Day	People Focus	Hub Country	Population	% Chr
1	Ahir	India	56,440,000	0.00%
2	Kurmi	India	25,750,000	0.00%
3	Kunbi	India	19,620,000	0.00%
4	Vanniyar	India	18,200,000	0.46%
5	Lingayat	India	17,900,000	0.00%
6	Nai	India	14,760,000	0.00%
7	Viswakarma	India	12,324,000	0.17%
8	Mahishya	India	11,500,000	0.01%
9	Koiri	India	10,700,000	0.00%
10	Vakkaliga	India	9,900,000	0.06%
11	Telaga	India	9,200,000	0.00%
12	Gujar	India	8,550,000	0.00%
13	Barhai	India	8,400,000	0.02%
14	Kamma	India	7,140,000	0.11%
15	Sonar	India	7,120,000	0.00%
16	Kapu	India	6,700,000	0.21%
17	Chotra Bansi	India	6,440,000	0.00%
18	Kalwar	India	6,000,000	0.00%
19	Kuruba	India	5,670,000	0.03%
20	Khandelwal	India	5,450,000	0.00%
21	Khandait	India	5,450,000	0.00%
22	Gola	India	4,900,000	0.04%
23	Bhuinhar	India	4,700,000	0.00%
24	Kachhi	India	3,900,000	0.00%
25	Mochi	Pakistan	3,400,000	0.42%
26	Lewa	India	2,750,000	0.00%
27	Kanet	India	1,730,000	0.00%
28	Kadwa Patidar	India	1,320,000	0.00%

• 700 Groups   • 4 Countries   • 450 Million People

10/40 Window Prayer Calendar

March
Least Reached Peoples of East Asia

Day	People Focus	Hub Country	Population	% Chr
1	Xiang Chinese	China	36,064,000	0.22%
2	Hakka	China	31,309,000	0.48%
3	North Korean	N. Korea	25,000,000	1.40%
4	Zhuang	China	15,800,000	0.29%
5	Manchu	China	12,666,000	0.00%
6	Tujia	China	7,353,000	0.41%
7	Yi Tribes	China	5,000,000	0.20%
8	Dan Chinese	China	4,296,000	0.35%
9	Bouyei	China	3,176,000	0.16%
10	Dong	China	3,000,000	0.05%
11	Bali Hindus	Indonesia	3,000,000	0.00%
12	Parsees	Iran	3,000,000	0.00%
13	Hmu	China	2,800,000	0.12%
14	Nosu	China	2,500,000	0.80%
15	Pinghu Chinese	China	2,338,000	0.34%
16	Miao	China	2,130,000	0.23%
17	Tay	Vietnam	1,500,000	0.00%
18	Li	China	1,500,000	0.07%
19	Hani	China	1,500,000	0.13%
20	Yao Tribes	Vietnam	1,500,000	0.33%
21	Iu Mien	China	1,230,000	0.12%
22	Ghao-Xong	China	1,200,000	0.42%
23	Muong	Vietnam	1,200,000	0.25%
24	Pingdi	China	1,100,000	0.04%
25	Mon Khmer Tribes	Vietnam	1,000,000	0.10%
26	Tai Tribes	Thailand	1,000,000	0.10%
27	Tibeto-Burman Tribes	Myanmar	1,000,000	0.10%
28	Nung	Vietnam	1,000,000	0.10%
29	She	China	820,000	0.12%
30	Nisu	China	780,000	0.18%
31	Gelao	China	670,000	0.11%

• 250 Groups • 8 Countries • 200 Million People

April
Buddhist Peoples

Day	People Focus	Hub Country	Population	% Chr
1	Chinese Buddhist	China	150,000,000	0.67%
2	Japanese	Japan	124,000,000	0.40%
3	Vietnamese	Viet Nam	65,000,000	0.77%
4	Thai	Thailand	32,000,000	0.78%
5	Burmese	Myanmar	27,000,000	0.11%
6	Isan	Thailand	16,300,000	0.00%
7	Sinhala	Sri Lanka	14,500,000	0.07%
8	Khmer	Cambodia	10,400,000	0.48%
9	Indian Buddhists	India	8,000,000	0.00%
10	Chinese Mongol	China	5,800,000	0.09%
11	Tibetan	China	4,500,000	0.00%
12	Lao	Laos	3,300,000	0.61%
13	Shan	Myanmar	3,200,000	0.00%
14	Mongolian	Mongolia	2,200,000	0.45%
15	Bai	China	2,000,000	0.00%
16	Drukpa	Bhutan	1,500,000	0.00%
17	Khampa	China	1,500,000	0.03%
18	Mon	Myanmar	1,300,000	0.00%
19	Thai Khmer	Thailand	1,200,000	0.00%
20	Arakanese	Myanmar	1,200,000	0.08%
21	Vietnamese Khmer	Vietnam	1,100,000	0.18%
22	Dai	China	1,000,000	0.00%
23	Amdo	China	1,000,000	0.00%
24	Newari	Nepal	900,000	0.00%
25	Parauk	Myanmar	730,000	0.00%
26	Taungyo	Myanmar	620,000	0.00%
27	Palaung	Myanmar	600,000	0.00%
28	Kalmyk-Oirat	Mongolia	560,000	0.00%
29	Chakma	Bangladesh	500,000	0.20%
30	Buriat	Russia	500,000	0.00%

- 150 Groups   • 15 Countries   • 500 Million People

May
West African Muslim Peoples

Day	People Focus	Hub Country	Population	% Chr
1	Hausa	Nigeria	23,000,000	0.04%
2	Nigerian Fulani	Nigeria	12,000,000	0.02%
3	Yoruba Muslims	Nigeria	4,000,000	0.05%
4	Bambara	Mali	3,700,000	0.27%
5	Yerwa Kanuri	Nigeria	3,700,000	0.03%
6	Wolof	Senegal	3,700,000	0.00%
7	Malinke	Mali	3,500,000	0.09%
8	Futa Jalon	Guinea	3,000,000	0.00%
9	Pulaar	Senegal	3,000,000	0.03%
10	Songai	Mali	2,500,000	0.02%
11	Adamawa	Cameroon	2,300,000	0.00%
12	Tazarawa	Niger	2,250,000	0.00%
13	Sokoto Fulani	Niger	2,000,000	0.00%
14	Tuareg	Niger	1,677,000	0.00%
15	Dyerma	Niger	1,650,000	0.00%
16	Maninka	Guinea	1,500,000	0.07%
17	Jula	Cote d'Ivoire	1,500,000	0.00%
18	Soninke	Mali	1,250,000	0.00%
19	Susu	Guinea	1,100,000	0.00%
20	Nupe	Nigeria	1,100,000	0.18%
21	Bidan	Mauritania	1,100,000	0.00%
22	Manga Kanuri	Nigeria	1,000,000	0.00%
23	Maasina Fulbe	Mali	1,000,000	0.00%
24	Adarawa	Niger	1,000,000	0.00%
25	Tukulor	Senegal	1,000,000	0.00%
26	Arewa	Niger	950,000	0.00%
27	Fulacunda	Senegal	950,000	0.00%
28	Bauchi Fulani	Nigeria	800,000	0.00%
29	Dagomba	Ghana	766,000	0.52%
30	Haratine	Mauritania	700,000	0.00%
31	Tem	Togo	350,000	0.00%

- 300 Groups   • 15 Countries   • 120 Million People

10/40 Window Prayer Calendar

June
Hindu Lower Caste Peoples

Day	People Focus	Hub Country	Population	% Chr
1	Chamar	India	47,300,000	1.09%
2	Pasi	India	7,290,000	0.13%
3	Dhobi	India	5,320,000	0.13%
4	Dusadh	India	5,190,000	0.81%
5	Namasudra	India	4,150,000	0.53%
6	Rajbanshi	India	4,130,000	0.04%
7	Bhambi	India	3,450,000	1.86%
8	Bagdi	India	3,350,000	0.20%
9	Pod	India	2,810,000	0.04%
10	Musahar	India	2,810,000	0.50%
11	Bauri	India	2,140,000	0.93%
12	Kaibarta	India	2,000,000	0.24%
13	Khatik	India	1,750,000	0.43%
14	Dhanak	India	1,520,000	1.78%
15	Ganda	India	1,140,000	1.66%
16	Bhovi	India	1,100,000	0.16%
17	Shilpkar	India	940,000	0.13%
18	Arunthathiyar	India	925,000	0.16%
19	Holiya	India	865,000	0.42%
20	Bairwa	India	785,000	0.32%
21	Hari	India	778,000	0.19%
22	Kondara	India	700,000	0.21%
23	Madari	India	665,000	0.50%
24	Thori	India	641,000	0.42%
25	Rajwar	India	590,000	0.28%
26	Kuravan	India	530,000	1.08%
27	Doom	India	528,000	0.54%
28	Basor	India	516,000	1.45%
29	Lohar	India	482,000	0.37%
30	Sunri	India	461,000	0.33%

- 300 Groups   • 4 Countries   • 200 Million People

10/40 Window Prayer Calendar

July
South Asian Muslim Peoples

Day	People Focus	Hub Country	Population	% Chr
1	Bengali Muslims	Bangladesh	120,000,000	0.04%
2	Punjabi Muslims	Pakistan	75,000,000	0.00%
3	Urdu Shaikh	India	24,400,000	0.00%
4	Jat Muslims	Pakistan	22,000,000	0.00%
5	Sindhi Muslims	Pakistan	18,500,000	0.00%
6	Bihari Muslims	India	17,700,000	0.00%
7	Siraiki	Pakistan	15,000,000	0.00%
8	Ansari	India	13,000,000	0.00%
9	Urdu Pathan	India	12,400,000	0.00%
10	Deccani Muslims	India	11,000,000	0.00%
11	Mappila	India	8,900,000	0.00%
12	Rajput Muslims	India	8,000,000	0.00%
13	Tamil Muslims	India	6,000,000	0.00%
14	Sylhetti	Bangladesh	5,000,000	0.00%
15	Urdu Sayyid	India	4,560,000	0.00%
16	Arain	Pakistan	4,500,000	0.00%
17	Gujarati Muslims	India	4,500,000	0.00%
18	Kashmiri	India	4,050,000	0.00%
19	Marwadi Muslims	India	4,000,000	0.00%
20	Nai Muslims	India	4,000,000	0.00%
21	Bahna	India	3,000,000	0.00%
22	Telugu Muslims	India	3,000,000	0.00%
23	Hindko	Pakistan	2,800,000	0.00%
24	Garia	India	2,700,000	0.00%
25	Labbai	India	2,540,000	0.00%
26	Teli	India	2,000,000	0.00%
27	Brahui	Pakistan	1,720,000	0.00%
28	Moors of Sri Lanka	Sri Lanka	1,500,000	0.00%
29	Nepalese Muslims	Nepal	1,200,000	0.00%
30	Oriya Muslims	India	820,000	0.00%
31	Maldivian Muslims	Maldives	300,000	0.00%

- 350 Groups   • 4 Countries   • 400 Million People

10/40 Window Prayer Calendar

August
East African Muslim Peoples

Day	People Focus	Hub Country	Population	% Chr
1	Somali	Somalia	12,000,000	0.00%
2	Badawi	Sudan	11,700,000	0.00%
3	Muslim Oromo	Ethiopia	4,200,000	0.00%
4	Baggara	Sudan	4,000,000	0.00%
5	Sudanese Arab	Sudan	3,700,000	0.00%
6	Ethiopian Somali	Ethiopia	2,800,000	0.00%
7	Makhuwa Muslims	Mozambique	2,500,000	0.00%
8	Kababish	Sudan	2,100,000	0.00%
9	Yao	Malawi	2,000,000	0.00%
10	Swahili Muslims	Congo	2,000,000	0.00%
11	Sidamo	Ethiopia	1,850,000	0.00%
12	Shuwa Arab	Chad	1,820,000	0.00%
13	Egyptian Nubian	Egypt	1,700,000	0.00%
14	Beja	Sudan	1,600,000	0.00%
15	Maay	Somalia	1,500,000	0.00%
16	Makonde	Tanzania	1,500,000	0.00%
17	Afar	Ethiopia	1,200,000	0.00%
18	Tigre	Eritrea	1,200,000	0.00%
19	Fur	Sudan	750,000	0.00%
20	Nubians	Sudan	700,000	0.00%
21	Hadiyya Muslims	Ethiopia	700,000	0.00%
22	Shirazi	Tanzania	670,000	0.00%
23	Zaramo	Tanzania	650,000	0.00%
24	Comorian	Comoro Is.	600,000	0.00%
25	Kenyan Somali	Kenya	520,000	0.00%
26	Mwera	Tanzania	470,000	0.00%
27	Zigula	Tanzania	460,000	0.00%
28	Kanembu	Chad	445,000	0.00%
29	Masalit	Sudan	440,000	0.00%
30	Fulani Hausa	Sudan	420,000	0.00%
31	Maba	Chad	360,000	0.00%

- 400 Groups
- 14 Countries
- 100 Million People

10/40 Window Prayer Calendar

September
N. African and Mid. East Peoples

Day	People Focus	Hub Country	Population	% Chr
1	Egyptian Arab	Egypt	62,000,000	0.00%
2	Turks	Turkey	57,000,000	0.00%
3	Algerian Arab	Algeria	27,000,000	0.00%
4	Yemeni Arab	Yemen	21,000,000	0.00%
5	Saudi Arab	Saudi Arabia	18,000,000	0.03%
6	Morrocan Arab	Morocco	16,000,000	0.00%
7	Syrian Muslims	Syria	14,000,000	0.00%
8	Iraqi Shiite Arab	Iraq	11,000,000	0.00%
9	Tunisian Arab	Tunisia	10,000,000	0.00%
10	Jordanian Muslims	Jordan	8,000,000	0.00%
11	Iraqi Sunni Arab	Iraq	5,000,000	0.00%
12	Israeli Jew	Israel	5,000,000	0.00%
13	Albanian Muslims	Albania	5,000,000	0.00%
14	Shilha	Morocco	4,500,000	0.02%
15	Palestinian Muslims	Palestine	4,000,000	0.00%
16	Kabyle	Algeria	3,500,000	0.00%
17	Libyan Arab	Libya	3,500,000	0.00%
18	Algerian Bedouin	Algeria	3,000,000	0.03%
19	Bosnian Muslims	Bosnia	2,500,000	0.00%
20	Omani Arab	Oman	2,000,000	0.00%
21	Egyptian Gypsies	Egypt	2,000,000	0.00%
22	Lebanese Muslims	Lebanon	2,000,000	0.00%
23	Riffi Berber	Morocco	1,800,000	0.06%
24	Jebala	Morocco	1,800,000	0.06%
25	Shawiya	Algeria	1,600,000	0.00%
26	Egyptian Bedouin	Egypt	1,300,000	0.00%
27	Turkish Arab	Turkey	1,200,000	0.00%
28	Kuwait Arab	Kuwait	1,000,000	0.00%
29	Emirati Arab	UAE	650,000	0.00%
30	Bahraini Arab	Bahrain	400,000	0.00%

• 250 Groups   • 19 Countries   • 320 Million People

10/40 WINDOW PRAYER CALENDAR

October
Tribal Peoples of South Asia

Day	People Focus	Hub Country	Population	% Chr
1	Gond	India	10,600,000	1.06%
2	Bhil	India	10,150,000	0.88%
3	Kori	India	3,500,000	0.64%
4	Banjara	India	3,100,000	0.62%
5	Bhil Mina	India	2,910,000	0.34%
6	Naikda	India	2,180,000	0.06%
7	Bhuiya	India	1,595,000	0.19%
8	Koli Mahadev	India	1,090,000	0.87%
9	Tipera	India	990,000	0.49%
10	Rabari	India	920,000	0.22%
11	Kawar	India	800,000	0.21%
12	Ho	India	800,000	0.94%
13	Varli	India	778,000	0.39%
14	Bhilala	India	760,000	0.27%
15	Bhumij	India	730,000	0.59%
16	Dubla	India	680,000	0.26%
17	Halba	India	658,000	0.68%
18	Dhodia	India	653,000	0.23%
19	Koya	India	653,000	0.90%
20	Kol	India	453,000	0.26%
21	Miri	India	448,000	0.77%
22	Thakur	India	444,000	0.07%
23	Yenadi	India	440,000	0.37%
24	Kolha	India	433,000	0.61%
25	Saharia	India	416,000	0.00%
26	Yerukula	India	413,000	0.74%
27	Paroja	India	393,000	0.76%
28	Baiga	India	369,000	0.66%
29	Dhanka	India	350,000	0.91%
30	Charan	India	340,000	0.00%
31	Bhottada	India	340,000	0.33%

- 200 Groups   • 4 Countries   • 100 Million People

10/40 Window Prayer Calendar

November
S. E. Asian Muslim Peoples

Day	People Focus	Hub Country	Population	% Chr
1	Sunda	Indonesia	32,000,000	0.07%
2	Malay	Malaysia	20,000,000	0.00%
3	Jawa Pesisir	Indonesia	18,600,000	0.02%
4	Madura	Indonesia	13,500,000	0.00%
5	Indonesian	Indonesia	10,000,000	0.01%
6	Minangkabau	Indonesia	8,100,000	0.00%
7	Pendalungan	Indonesia	6,500,000	0.00%
8	Bugis	Indonesia	3,800,000	0.08%
9	Aceh	Indonesia	3,500,000	0.00%
10	Banjar	Indonesia	3,000,000	0.00%
11	Thai Malay	Thailand	2,500,000	0.00%
12	Sasak	Indonesia	2,345,000	0.02%
13	Makassar	Indonesia	2,240,000	0.02%
14	Melayu Riau	Indonesia	2,000,000	0.00%
15	Lampung	Indonesia	1,500,000	0.00%
16	Rohingya	Myanmar	1,400,000	0.00%
17	Tausug	Philippines	1,000,000	0.00%
18	Maranao	Philippines	1,000,000	0.01%
19	Magindanaon	Philippines	1,000,000	0.01%
20	Gorontalo	Indonesia	900,000	0.03%
21	Jambi	Indonesia	800,000	0.00%
22	Komering	Indonesia	800,000	0.00%
23	Sama	Philippines	700,000	0.01%
24	Pasemah	Indonesia	650,000	0.00%
25	Palembang	Indonesia	625,000	0.00%
26	Mandailing	Indonesia	400,000	0.08%
27	Cham	Cambodia	350,000	0.00%
28	Brunei Malay	Brunei	300,000	0.00%
29	Ogan	Indonesia	300,000	0.00%
30	Muna	Indonesia	230,000	0.00%

- 300 Groups • 7 Countries • 200 Million People

10/40 WINDOW PRAYER CALENDAR

December
Upper Caste Peoples of South Asia

Day	People Focus	Hub Country	Population	% Chr
1	Mahratta	India	28,540,000	0.00%
2	Sikhs	India	24,000,000	0.00%
3	Bhojpuri Rajput	India	16,700,000	0.00%
4	Kayastha	India	12,000,000	0.00%
5	Hindi Brahmin	India	10,700,000	0.00%
6	Marwadi Bania	India	8,800,000	0.00%
7	Bhojpuri Brahmin	India	7,100,000	0.00%
8	Punjabi Jat	India	7,000,000	0.00%
9	Bengali Brahmin	India	6,600,000	0.00%
10	Nayar	India	6,300,000	0.11%
11	Hindi Rajput	India	6,300,000	0.00%
12	Hindi Bania	India	5,500,000	0.00%
13	Marwadi Brahmin	India	4,600,000	0.00%
14	Bhumihar Brahmin	India	4,100,000	0.00%
15	Marathi Brahmin	India	4,100,000	0.00%
16	Arora	India	3,800,000	0.00%
17	Telugu Bania	India	3,600,000	0.00%
18	Telugu Brahmin	India	3,500,000	0.00%
19	Chhetri	Nepal	3,500,000	0.00%
20	Jains	India	3,500,000	0.00%
21	Gujarati Bania	India	3,400,000	0.00%
22	Marwadi Rajput	India	3,300,000	0.00%
23	Haryanvi Jat	India	3,300,000	0.00%
24	Awadhi Brahmin	India	3,000,000	0.00%
25	Sindhi Hindus	India	3,000,000	0.00%
26	Gujarati Brahmin	India	2,700,000	0.00%
27	Nepali Brahmin	Nepal	2,500,000	0.00%
28	Kannada Brahmin	India	2,300,000	0.00%
29	Tamil Brahmin	India	2,200,000	0.00%
30	Gujarati Rajput	India	2,100,000	0.00%
31	Oriya Brahmin	India	2,100,000	0.00%

- 400 Groups   • 4 Countries   • 200 Million People

Appendix B: Frontier Mission Fund

The purpose of the Frontier Mission Fund is to accelerate what is being done to reach all remaining unreached peoples with the gospel. The goal is to ensure that every unreached group has a disciple-making movement in the next ten to fifteen years. Most of the funds will be focused on the least reached mega-peoples of the 10/40 Window. The remaining funds will be used to reach the smaller unreached tribal and minority people groups in every country. Centers of research, training, publishing, community development and inter-agency partnership are being established for every unreached group, or cluster of related groups, throughout the world. About 500 centers are being established in strategic locations. Indigenous leaders are being trained and equipped to operate these centers and continue the development of evangelistic and discipleship resources and the multiplication of disciple-making fellowships among their group.

To contribute to the Frontier Mission Fund and to receive updates about how your giving is benefiting the least-reached peoples of the world, write to:

Frontier Mission Alliance

1443 E Washington Bl. #308
Pasadena, CA 91104-2721

Or send an email to fmf@finishthetask.org

To give by check, make checks payable to: Frontier Mission Fund. To give by credit-card, automatic-debit, or wire-transfer, go online to www.fmalliance.org for more information.

NOTES

Chapter 1: Getting Perspective

1. Holly Peters, "Evangelicals on the Decline," *Biola Connections*, Fall 2002, 12-16.
2. Global Mission Database, compiled by the Frontier Mission Alliance, available online at www.research.ms.
3. Ibid.

Chapter 3: Eternal Glory

1. Vinita Hampton and Carol Plueddemann, *World Shapers*, (Wheaton: Harold Shaw Publishers, 1991), p. 20.
2. 1 Thess. 5:16-18.

Chapter 4: The Real Danger

1. Global Mission Database.
2. Pastor John Piper, Bethlehem Baptist Church, 2002.

Chapter 7: Satan's Final Defeat

1. David Taylor, "Operation World 2001 Reveals Emerging Global Trends," *Mission Frontiers*, December 2001, 30-32.
2. Matt. 7:15; Mark 13:22; Acts 20:29; 2 Cor. 11:13-15; 1 Tim. 4:1-2; 2 Pet. 2:17-19; 1 John 2:18-19; Jude 1:12-13.

Chapter 8: Bringing Back the King

1. The full details of this fascinating war can be found on the official website of Israel's Defense Forces: www.idf.il.
2. Phil. 4:13; Luke 10:19; Isa. 54:17; Deut. 11:25.

Chapter 10: Courage Under Fire

1. Heb. 11:4.
2. Barbara Basler, "AARP At Your Service," *AARP Bulletin*, July-August 2002, 19.
3. Bob Smietana, "Chicago's Holy Fire," *Christianity Today*, February 2004, 34.
4. Matt. 25:41; Matt. 25:12; Matt. 25:30.

Chapter 12: Just Ask

1. Matt. 7:8, 18:19, 21:22; John 14:13, 15:16, 16:23; 1 John 5:15.
2. Wesley Duewel, *Touch the World through Prayer*, (Grand Rapids: Zondervan Publishing House, 1986), p. 60.
3. Rom. 15:30-32; 2 Cor. 1:8-11; Eph. 6:19-20; Phil. 1:18-19; Col. 4:2-4; 2 Thess. 3:1-2.

NOTES

Chapter 13: Spiritual Realities

1. Mrs. Howard Taylor, *Behind the Ranges*, (London: China Inland Mission, 1944), p. 1.

Chapter 14: Growing In Faith

1. John McComb Roots, *Chou: An Informal Biography*, (New York: Doubleday, 1978), pp. 33-35.

Chapter 15: Satan's Top 5 Lies

1. Brother Andrew, *And God Changed His Mind*, (London: Marshall Pickering, 1990), p. 22.
2. SBC missionaries to Tanzania, Doug and Evelyn Knapp. For fascinating missionary biography read their book, *Thunder in the Valley*, (Nashville: Broadman Press, 1986).
3. Marc Cerasini, *The U.S. Special Ops Forces*, (Indianapolis: Alpha Books, 2002), p. 136.

Chapter 17: I Am Resolved

1. Frank Bettger, *From Failure to Success in Selling*, (Englewood Cliffs: Prentice-Hall, 1966), p. 25.

Chapter 18: Final Countdown

1. Acts 20:24; 1 Cor. 9:24, 9:26; Gal. 2:2, 5:7; Phil. 2:16; 2 Tim. 4:7; Heb. 12:1.

For the full bibliography and additional comments go to
www.taylorpublishing.info/eternalvision.htm

Mission Resource Center

10/40 Window Prayer Calendar-*Booklet* (36 page booklet)
Use this prayer calendar to pray daily for the unreached peoples of the 10/40 Window throughout the year. Set of 10. $4.95 per set

10/40 Window Prayer Calendar-*Sheet* (1 sheet, front and back)
Designed for mass-distribution, lists the entire prayer calendar on 2 pages. Also available for free download at www.prayeralliance.org/calendar Set of 200. $4.95 per set

Light the Window Prayer Journal (monthly magazine)
Exciting monthly prayer updates from the 10/40 Window and challenging articles to inspire your commitment. 1 Year Subscription is $12.00

Light the Window Prayer DVD (monthly video)
Monthly video update on what God is doing among the affinity bloc being prayed for in the 10/40 Window Prayer Calendar. 1 Year Subscription is $12.00

Operation 10/40 Window (450 pages)
Introducing the largest, least reached peoples of the 10/40 Window. One page profiles of each group, including maps and pictures. $15.00 each

Eternal Vision-*Leader's Edition* (352 pages)
Seeing life from heaven's perspective. $9.95 each. 3 or more, $8.95 each

Eternal Vision-*Class Edition with Study Guide* (220 pages)
Shorter chapters for use in Bible studies. $8.95 each. 3 or more, $7.95 each

How To Order:
Online orders can be placed at www.fmalliance.org. Or photocopy this page and send to Frontier Mission Alliance, Pasadena, CA 91104.   1443 E Washington Bl. #308
Pasadena, CA 91104-2721

Name: _____

Shipping Address: _____

_____

Phone: _____ Email: _____

Type of Payment: ___ Credit Card ___ Check *(Frontier Mission Alliance)*

Credit Card #: _____ Expiration: ____ / ____

Items	Qty.	Sub-Totals
	Shipping	
U.S. orders add 10% for shipping (outside of U.S., 20%)	**Total**	